Studies in Australian History
Series editors: Alan Gilbert and Peter Spearritt

The Origins of Australia's Capital Cities Pamela Statham (editor)
Convict Workers Stephen Nicholas (editor)
A Military History of Australia Jeffrey Grey
The Invisible State Alastair Davidson
The Price of Health James A. Gillespie

The Rule of Law in a Penal Colony

Law and Power in Early New South Wales

David Neal

CAMBRIDGE UNIVERSITY PRESS
Cambridge
New York Port Chester Melbourne Sydney

CAMBRIDGE UNIVERSITY PRESS
Cambridge, New York, Melbourne, Madrid, Cape Town, Singapore, São Paulo

Cambridge University Press
The Edinburgh Building, Cambridge CB2 8RU, UK

Published in the United States of America by Cambridge University Press, New York

www.cambridge.org
Information on this title: www.cambridge.org/9780521372640

© Cambridge University Press 1991

This publication is in copyright. Subject to statutory exception
and to the provisions of relevant collective licensing agreements,
no reproduction of any part may take place without the written
permission of Cambridge University Press.

First published 1991
First paperback edition 2002

A catalogue record for this publication is available from the British Library

National Library of Australia Cataloguing in Publication data
Neal, David, 1950–
The rule of law in a penal colony: law and power in
early New South Wales.
Bibliography.
Includes index.
ISBN 0 521 37264 X
1. Rule of law – New South Wales – History. 2. Law –
New South Wales – History and criticism. I. Title. (Series:
Studies in Australian history (Cambridge, England)).
340.09944

Library of Congress Cataloguing in Publication data
Neal, D. J. (David J.)
The rule of law in a penal colony: law and power in
early New South Wales / David John Neal.
    p.   cm. – (Studies in Australian history)
Based on the author's thesis (Ph.D.).
Includes bibliographical references and index.
ISBN 0 521 37264 X
1. Criminal justice, Administration of – Australia –
New South Wales – History. I. Title. II. Series.
LAW.
345.944'05–dc20
[349.44055]

ISBN 978-0-521-37264-0 hardback
ISBN 978-0-521-52297-7 paperback

Transferred to digital printing 2007

For Kin Tow, Raie Neal and David L. Neal

Contents

List of illustrations	viii
Abbreviations	ix
Preface	xi
1 Great Changes	1
2 Free Society, Penal Colony, Slave Society, Prison?	27
3 The Rule of Law	61
4 The Courts	85
5 The Magistracy	115
6 Policing a Penal Colony	141
7 The Campaign for Trial by Jury	167
8 Conclusion	189
Appendices	198
Notes	202
Bibliography	249
Index	264

List of illustrations

Norwich Castle Jail	x
Writ in Kables' case	26
Mounted Police escorting prisoners	60
Sir Francis Forbes	84
Hartley Court House	114
Emancipist petition of 1819	166
William Charles Wentworth	188

Abbreviations

AONSW	Archives Office of New South Wales
BL	British Library
CO	Colonial Office
DCL	Derby Central Library
Hist. Studs.	*Australian Historical Studies*
HO	Home Office
HRA	*Historical Records of Australia*
HRNSW	*Historical Records of New South Wales*
IUP	Irish University Press
JRAHS	*Journal of the Royal Australian Historical Society*
L.R.	*Law Review (e.g. Melb. Univ. L.R.)*
ML	Mitchell Library
NLA	National Library of Australia
PRO	Public Record Office
SRO	Scottish Record Office

Inside the walls of Norwich Castle, ca. 1785. Artist's impression, based on contemporary plans, by Nick Arber. The drawing shows the felons' yard with dungeons opening onto it. The rooms above the dungeon were occupied by better-off debtors. Reproduced by kind permission of the artist.

Preface

The European discovery of the east coast of Australia caused great excitement among natural scientists. For Sir Joseph Banks and the Royal Society, Australia formed a natural, isolated laboratory from which they reaped a rich harvest of specimens and ideas. It provided part of the background against which one of its very famous scientific visitors, Charles Darwin, formulated his theory of evolution.[1]

The white settlement of New South Wales seems to have proved less interesting to social and political thinkers than it did to natural scientists. Certainly Jeremy Bentham – obsessed with social engineering and the philosophy and techniques of punishment – took an avid interest. But for the most part, then and since, the formation of New South Wales has not drawn much attention from those interested in the history of social and political ideas. Yet the story of New South Wales – like the stories of the foundation of European settlements in the new world[2] – offers social scientists and historians the opportunity to study the development of a new society in close to laboratory conditions.

Of course the social laboratory analogy cannot be pushed too far. New South Wales was not a *tabula rasa*. Despite the legal fiction that New South Wales was deserted – *terra nullius* – the Europeans ecountered an Aboriginal population with its own social and economic system.[3] As part of their cultural baggage, the white settlers – both convict and free – brought with them the major contemporary social and political ideas of the late eighteenth century. These ideas interacted with the strange conditions of the new colony and the changing ideas of those 'at home' about penal practices, colonisation, slavery, social arrangements and politics.

Law formed an important part of this cultural baggage. The convicts had first-hand experience of the criminal law. But all the

British colonists came out of a political culture which laid heavy stress on the rule of law as the guarantee of its fundamental political value, British liberty. Sir William Blackstone, in his *Commentaries on the Laws of England* – published just twenty years before British settlement of New South Wales – set out to instruct 'the rising generation in the wisdom of our civil polity'.[4]

Blackstone's four volumes are a paean to English law and the English constitution. Its fame made Blackstone a public figure; British colonists around the world cited their favourite passage from Blackstone, the one that goes, '. . .if an uninhabited colony is discovered and planted by English subjects, all the English laws are immediately there in force. For as the law is the birthright of every subject, so wherever they go they carry their laws with them'.[5] But this applied only insofar as the circumstances of the colony permitted. What would the rule of law mean in the circumstances of a penal colony?

This work sets out to answer that question. While a great deal of recent work by historians of eighteenth-century Britain has given the rule of law pride of place, little attention has been given to its impact on the early history of New South Wales. General histories of early Australia have either ignored or misunderstood this aspect of English political culture. A sort of disciplinary apartheid has been practised whereby law and the constitution are confined in a separate category of historical enquiry. For their part, the constitutional and legal histories concentrate on the legal frameworks at the expense of the people and the passions that excited them to battle with their governors, to haul their opponents into the colony's courts, and to insist on their rights as Britons to their colonial masters.

The argument that I will develop is that the rule of law – a set of concepts encompassing legal rules, institutions, processes of reasoning and powerful symbols – played a prime role in changing New South Wales from a penal colony to a free society. The colonists used the imported rule of law ideology to settle the terms on which authority would be exercised in the colony and to force the colonial power to grant its penal colony the institutions and conditions of a free society.

This has been a long project and I have incurred many debts. The first one, as will be apparent from the body of the work, is to generations of Australian historians who have gone before me. To a greater extent than is conventional in Australian historiography, I have built on the fine work of my predecessors.

I acknowledge in particular the seminal work on the rule of law in eighteenth-century England by Edward Thompson and Douglas

Hay [6] Their ideas started me thinking about the late-eighteenth-century extension of the English criminal justice system at Botany Bay. My researches eventually led to Herbert Evatt's *Rum Rebellion*. This book was written in the 1930s and has been read widely ever since. Evatt makes the clearest possible statement about the political role of the courts up to the Rum Rebellion in 1808. Yet his brilliant insight about the interaction of law and politics in early New South Wales has not been grasped. His book convinced me that there was an important story to be told about the rule of law in New South Wales. As I read more, the language of the rule of law – Magna Carta, British law and British liberty, Blackstone, the Bill of Rights, the independence the judiciary – seemed to occur all the time. This is particularly true of the colonial newspapers in the 1820s. So many of the great issues of the times were fought out in the colony's courts. Currey's biography of Chief Justice Francis Forbes gave me an invaluable entrée to many of these legal battles.[7] Alex Castles, both personally and through his book, *An Australian Legal History*, has been extremely helpful with guidance to sources and generous with his encyclopaedic knowledge of early Australia.

Among the general historians, I thank John Hirst. Although I have fundamental disagreements with the arguments in his *Convict Society and Its Enemies*, those arguments made me think extremely hard about my interpretation of early New South Wales. His book has broken with some narrowing conventions of Australian historiography. Too much Australian history proceeds as if no other historians had written about the topic in hand, and as if New South Wales, with the Colonial Office in the background, developed in isolation from the rest of the late eighteenth, early nineteenth-century world. While there is a fund of excellent works from primary sources, there are very few works of interpretation, argument and debate. John Hirst's approach, his willingness to engage with the work of other historians, and his comparisons with the slave societies in America and the West Indies, will lead to a richer, more cumulative and less parochial historiography.

I also owe a debt of thanks to many colleagues who have assisted in the best traditions of the academic community. Martin Krygier now knows more about Australian history than he ever wanted to know – his ideas, support, friendship and encouragement throughout have been much appreciated. I have also enjoyed and benefited enormously from long discussions with David Philips about the English criminal law and the recent literature about it. David Lieberman introduced me to some excellent work on eighteenth-century English legal and political thought, and Sandy Blair provided perceptive criticisms from her detailed knowledge of the historical literature on New South Wales. Alan Atkinson, David Brown, Martin Chanock, Barrie Dyster, Mark Finnane, Michael Hammond, Peter Fitzpatrick, Michael Sturma, Ian Tyrell and Richard Wasserstrom read and commented on drafts of various chapters. Montserrat Gorina, Reg Graycar, Owen Jessep and Mariana Olubas helped with the proof-reading. The annual Law in History Conferences, organised at La Trobe University by Ian Duncanson and Chris Tomlins, have provided a valuable forum in which to try out some of my ideas. Elaine Jackson, Penny Campion, Barbara Hook, Elizabeth Thomson and Mark Polden worked for me as research assistants at different times; I have benefited greatly from their work and interest. The burden of the typing and my deadlines has fallen on Mary Johnson, Bernadette Dattatreyan, Julie Freeman and Margo Martinez. I thank them especially for their cheerful tolerance and assistance. I also gratefully acknowledge my institutional support: the Law Faculty of the University of New South Wales, Sydney, Australia, and the Jurisprudence and Social Policy Program at the University of California, Berkeley, USA, and the Beckwith Foundation. Permission to quote from the Catton Papers was granted by Mr D. Neilson.

This book began life as a doctoral thesis. Very special thanks to the chair of my thesis committee, Sheldon L. Messinger. As a supervisor he has given me a standard which I can only hope to maintain for my own students. His suggestion that I should read Hay and Thompson set me off along the road to this book. That suggestion cost him long hours of reading drafts and discussing them. I cannot imagine a better supervisor. Philip Selznick agreed to serve on my thesis committee when he was about to retire and could have called all his time his own. He makes his students reach for the deeper understandings and I consider it a privilege to have worked under him. Tom Laqueur also served on the thesis committee. His diverse interests and perspectives have made this a much broader and more creative work than it would otherwise have been.

My deep personal thanks go to my parents, whose concern for education led them to make great sacrifices on behalf of their children. Finally, my deepest debt is to my wife, Kin Tow. This work has imposed an enormous strain on her but her faith in the project and in me was sustaining. I thank her for her love and support. Now it's her turn.

David Neal

CHAPTER 1
Great Changes

In 1786 Susannah Holmes gave birth to a son in Norwich Castle Jail. Both the child's parents had been sentenced to death. Susannah had been in the jail since 1783, convicted of breaking into the house of Jabez Taylor and stealing 'one pair of linen sheets value 10 shillings, one linen gown value 5 shillings, one linen shift value 2 shillings, four yards of Irish linen cloth value 6 shillings, three linen handkerchiefs value 3 shillings, one silk handkerchief value 2 shillings, three muslin neckcloths value 18 pence, two black silk cloaks value 10 shillings, two silver tablespoons value 12 shillings, two silver teaspoons value 2 shillings, goods of said Jabez'. The law prescribed the death penalty for burglary and the Norfolk assize judge, Mr Justice Nares, put on his black cap and sentenced Susannah to death.

It must have been awesome to stand in court as a defendant and have the death sentence imposed. But Susannah probably knew that she would be included in the judge's list of those who would be recommended for reprieve. After the court room rituals had been completed, the judge stayed the punishment and wrote the standard letter. '. . . [S]ome favourable circumstances appearing on her behalf . . .', the judge wrote to the king, '[I] humbly recommend her to Your Majesty, as a proper object of Your Majesty's Royal Mercy upon the several conditions following . . . being transported as soon as conveniently may be to some of Your Majesty's Colonies or Plantations in America for the term of Fourteen Years'. Susannah had been fortunate enough to have her name included in the judge's letter along with one other woman and nineteen men who had been convicted of capital offences on the Norfolk Circuit in March 1784. Those whose names were not included in this deathly form letter might use whatever patronage connections they had to approach the king. Friends and neighbours petitioned on behalf of Thomas Dunn, for example, convicted of stealing two fat sheep from his employers. But when the king asked the trial judge whether Thomas might be deserving, the judge replied that his character and position of trust aggravated rather than mitigated his crime. His Majesty was 'graciously pleased to extend his Royal Mercy' to Susannah. Death waited for those, like Thomas Dunn, whose names did not move the monarch to suspend the seemingly inexorable processes of the law.[1]

Susannah was 19 at the time of her crime in 1783. The baby's teenage father, Henry Kable, had also been convicted of housebreaking. Early in 1783, Henry, Henry senior (the child's grandfather), and a friend, Abraham Carman, had stolen goods from a Norfolk country house. They were all convicted and sentenced to death. The trial judge, Baron Eyre, wrote the standard letter seeking the King's mercy on behalf of young Henry and fourteen others convicted at those Norfolk Lent Assizes in 1783. The names of Henry's father and their friend did not appear on the letter. Nor do they seem to have had people who could or would petition the King on their behalf. They were hanged outside the jail, just near the market place, on Saturday, 5 April 1783. Perhaps Henry's youth – he was 17 at the time of his crime – had engaged Baron Eyre's sympathy; perhaps the older men had prior convictions. The letter did not say why some would live and others would die. Henry Kable, the younger, had his sentence commuted to transportation to America for seven years.[2] But the American War meant that transportation to America was no longer possible. So Henry was returned to the Norwich Jail where he had been held since his arrest.

Norwich Castle Jail was a makeshift affair, like many other jails in eighteenth-century England. These were not the high security, single-cell prisons of the nineteenth and twentieth centuries. There was a great deal more coming and going both between the prisoners within the jail and between the jail and the outside world. In the eighteenth-century jails, prisoners often relied on family and friends to supplement their rations. The mediaeval castle at Norwich had been converted into a jail with rough shelters built up against the castle walls for some of the inmates. The jail was crowded too and food was in short supply. The local residents of Norwich took pity on the prisoners that winter and sent in special food for the festive season. But the numbers of people building up in their local jail since the war had ended transportation to America worried the good citizens of Norwich and they petitioned the government to do something about it.[3]

In the midst of all their troubles – their trials, the convictions, having the death sentence imposed, their reprieves, the execution of Henry's father and the pitiless conditions of Norwich Jail – Henry and Susannah met. Maybe they had known each other before. Maybe love blossomed in their bleak circumstances. Maybe they provided each other with solace in a fearful time. Whatever the case, they formed a relationship and Susannah gave birth to Henry's child in the jail in 1786. They applied for permission to marry but this was refused.

In that year, a fleet of ships was being prepared to transport 750 convicts to a place called Botany Bay. Cook had landed there sixteen years earlier and explored the east coast. Now the British government planned to establish a colony there. Prisoners were being mustered from the overcrowded jails into old ships moored in ports around England. When it was discovered that there were insufficient women prisoners for the fleet, the order came from London to transfer the female convicts at Norwich Jail to the hulks at Plymouth. From there they would be loaded onto the ships bound for Botany Bay. Susannah Holmes was one of these women.[4] Henry Kable's distressed pleas to be allowed to marry Susannah and accompany her to New South Wales fell on deaf ears.

Worse was to come. When Susannah and her breast-fed child were delivered to the hulk *Dunkirk* at Plymouth on 5 November 1786, the captain refused to accept the child on the ground that he had no lawful authority to do so. To his eternal credit, the prison turnkey, Mr Simpson, who had ferried Susannah out to the hulk took the baby into his care. More than that, he decided to take matters into his own hands. With the infant on his lap, he travelled to London to confront Lord Sydney, the Home Secretary. Undeterred by the refusals of a personal interview from Lord Sydney's staff, he decided to wait at the house until his Lordship did appear. When a no doubt surprised Lord Sydney descended the stairs, Simpson seized his opportunity and persuaded him to order that mother and child be reunited. Nothing daunted, Simpson also secured permission from Lord Sydney for Henry to be allowed to marry Susannah and accompany her and the child to New South Wales. Simpson took the news back to Henry at Norwich and then escorted him to the ship at Plymouth where, according to the captain's report, the family was reunited after 10 days separation. The captain recorded the joyful reunion sourly:

> Plymouth Dock Nov 16 1786
> Sir, I beg leave to acquaint you that I yesterday afternoon received on board His Majesty's Ship Dunkirk (in obedience to Lord Sydney's commands) a Male child, said to be the son of Susannah Holmes, a woman under my Custody, and at the same time Henry Cabel, a convict from the Gaol at Norwich was delivered to me.
> I am very respectfully Sir Your Most Obedient and Most humble Servant
> Henry Bradley

Simpson's mercy dash, a round trip of some seven hundred miles by coach, and the story of the Kables attracted the attention of the press. The *Norfolk Chronicle* was pleased to report that 'the laws of England, which are distinguished by the spirit of humanity which framed them, forbid so cruel an act as that of separating an infant from its mother's breast. . . . it cannot be but a pleasing circumstance to every Englishman to know, that, though from the very nature of the situation of public Ministers, they must, on most occasions, be difficult of access, . . . when the object is humanity, and delay would materially affect the happiness of even the meanest subject in the kingdom, the Minister himself not only attends to complaints properly addressed, but promptly and effectually affords relief'. The London newspapers were equally fascinated by the story of 'John Simpson, the humane turnkey'. It attracted the attention of Lady Cadogan who organised a public subscription which yielded the substantial sum of twenty pounds – about twice the annual salary of a labourer at that time, and four times the value of the goods Susannah had stolen – enough money to buy clothes and other items for their new life in New South Wales. Their parcel was loaded onto one of the transport ships, the *Alexander*, before they set sail in 1787.[5]

The convict ships arrived in Sydney harbour in January 1788; the voyage took eight months. They went ashore in row boats. There was no dock. There were no buildings either so they lived in tents. But the absence of buildings was not going to delay the landing of British institutions, marriage and the Anglican church among them. Along with several other couples, Henry and Susannah were married that February by the Anglican chaplain, in one of the first weddings in the new settlement. But the parcel sent to assist them in beginning their new lives was missing.

On the first of July 1788, a writ in the names of Henry and Susannah Kable was issued from the new Court of Civil Jurisdiction in New South Wales (see illustration p.26). The writ recited that the parcel loaded onto the *Alexander* had not been delivered to the Kables in Sydney despite many requests, and sought delivery of the parcel, or its value. It named the ship's captain, Duncan Sinclair, as defendant. The court, consisting of Judge-Advocate David Collins and two civilians, issued a warrant to the provost marshall ordering him to bring the captain before the court the next day to answer the complaint against him.

On the day of the hearing the court received evidence that the parcel had been loaded on the ship but – with the exception of some books which probably neither Henry nor Susannah could read – the contents of the parcel could not be found. Henry Kable swore that the missing goods were worth fifteen pounds. The court found for the plaintiff and entered a verdict for that amount.

This was the first civil case ever held in Australia. It is extraordinary in many ways. In the first place the whole story of the Kables is extraordinary. Their conditions of imprisonment at Norwich jail allowed the opportunity to conceive the child. The intervention of Simpson, his ability to gain access to the relevant minister, and the fact that the plight of Susannah, Henry and the baby could move the minister in an age usually noted for great social distances and lack of sympathy for criminals is also extraordinary. Some were not so fortunate. In 1819, Bennett described the case of a woman whose baby was ripped from her breast at the hulk.[6] The fact that the case of Susannah and Henry Kable was taken up in the press and moved people to contribute to a public subscription also speaks of a sympathy not usually associated with the eighteenth-century English views on crime and the dangerous classes. The fact that they went out to Botany Bay together and were allowed to marry also runs counter to stereotyped views about the treatment of convicts. It was not unusual for convicts to be accompanied by their spouses, though usually the spouse was free. Their subsequent history is also quite extraordinary. A couple of years later, Henry became a constable of police, and later chief constable in the new colony and was involved on the prosecution side in criminal cases. After a stint in the police, he moved on to even better things as a merchant and ship owner. Like others in the colony, and perhaps because of his early success, Henry used the courts to ruin his opponents. He seems to have prospered; in 1808 shipping records show Kable and two partners as principal ship owners in the expanding commerce of the colony. The partnership dissolved in some bitterness shortly afterwards but not before Henry had managed to divest himself of a good deal of his property in order to avoid the consequences of any court order.[7]

Legally, the Kables' case is quite extraordinary too. In the place where a writ would usually describe the plaintiffs' occupation, the words, 'New Settlers of this place', have been crossed out and nothing has been substituted. To have described them as convicts would have been fatal to their case. Felons were regarded as if they had already been executed in English law and therefore unable to sue. The fact that Henry and Susannah were convicts and the legal consequences of that fact must have been obvious to some of those concerned; maybe the description 'New Settlers' was too close to a fabrication, and hence this part of the writ was altered in order to maintain a discreet silence.[8]

Whatever the reason, the omission allowed the case to proceed and the governor gave the orders for the royal letters patent which constituted the new court to be read, convening the court for the first time. Thus, the first sitting of a civil court in Australia and the first civil case to be heard, occurred at the behest of two convicts under sentence. Moreover, it named an important figure in the colony, a ship's captain, as defendant, subjected him to the power of the court's jurisdiction and officers, and made an order against him. It vindicated the property rights of two convicts and publicly demonstrated the ability even of convicts to invoke the legal process in the new colony. Nor was it to be the last time that convicts used the legal system to assert their rights in the colony, despite English law which regarded felons and former felons as civilly dead (i.e., unable to sue, unable to be a witness, to hold property, make contracts, etc.) or, as Blackstone graphically puts it, 'no longer fit to live upon the earth, . . . to be exterminated as monster and a bane to society, . . . by an anticipation of his punishment, he is already dead in law.'[9] For the situation to have been otherwise in a colony overwhelmingly composed of convicts and former convicts would have created enormous difficulties in the conduct of the colony's commercial and legal affairs. Indeed when this spectre was malevolently raised thirty years later by a legally qualified judge who was prepared to break the tacit colonial amendment of the laws relating to attainder, as it was known, the colony was thrown into uproar.[10] By that point, former convicts, including Henry Kable, dominated the mercantile class in Sydney, and held more property than the free settlers. The prospect that they might not be able to rely on the legal system to support their property rights or use the courts to enforce their contracts, rights assumed since the Kables' case in 1788, shook the foundations of the colony's legal, commercial and social order.[11]

Henry and Susannah Kable might easily have become Americans. As we have seen, their reprieves specified that they be transported to America. But the great events of the American Revolution meant that England had not been able to send convicts to the American colonies for some years. John Howard's 1777 report on the overcrowding and appalling conditions in English prisons increased the pressure on the government to find an alternative to places like Norwich jail. The residents of Norwich were by no means the only ones to petition the government about overcrowded jails.[12]

As Home Secretary, Lord Sydney had responsibility for law and order, which included prisons. It was an important responsibility but by no means his only duty. The Home Office still administered most domestic issues at the end of the eighteenth century, while the other great department of government, the War Office, conducted foreign affairs.[13] However, in the early 1780s, the state of prisons was becoming a critical issue. A flood of petitions urged the Home Secretary to take action to relieve the pressure on the jails and bridewells now filled to overflowing with long-term prisoners whose death sentences had been reduced to terms of transportation. England's eighteenth-century prison establishment traditionally only catered for prisoners awaiting trial and those sentenced to short-term imprisonment. Corporal punishments – hanging, flogging, branding, the stocks, the pillory, etc. – had formed the central core of the penal system up to and including the eighteenth century, supplemented by short-term imprisonment, transportation and extensive use of the prerogative of mercy.[14]

After the loss of the American colonies, the government had adopted the temporary expedient of contracting with private operators to 'warehouse' convicts in old ships ('the hulks') moored at various ports around the English Coast. Susannah Holmes was taken to one of these hulks at Plymouth. However, by the mid-1780s the capacity of the hulks had also been exceeded and hundreds of humble petitioners from all over England voiced their fears that the jails would burst asunder and spread the convict contagion throughout 'England's green and pleasant land'. The horror of the meeting between young Pip and the convict who had escaped from the hulks in Charles Dickens' *Great Expectations* conveys something of the fears and urgency of the petitions concerning prison overcrowding. The

Sheriff of Norfolk and the Grand Jury sitting at Norwich Castle in 1786 petitioned the king about the 40 prisoners held in the Castle:

> ... your petitioners are well informed and have every reason to believe and fear that the Confinement of so large a Number of Prisoners in the said Gaol may prove extremely dangerous as well because the size and strength of the Gaol are not adapted to their Reception, as also because the present season of the year is likely to produce Infectious Diseases amongst them, and the Apprehensions of your Petitioners are more particularly excited by these Circumstances, because they are credibly informed that Attempts have already been made for the Escape or Rescue of some of the Prisoners notwithstanding additional guards have been lately added, and because one or two of the Prisoners are now ill of the fever.[15]

Despite a lobby to build new-style penitentiaries in England, Pitt's government judged that transportation to a new colony would be a more effective, speedy and economical solution to the convict problem. Trade and naval strategy influenced the eventual decision to found the colony in the Antipodes, but penal purposes provided, and continued to provide over the next fifty years the predominant rationale for the British settlement of New South Wales.

And it was a big decision for the British government. By comparison with transportation to America, the new penal colony was a huge undertaking. Under the system used for transportation to America, the government simply contracted with private shippers who took over responsibility for the convicts and, on arrival, assigned them for the period of their sentence to settlers in already-established and financially independent colonies.[16] By contrast, the plan for New South Wales called for the British government to undertake direct responsibility not only to mount the expedition, but also to establish and maintain the colony itself. In an age of ultra-small government, this meant that the Home Office, with a staff of thirteen for *all* its business, had to decide which convicts to transport, muster them into the hulks from the haphazardly-organised, locally-administered jails, co-ordinate with other departments to mount the fleet of ships (e.g. the Admiralty for the transport ships and escorts, the Treasury to pay for provisions, fitting out, etc.), make the necessary legal arrangements for establishment and administration of the colony, find and appoint civil officials to run it, and so on through a thousand and one details necessary to establish a settlement on the other side of the world.[17]

This minimalist approach to government also had a bearing on the internal dynamics of development in New South Wales. Only nine government functionaries accompanied Governor Phillip to assist in administration in New South Wales. The government also sent a company of 212 marines as a garrison to defend the colony against threats from the French, the Aborigines, or both. According to an English tradition of separating military and civil affairs, the marines expected not to be involved in day-to-day administration. Whether this was intended for New South Wales or not, the marines made it clear from the outset that they would not stoop to the policing and superintendence of convicts.[18] This, coupled with the absence of free settlers, meant that from first settlement in 1788, and for many years afterwards, many public tasks in New South Wales had to be performed by the convicts themselves, people like Henry, Susannah and the 757 other convicts who accompanied them on the First Fleet. This is how Henry found himself appointed constable in 1789 and then chief constable for the town of Sydney in 1794. As we will see in chapter 6, convicts, ticket-of-leave holders and former convicts made up a large part of police numbers throughout the transportation period. By necessity, these people performed a variety of tasks as minor government functionaries, and where there was no free person with the requisite skills, they performed more important functions too. In the early days, convict attorneys were much in demand with the government and free people; Sydney's finest public buildings from the early period were designed by a convict architect, Francis Greenway. This situation continued throughout most of the convict period.

So what sort of place was New South Wales?

The best description is that it was a penal colony at the start and, little by little, it came to be a free society by the end of the transportation period. I say why I think those are the correct characterisations in chapter 2. Why did it change? Obviously for a lot of different reasons. But *not* because the British government planned it that way. Many of the changes came about despite rather than because of the British government. This applied, for example, in the sphere of commercial development. Trade in the Pacific was dominated by the East India Company's monopoly; Sydney's merchant traders battled stubbornly to maintain their operations in the face of English legislation and opposition from the Company.[19] Political and legal reforms came at the cost of long campaigns, mainly fought by people who started off with multiple disadvantages: they were arguing for the political liberties of ex-convicts, within a colony which London saw primarily as a place for dumping convicts, and at a time when most British people could not vote.

A number of factors affected the British government's receptivity to proposals for change from the colony. In the first place, the French and American Revolutions had confirmed Tory opinion about the dangers of democracy. The penal colonies were the first example of colonies founded without representative institutions.[20] These factors worked against New South Wales. Denial of trial by jury and local legislative councils came about in part because of the potential of these institutions to provide sites of opposition to imperial policy, as they had in America and the West Indies.[21] But the loss of the American colonies reconciled England to the practical limits on its power to rule distant colonies. British governments determined to avoid the pitfalls of the American situation. The expense and difficulties of conducting the war across the Atlantic against the Americans had been forcibly drawn to the attention of the government by critics of the New South Wales plan, among them Jeremy Bentham.[22] Political actors in New South Wales were prepared to threaten a Botany Bay tea party against British governments which, while prepared to delay, ultimately were not prepared to refuse change outright.[23] While some in the colony were frustrated by what they saw as long delays in the granting of free institutions, they were granted at a time when the majority of the population was still convict or ex-convict. Indeed, given New South Wales' character as a penal colony – even without the other factors mentioned – the transition to a free society in fifty years can be seen as a remarkably speedy one.

A second important change in English thinking flowed from America, and was bolstered by the French Revolution. Both revolutions carried with them ringing declarations of the universal rights of man. The egalitarian, democratic ideas associated with these declarations put great pressure on English ideas of civic competence based on the ownership of wealth, preferably landed wealth.[24] The right of men to vote or stand for Parliament was tied to the ownership of property not to the fact of adult personhood. Once again, for New South Wales this was a double-edged sword, but one which in the end operated in favour of the liberal cause. Ironically, many of the emancipated convicts were wealthy and would have satisfied a property qualification. But they hitched their cause to the fundamental rights of individuals, rights which revived after the civil death of convicthood. To eighteenth-century English eyes, especially those of a Tory hue, the democratic republican ideas of the two great eighteenth-century revolutions were anathema. Emancipists and liberals in the colony were accused of being covert Yankee sympathisers. Democratic ideas and abolition of social distinctions were associated with subversion of the natural order based on rank and wealth. Edmund Burke, for example, firmly associated universalist declarations of rights with the Terror in France; Jacobin sympathisers, trade union and radical political associations in Britain met a barrage of repressive laws and practices.

The French Revolution certainly struck terror into the hearts of England's ruling class. There were riots and spies about looking for Jacobins. Some of those caught up in the repression that followed were transported to New South Wales. Four Scottish Jacobins associated with the London Corresponding Society – the Scottish martyrs – were transported to New South Wales in 1794. Fears that they would introduce their radical creed there and join forces with the rebellious Irish convicts caused tension in the colony. Ownership of a copy of Tom Paine's *The Rights of Man* was grounds for suspicion and persecution by members of the garrison.[25] The Scottish martyr, Maurice Margarot, and the Irish rebel leader, Joseph Holt, although allowed leniency in their association, were suspected by the governor of hatching plots against his government. As we shall see, however, universalist declarations and revolution did not prove to be the strategy in New South Wales.

Despite the repression, the ideas of the French and American Revolutions were beginning to percolate into English politics. The first, and for the purposes of this story, most important manifestation of these ideas in England was the anti-slavery movement. The arguments against slavery depended heavily on universalist arguments about the rights of man.[26] In January 1788, English anti-slavery lobbyists had 100 petitions before Parliament and, though baulked on this occasion by the French Revolution, they had sufficient influence to have legislation passed banning the slave trade in 1806. From then on, slave societies in the Americas and the West Indies would have to replace their slaves by reproduction. This popular opposition to the slave trade, coinciding with the United States Declaration of Independence, the French Revolution and the settlement of Botany Bay, formed just the first stage of the anti-slavery campaign.[27] In the succeeding fifty years anti-slavery campaigners battled British planter interests over the abolition of slavery in British colonies, especially in the West Indies. Drawing on the rhetoric of freedom and the rights of man, evangelicals like Wilberforce ran a political campaign that produced thousands of tracts, enormous public meetings and hundreds of petitions. Petitions against slavery in the 1830s attracted more signatures than even the widely-supported Chartist petitions in favour of the rights of English workers![28] Legislation for the abolition of slavery in the West Indies eventually came in 1832, pre-dating the decision to end transportation to New South Wales by only a few years. Anti-transportation campaigners drew the analogy between slaves and convicts assigned to private masters in New South Wales, tapping the fund of values and arguments which had developed around slavery. Changing ideas about punishment and especially the move towards penitentiary-style imprisonment – ideas propounded by those same anti–slavery, anti-transportation campaigners – intersected with the other arguments against transportation.

The combination of egalitarian political ideas and their embodiment in the anti-slavery movement changed the terms of political argument in England. Old measures of civic competence – the property qualification both for the right to vote and to sit in parliament – were challenged. In England – where social and economic mobility were relatively limited and wealth could conveniently be equated to virtue – the changes were slower in coming. But in New South Wales with its large number of wealthy former convicts, questions of merit were much more difficult. While the Emancipists – ex-convicts and their sympathisers – argued for the traditional measure of civic competence – wealth – their conservative opponents, the Exclusives, strived to develop counterarguments for the political disqualification of former convicts based on their prior convictions. But the English political climate of the 1830s – the era of the new industrialism, the first *Reform Act*, the ascendancy of Whig governments, reform of the criminal law and the abolition of slavery – was not conducive to arguments proposing new forms of political disenfranchisement.

The fifty years between the founding of New South Wales and the end of transportation also saw radical changes in English thinking about crime and punishment. These too had profound effects on New South Wales. The principal weapon in the eighteenth-century criminal law was the death penalty, or at least the threat of it. Some 200 offences carried the death penalty. As we have seen in Norfolk, for the unlucky few the capital sentence was carried into effect. In rural areas of England it was the climax of the elaborate assize court rituals.[29] In London, court proceedings were much more mundane, though executions were public spectacles.[30] For the majority of capital offenders, however, the royal prerogative of mercy and the *Transportation Acts* gave the option of punishments short of death.

Exemplary capital punishment stood at the centre of eighteenth-century English penal policy. The government could not execute everyone convicted of a capital offence: that would have led to a slaughter. But suitable alternatives were hard to find. From 1715, transportation to America provided the alternative for some but many were still released after some form of corporal punishment. Prisons primarily served as places for holding those awaiting trial, debtors and some short-term prisoners. Imprisonment – the principal element in the penal thinking of the nineteenth and twentieth centuries – played only a minor part in the eighteenth. Penal policy depended on the awful spectacle of the gallows to deter rogues from crime.[31]

However, by the middle of the eighteenth century this policy was coming under attack. The Italian criminologist, Cesare Beccaria, argued for a more rational policy of deterrence based on certainty of apprehension, conviction and punishment. Moreover, the punishment should be tailored the seriousness of the crime rather than the one punishment – death – for all serious crimes, a punishment which everyone knew would not be carried into effect on the majority of occasions. Beccaria's theory gained currency in England through the publication of Blackstone's *Commentaries* in the 1760s. Later in the century, Bentham's campaign for penitentiary-style imprisonment would provide a punishment mechanism by which some of these ideas could be put into effect and elaborated.[32]

The English criminal justice system breached Beccarian principles in two important ways. In the first place, the absence of professional police forces meant that apprehension was very uncertain. The system of local constables supervised by amateur gentlemen justices of the peace did not produce the degree of certainty envisaged in the Beccarian scheme. Despite serious concern about crime and public disorder, the English ruling gentry strongly resisted attempts to establish professional police forces. For Members of Parliament, paid police forces conjured up folk memories of Cromwell's standing army and the French spy system, both much detested as threats to English liberty. Moreover, the arguments carried an implied criticism of the justices of the peace, themselves often members of the very parliament asked to establish police forces.[33] These attitudes about justices of the peace and police flowed through to the colony, as will be seen in chapters 5 and 6.

Uncertainty of apprehension was matched by uncertainty of punishment. Because it was so draconian, the argument ran, the death penalty could be used only sparingly even against those criminals who happened to be apprehended. The examples we have already encountered from the Norfolk circuit confirm this. Although burglars and sheep stealers were liable to be hanged, robbery and burglary would usually earn the culprit fourteen years transportation, while theft of goods or animals was a seven-year offence. Our friend

Henry was lucky to get only seven years for his burglary; Susannah's sentence of fourteen years was more usual and Henry's father and their friend went to the gallows. Bentham's penitentiary offered a system where the punishment could be better measured to fit the crime and would be carried out in every case.

Yet, the arguments for penitentiaries also encountered a great deal of resistance. Expense played a big part in the argument. However, as Bentham was quick to point out, transportation to Botany Bay proved to be very expensive too. But opposition to the impersonal precision of the penitentiary system lay deep within a system of paternalistic power which depended on discretions and patronage to adjust delicate local problems and regulate the relationships between central government and the local gentry. England's rulers preferred a system of terror and discretion which they controlled at many points to one based on impersonal certainty. The ability to manipulate the ideology, instruments and symbols of the criminal law put a powerful rhetorical device in the hands of the gentry, a device which they understood and used to maintain and enhance their political authority. Certainty strained too hard against the intuitions of paternalism.[34]

Transportation to New South Wales, however, was on the cusp between the old and the new penal systems. From the outset, it served as the butt of Jeremy Bentham's campaign to establish the penitentiary as the main form of criminal punishment. The distance, discretion and arbitrariness involved in the transportation system offended almost every Benthamite principle. However, the old ideas were a long time dying. England did not establish its first modern police force until the late 1820s, about the same time as Bentham's disciples in government began to abolish the death penalty for a long list of offences. The penitentiary would become the principal instrument for criminal punishment but the real developments took place in the 1830s. These changes in the criminal justice system had profound effects on New South Wales. They led to the termination of its penal phase and cleared the way for political institutions consistent with its emerging status as a free society.

We have been discussing the English background to events in New South Wales. They form a crucial context for the development of the colony but they do not constitute the primary focus of this work. The punishment of convicts dominated England's purposes for the colony. But events in New South Wales forced an alteration. The dynamics of that change occupy centre stage in this story. The possibilities and pace of change were affected by the great events of the times. But the initiatives for the changes in the status of New South Wales came from the colony itself.

Within the colony several major forces for change were at work, and they were linked. One of them was simply the growth and changing composition of the population. Throughout the period England transported 80,000 convicts to New South Wales. More convicts arrived there in the last decade of transportation than in any other. The percentage of the European population which was convict ranged from 74 per cent in the first decade, dipping to 36 per cent in 1804, to 45 per cent in 1820, to 30 per cent in 1840 at the end of transportation, a rough working average of 40 per cent. If convicts, emancipists and their children are taken together, they made up 87 per cent of the population in 1828 and 63 per cent in 1841.

The overall population of the colony remained quite small for the first few decades. The original 1,000 grew to 11,000 by 1810 and doubled to reach 23,000 in 1820. Very few free people felt inclined to launch themselves on a 12,000-mile journey to the edge of the eighteenth-century world, there to share their lives with convicts and, probably, never see England again. But there were free people in New South Wales. Children of convicts, unlike the children of slaves, were born free in the colony. Henry and Susannah Kable's son, Henry, was one of them; so were their ten colonial-born children. The wives of the governors, government officials, the military and, sometimes, of the convicts, also came to the colony. As sentences expired, emancipated convicts mostly stayed in the colony and added to the numbers of the free. Once in the colony, some of the soldiers saw economic opportunities and decided to stay and settle on the land granted them. But only a few people went to New South Wales for the purpose of settling there before 1820.

By 1820, as the population grew and stories of the fortunes that had been made there started to filter back to Britain, free settlers began to emigrate but they were still vastly outnumbered. Free emigration to the colony became more significant in the 1830s but the greatly increased number of unfree settlers transported in that decade more than matched this increase. In the 1830s, Britain transported 34,000 convicts to a colony that numbered 46,000 people at the beginning of the decade and 129,000 at the end.[35]

The second force for change was economic. The development of agriculture and trading prompted colonists to assert their economic, political and social interests against England's interest in running a penal colony. As recent historians of early New South Wales have pointed out, the tension between economic and penal interests resulted in the colonists laying England's interests to one side. While England tried more than once to restore conditions more consistent with punishment of offenders, the masters of assigned convicts were more interested in getting the best out of their workers even if that meant defying the regulations by granting indulgences.[36]

Distance between New South Wales and England also served as a force for change. It took Henry and Susannah Kable eight months sailing to reach their destination 12,000 miles away. Improvements in ships and navigation cut this time down by two or three months during the convict period. It took a similar time to sail back. Where a governor's instructions were unclear or the vagaries of running a penal colony called for quick responses, those on the spot had to make immediate decisions. This conferred a great deal of practical autonomy on the governor. Governor Bligh, true to his *Bounty* image, overstated the case when pricked: 'Damn the Secretary of State! He commands at home, I command here!' But there was more than a grain of truth in what he said.[37] When a governor wanted directions from London, sailing time alone took twelve to eighteen months, assuming ships arrived and departed on demand, which, of course, they did not. Time was needed in England to consider the problem and formulate a response. To give but one example, when the newly-arrived judge of the New South Wales Court, Jeffery Bent, refused to open the Supreme Court because of his opposition to emancipist attorneys, the court stayed closed for two and a half years. In many other instances a practical expedient was adopted: when English instructions arrived they had often been overtaken by events. This heightened the strategic importance of local political institutions – including the courts – in resolving issues without resort to England, or framing them for presentation to the metropolitan power.

The emancipation of convicts provided the other major force for change. The unusual state of society in New South Wales meant that for a long time the relationship between free and freed settlers was uncertain. On the one hand, governors like Bligh and Macquarie saw the colony as a place primarily for convicts and emancipists. On the other, free settlers chafed at the restrictions placed on them because of the penal purposes of the colony. A new social hierarchy had to be hammered out. But what caste does a society assign to the majority of its population who are ex-convicts and their families? How does an eighteenth-century officer and gentleman behave towards his fellow officer's convict mistress? Who was a fit person to hold the public offices in the new settlement? Would emancipated convicts be entitled to own land, make contracts and enforce them in the courts? Would the colony have the hallowed form of trial by jury; if so, who would serve on those juries? Would the colony have political institutions and, if so, who would be entitled to participate in them? Would the English class system be recreated in New South Wales or would the winds of equality blow those distinctions before them? The unique nature of New South Wales as a penal colony made these questions – questions faced to some extent by all new societies – all the more difficult. As one settler wrote in 1839, 'Every man does not know his own position so well as at home.'[38] And by what mechanisms would these difficult problems be resolved?

People in the colony divided into three groups. For one of them – the Aborigines – the white invasion brought revolutionary change. The Aboriginal inhabitants occupied an ambiguous position in the new white polity. Colonisation proceeded on a legal myth: that New South Wales was *terra nullius*, a land that no one owned, either because no one lived there or those who did were uncivilised. The governors were instructed to conciliate and protect the Aboriginal natives. But that did not extend to recognition of their right to the land they lived in. On the one hand, the Aborigines were entitled to the protections of the legal system; on the other, because they did not believe in God, they could not take the oath and give evidence in court, thus rendering a fairly marginal protection even less effective. The truth of it is that for the first fifty years the colonial legal system had trouble deciding whether the Aborigines should be treated as subjects of the Crown or foreign enemies who could be hunted down in reprisal raids and shot. The New South Wales Solicitor-General in the 1820s, Saxe-Bannister, proposed a truly legalistic solution to this problem. Governor Darling should halt the military raiding parties in the Hunter Valley until martial law could be declared. Then he, Saxe-Bannister would lead the troops![39] As late as 1836, counsel for an Aboriginal defendant – charged with the murder of another Aborigine – argued that Aborigines did not come under the jurisdiction of the white laws and that New South Wales was not a settled colony. The judge rejected the submission but, significantly, it had taken forty-eight years to determine the issue authoritatively.[40] For the white settlers, the Aborigines occupied a status appropriate to the English legal designation of the colony, *terra nullius*, a no-man's land. While the governors were instructed to conciliate and protect them, the Aborigines were mentally and often geographically peripheral to white purposes for the colony. The one thing that was clear about their position was that the whites wanted their land. When they resisted they were met with force. While the rule of law proved an effective instrument for groups and individuals within white society, for the Aborigines the protections it promised came to little. More than this, the law played a major ideological role in the expropriation of the original owners.[41]

Two major political groups emerged from the ranks of the colonisers: Exclusives and Emancipists. The main line of cleavage was a criminal conviction. Those who came to the colony free, especially the wealthy ones, distinguished themselves sharply as 'respectable'. The nucleus of this group was formed by John Macarthur and former officers from the New South Wales Corps. Its numbers were swelled by the arrival of new wealthy free settlers, officers of the military garrisons sent out to the colony and colonial officials. Variously referred to as the Exclusives, the Settlers, the Emigrants and the Pure Merinos, the unifying feature of this group was its determination to exclude those with the convict taint from positions of status and power. This taint extended to convicts, emancipists and their children.[42] The ranks were not rock solid. Henry Kable, for example, allied himself with Macarthur in the Rum Rebellion. As wealthy traders, they both had strong economic reasons to dispose of Governor Bligh. Two of Henry and Susannah's daughters married men from the Exclusive group. The great wealth of some emancipists could confuse social boundaries, especially if business called. Opposition to Whig and radical views also provided common ground. Many commentators, however, testified to the entrenched nature of the factions, and the fervour with which they practised their opposition. As free settlers came in larger numbers in the 1830s, and with the end of transportation, the old groupings began to fall apart and be replaced by more traditional factors, such as wealth. Post-transportation, the Emancipist leader Wentworth found he had more in common with other wealthy landowners; the Exclusive leader, James Macarthur no longer feared an Emancipist ascendancy.[43]

The other group, the Emancipists, did not in fact restrict itself to former convicts. In order to reflect this point, I have capitalised the 'e' in emancipist to indicate a reference to the political group which included non-convicts; the lower case 'e' is used for references to people who were former convicts. The early seeds of the Emancipist group can be traced to resentment among the less wealthy free settlers of the treatment meted out to them by the rum traders in the New South Wales Corps, the officers' abuse of their position on the bench in the colonial courts, and the degree of influence they exercised in England.[44] Opposition to the Exclusives united these people with the ever-growing group of emancipated convicts, some of whom quickly became very wealthy. Emancipists dominated the colony's commerce due to the ironic fact that, as gentlemen, the officers could not be seen to engage in trade. In the early 1820s, the Emancipists – whose leadership included three lawyers, two free and one an ex-convict, W. C. Wentworth, Robert Wardell and Edward Eagar – began a campaign to expand the colony's political and legal institutions to make them more consistent with their 'British birthrights'. Trial by jury and representative councils were their primary objectives. But it was the more radical plank of the platform – the insistence that former convicts who satisfied the general property qualification would be eligible to participate equally in these bodies – which formed the heart of the conflict with the Exclusives.

Aside from the free settlers who had suffered at the hands of the Exclusives, the Emancipists had some powerful sympathisers: governors like Macquarie and Bourke, some government officials and those of a liberal, Whig or radical viewpoint, like the wealthy knight, Sir John Jamison and E.S. Hall, the editor of the third newspaper, the *Monitor*. The Emancipists campaigned vehemently through the 1820s and 1830s in the colony and in England to secure their share of political power in the colony. As the Emancipist group grew in numbers and wealth, and the prospect of a new constitution drew nearer, conflict between the Emancipists and the Exclusives sharpened. Emancipists sought equality in all spheres, especially legal and political equality. Their opponents, the Exclusives, tried to impose an hereditary, inferior status.

New South Wales was a prickly society. Necessity forced everyone – bond, freed and free – to mix closely in daily life. Equality was foreign to men such as the Exclusives, whose social and military backgrounds emphasised hierarchy. Equality with former convicts was anathema! They were extremely conscious of rank and station in social life, the more so since many of them had slim claims to gentry status according to English criteria, a fact not lost on the wits of Sydney who dubbed John Macarthur 'Jack Bodice', in case he forgot his family connection to the stay-making trade. These sensitivities produced a comedy of manners rivalling anything written by Jane Austen. The veneer of harmony could be easily pierced by the slightest breach of etiquette or failure to observe rigid social conventions and tacit understandings about life in the colony. Officers could live with convict mistresses, so long as they did not bring them into polite society. To omit 'esquire' on a letter to a gentleman would surely give umbrage. For Governor Macquarie to attempt to 'force' emancipists on dinner guests at Government House or at the officers' mess betrayed lack of feeling for social proprieties, according to the Commissioner sent to the colony in 1818 to report on its state and progress.[45]

But these concerns were not ridiculous. They were intimately connected to the question of who would exercise power in the colony, who would have access to official positions of status such as the magistracy, the jury and, eventually, the legislature. Political power was an open question in New South Wales. Would landed wealth be the sole criterion of political competence, or would the convict taint be an added bar to participation? The two factions, Exclusives and Emancipists, had dramatically opposed answers to that question. As various governors found, depending on which faction they favoured, both groups could fiercely and effectively contest the seemingly autocratic powers of the governor, even without the traditional instrument of a colonial legislature. The Exclusives campaigned against the pro-emancipist Governor Macquarie and were eventually able to have him recalled. The Emancipists kept up an incessant barrage against Governor Darling whose sympathies lay with the Exclusives.

By 1819, the first significant expressions of desire for political autonomy began to be aired. That year the man who would become the Emancipists' most articulate spokesman, W.C. Wentworth, published his account of conditions in New South Wales. He nominated two principal political objectives: a legislative assembly and trial by jury.[46] In that year too, as detailed in chapter 7, trial by jury took pride of place in the first ever Emancipist petition to their monarch. It continued to be one, if not the most, important political issue in the colony for the remainder of the transportation period.

The petition of 1819 marked the emergence of the Emancipists as recognizable group in the public life of the colony and ushered in an age where politics in general took on a more explicit and recognizable form. The enquiries of Commissioner Bigge from 1818 on presaged changes in the colony's governance and the interested parties started jockeying for position. Newspapers entered the fray. The *Australian* – edited by the Emancipist leaders Wentworth and Wardell – commenced publication in 1824 and ran a pro-Emancipist, 'loyal opposition' editorial line. The *Australian* competed with the established, pro-government *Sydney Gazette*, which had started life as the official organ of the government, a heritage played on by the *Australian*. The third newspaper, the *Monitor*, took a radical viewpoint. The newspapers added a very important dimension to politics in the colony. Not only did they amplify the political activity taking place in other forums – including the courts where Wentworth and Wardell carried many of the political contests – but they constituted an important political forum in their own right. More newspapers, more petitions about various issues, public meetings, lobbying in London and the appointment of parliamentary representatives in England marked a new phase in the political life of the colony as the prospects for devolution of some sort of political power increased.

Theoretically, the early governors of New South Wales were autocrats. But in practice, the absence of the usual political forums squeezed political action into different shapes and patterns. Opposition found its forms. The earliest opposition came from the ranks of the garrisons sent to guard the colony, especially the New South Wales Corps. And who did they oppose? The colony's governors. The marines told the governor that they would only obey his *lawful* orders.[47] Whether they would perform police functions, whether they would serve on the civilian courts, and whether they were subject to civil laws and the jurisdiction of the colony's civil courts, all became matters of hot contention in the first decade of settlement.[48] By the end of the second decade, the New South Wales Corps (alias the Rum Corps) – aided and abetted by John Macarthur, its former paymaster, and other commercial interests – concluded a long period of peaceful opposition in the courts and elsewhere by armed rebellion against Governor Bligh, who had stood in the way of their commercial advantage. Significantly for this story, the coup took place just as Bligh seemed to have finally outmanoeuvred Macarthur in the courts.[49]

The most striking feature about politics in the colony's early period is the extent to which politics took a legal form. The courts served as a *de facto* parliament. No one has seen this more clearly than H.V. Evatt in his account of the years leading up to the Rum Rebellion in 1808:

> At first sight it might seem difficult to understand why mere legal contests should be regarded as having such importance as I ascribe to them. But the key places on the Criminal Court of the colony were occupied by the military officers. Through the adroit, if unscrupulous handling both of the Criminal Court and the military Courts Martial, Macarthur, whilst an officer of the Corps, had succeeded in discrediting both Hunter and King. He had not lost his skilfulness in employing such instruments.
> Moreover, the Courts were the true forum of the little colony. They had

no competitors as a means of expressing individual or public grievances. There was no legislature, no municipal government, no avowed political association or party, no theatre and no independent press. On the one hand there was the legal dictatorship of the Governor as the sole legislative and executive authority and the final authority in the civil jurisdiction, and this dictatorship was being exercised by Bligh in favour of the agriculturalists and poor settlers and against the wealthy traffickers and monopolists. On the other hand, the military officers had the real control of the criminal judicature, and, as the leading phalanx of the rum traffickers and monopolists, their economic power, previously uncontrolled, was threatened.

Thus there was always a distinct possibility that Bligh's exercise of political power would provoke an open clash solely because it struck at the heart of the military and economic dictatorship which either had to yield or fight. Meanwhile, bitter skirmishes between the opposing interests almost necessarily assumed the form of legal contests, because they could not be fought elsewhere.[50]

The courts provided an invaluable, strategic and legitimate means of political expression in the colony. They provided a public forum both for opposition to the governor's policy, and for the governor to have his authority underlined. They provided a State-backed means of harassing opponents and, for convicts and emancipists – people like the Kables – a site from which to establish the bench-marks of the new hierarchy. But Evatt's insight must be extended temporally and conceptually. The heightened political importance of the legal system continued long after the Rum Rebellion: indeed, it continued so long as the colony lacked its own elected legislative bodies. This is not to subscribe to a view of courts as apolitical in New South Wales post-1840. The stress on the courts, however, in the pre-1840 period arose because of the peculiar political form given to New South Wales by its colonial author.

Second, Evatt's point about the importance of courts states the issue in too narrow and cryptic a way. The courts form one element of an ideological and institutional complex encapsulated in the phrase, the rule of law. Wittingly or not, whoever allowed it or however it came about, that first civil suit in the colony brought by the Kables, two convicts, signalled the establishment of the rule of law in the penal colony and imported a configuration of power that proved to be a most important source, and the most important *medium* of change in the transportation period.

This is a history of the transportation, not of convicts but of ideas and ideals. In particular, it is a history of a special set of ideas referred to as the rule of law. England in the late eighteenth century prided itself on a system of political liberty secured by the rule of law. As one historian has put it, '. . .the law assumed unusual pre-eminence in that century as the central legitimizing ideology, displacing the religious sanctions of previous centuries. It gave way, in its turn, to economic sanctions and the ideology of the free market and of political liberalism in the nineteenth. Turn where you will, the rhetoric of the eighteenth century is saturated with the notion of Law'.[51] Maybe we should not be too surprised that settlers in the penal colony of New South Wales continued to draw on that political idiom. But this was not a foregone conclusion. Convicts might have been cynical about the legal system. Irish convicts, Jacobins and those who saw the way to the future in the American model knew the other options. The choice and execution of a political strategy so heavily framed in legality are important parts of this story.

But unlike Britain, within the colony the rule of law model was also called upon to perform new tasks. One task was to prise political power from Britain. The other task was to settle the terms on which the main political actors, the governor, the Exclusives and the Emancipists, would exercise that power.

Within fifty years, the new settlers had persuaded England that what it saw as a penal colony should be regarded as a free society, entitled to its own elected political institutions. This was a quite radical transformation. Throughout the period, England continued to transport convicts to New South Wales. In the decade before a partially elected legislature was granted in 1842, more convicts than ever before were transported. At this time too, as we have seen, convicts, emancipists and their offspring made up the majority of the population. In very large measure, the political ideas and language the colonists drew on, both for struggles among themselves and against the metropolitan power, were based on their English legal inheritance. Rather than the universalistic, abstract language of the French and American revolutions, they claimed no more than their rights as free-born Britons, rights guaranteed by the Magna Carta, Habeas Corpus, the Bill of Rights, the Act of Settlement and the great synthesis of that inheritance, Blackstone's *Commentaries*.

Although Evatt's book has had a wide readership, the historiography of early Australia does not reflect his insight about the importance of rule of law in the colony's politics. The campaign for trial by jury and the controversy over emancipists in magistracy are, when noticed, treated as marginal disputes over civil liberties or contests for minor civil offices.[52] Judges who refused to acquiesce to the governor's wishes are portrayed as self-interested, pedantic or incapable of seeing that those military men of action, the governors, knew what was in the best interests of the colony. This seriously misunderstands the importance of the rule of law tradition in English political life.[53] The English had fought a civil war and staged a revolution on this theme in the seventeenth century. It was no less important in the eighteenth.

The elite in New South Wales knew this history intimately. Their letters to the colonial newspapers are studded with references to Magna Carta, Habeas Corpus, the Bill of Rights and quotations from Blackstone about their British birthrights.[54] The colony's military governors understood it too, although it did not sit easily with their ideas of order and discipline. Two years before the settlement of New South Wales, Governor Mostyn of Minorca had been successfully sued in England for illegal detention of a colonist. Lord Mansfield awarded 6,000 pounds damages against the Governor.[55] The case was well known; Governor Macquarie feared a similar fate from disaffected colonists on his return to England. The non-elite in the colony also had a more intimate knowledge of the law than most. While prepared to mimic, mock and break the law, they also used it extensively before magistrates against their masters, in civil litigation.[56] Rule of law claims – the right to jury trial and the right to bring law suits – formed the principal subjects of the first two Emancipist petitions to England.

Law became the means of expressing and contesting the differing conceptions of social and economic relations in the colony. When the conflict spilled over to England, the fact that it was couched in the familiar English forms and arguments gave the Emancipists their best chance of successfully asserting their claims for a devolution of political power and for equal status. A home government dependent on the rule of law for its own legitimacy could scarcely be unreceptive to arguments couched in those terms from its colony. Because of the penal nature of the colony, England resisted those arguments for a time, and sometimes failed to see them. But ultimately it yielded.

The history of New South Wales would have been radically different without the courts provided by the colonial power. A far more autocratic system would have prevailed, more akin to the governance of a prison or a military garrison. Other means would have had to have been found to have dealt with the conflicts and problems of status which arose. But this was not necessary. The courts in early New South Wales served as a vehicle through which a very complex scheme of social and political arrangements were hammered out. The Kables' case immediately introduced a change into the inherited legal framework. By dint of expediency, or serendipity, or oversight, convicts in New South Wales would enjoy the right to hold property and to sue in the colony's courts to protect that property. They would not have been able to do so in England. Just how far the peculiar circumstances of the colony would justify further departures from English law proved to be a point of contention and creative ambiguity for many years. This was a decision that judges had to make and it committed considerable political power to their hands.

With the exception of the abortive Castle Hill uprising and the Rum Rebellion, one of the salient features of this story is the choice of political strategy. The American and French revolutions gave political actors in New South Wales recent models for political change. Neither the ideology of universal rights nor the strategy of armed revolution was adopted in New South Wales. The presence of Jacobins, Irish rebels and political leaders who were well-versed in those ideas and strategies meant that the strategies actually adopted were not adopted in ignorance of other possibilities. Indeed, Wentworth was prepared to threaten the possibility of an American solution to English intransigence. However, because of some of the events already outlined, extreme measures did not become necessary.

Instead, the terms of political debate in New South Wales proceeded on very traditional lines. The protagonists relied on their British birthrights and deployed the language of the rule of law to secure them and to forge new social and political order out of the penal colony at Botany Bay.

26 THE RULE OF LAW IN A PENAL COLONY

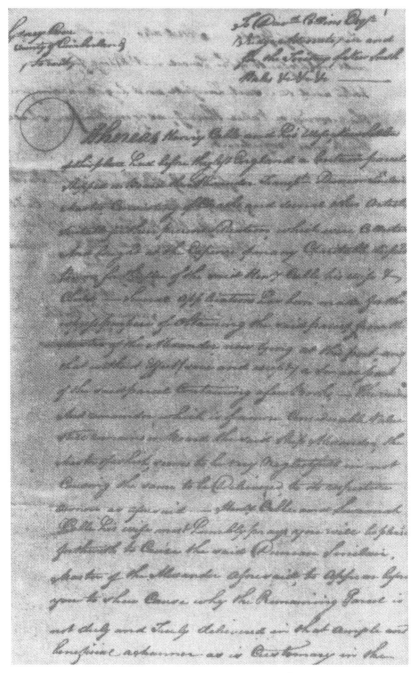

Copy (extract) of the writ in the Kables' case. Archives Office of New South Wales.

CHAPTER 2

Free Society, Penal Colony, Slave Society, Prison?

... the end of law is not to abolish or restrain but to preserve and enlarge freedom; for in all the states of created beings capable of laws, where there is no law, there is no freedom. For liberty is to be free from restraint and violence from others, which cannot be where there is no law; but freedom is not, as we are told, a liberty for every man to do what he lists – for who could be free, when every other man's humour might domineer over him? – but a liberty to dispose and order as he lists his person, actions, possessions, and his whole property within the allowance of those laws under which he is, and therein not to be subject to the arbitrary will of another, but freely follow his own.

Locke[1]

... The people are taught by the papers to talk about the rights of Englishmen and the Free Institutions of the Mother Country, many of them forgetting their actual condition. Besides, this is evident, altho' this is an English colony, there is no similarity whatsoever in its composition to that of England.

The Free Institutions of Great Britain may be very applicable to its Inhabitants and, at the same time, be extremely inapplicable to the inhabitants of New South Wales, though born in England.

But their pretensions seem totally inadmissable [sic] – the Colony is still in its infancy and is by no means prepared for such an Institution as a Legislative Assembly.

Governor Darling, 1827[2]

Talk of the free world and free societies – until recently contrasted to the unfree Eastern bloc countries – is a taken for granted part of contemporary political parlance, especially for those who live in one of the Western democracies. We think we understand what we mean by a free society and talk rather easily about the virtues of free institutions. In the daily round, not much is made of them, perhaps because they are not seriously challenged; even at elections people will talk dismissively about the meaninglessness of their vote. But it would be an entirely different matter to be told that you are not entitled to vote or that you are no longer free to do as you 'list', to borrow Locke's old word. Time and context vitally determine the salience of issues such as these. Blacks in contemporary South Africa, for example, regard their freedom and their enfranchisement as burning issues.

But what of people – convict and free – in New South Wales during the transportation years? What was it like to live in New South Wales for the Kables and thousands of others like them? How can people in the late twentieth century understand what it meant for them to be sent to live there as convicts, to live on there afterwards as emancipists, for their baby to grow up there as the child of convict parents, for the captain of their ship and other free people like him to be hauled before the colony's courts by convicted felons? What sort of society was it and what were the salient issues for its inhabitants? Why did Governor Darling regard the 'Free Institutions of Great Britain' as 'extremely inapplicable to the inhabitants of New South Wales, though born in England'? Was Botany Bay the brutal place so vividly described recently by Robert Hughes? Or was it a much more benign settlement, as argued in some recent revisionist histories of New South Wales? Has the focus on convictism blurred our understanding of what it was like to live in New South Wales in the early part of the nineteenth century? Were conditions there so different from those experienced by free workers in England at the time, or by other emigrants, or by people in the free societies we live in today? Was it a fairly unremarkable place with somewhat unusual origins in penality – a free society from the outset, as one historian has recently claimed – or did the penal stamp cut deeply into the social fabric? Is this the blood-curdling story of the chain gang and the lash or is it the more prosaic triumph of *homo economicus* over the penal designs of those administering a bloody criminal code? If we may resort to a few convenient labels to summarise some of this, was New South Wales a penal colony that became free, or was it a free society from the outset?

At stake here are important questions about how people experienced life in the colony, what they saw as the major issues in their lives, and the objectives they valued enough to struggle for. Also at stake is our ability to understand their concerns – especially the desire for freedom – in the age of the French and American Revolutions, an age when the abolition of slavery was a major public issue and at a time when half to three-quarters of the population of New South Wales had first-hand experience of bondage. When we adopt labels – in this case 'free society' and 'penal colony'– as shorthand to discuss such questions, we run the risk of misunderstandings and descent into semantic argument. But the way we characterise a place and time colours our whole understanding of it. If we think of early New South Wales as a penal colony where people struggled to establish a free society, that is an entirely different story from one in which the society was free from the outset, requiring only the effluxion of time and the birth rate to sort out anomalies caused by the unusual number of convicts in the early years. As will become clear, I do not accept the latter, evolutionary account. The story of early New South Wales is a story about struggles for important changes in the pattern of social life for people in the colony. It is a story about people who felt their lack of freedom keenly at a personal and political level. And it is a story about how they transformed their society from a penal colony to a free society and how they were able to use the rule of law to achieve their objectives.[3]

Many of New South Wales' inhabitants, the convicts, were subject to the will of others, but not quite the arbitrary will to which Locke refers. As the Kables had demonstrated, and Blackstone confirms, law operated however imperfectly, in the British colony of New South Wales from the outset; even convicts had rights under it.[4] While a convict, like a slave, had some legal rights, he or she, certainly did not have the 'liberty to dispose and order as he lists his person, actions, possessions and his whole property, . . . ' Convicts forfeited many of those rights on conviction. By virtue of the same law which, according to Locke, guaranteed freedom, convicts lost it. Contrary to common misconceptions, convicts (and slaves) had rights. But they were fewer and narrower than those of free citizens. The distinction between bond and free is a distinction of degree, not a distinction between those with some rights and those with none at all. Had it been suggested to Henry and Susannah Kable after their court victory that because they had some rights they were free, they would have regarded the suggestion as more than faintly ridiculous. The rights and freedoms they experienced both in Norwich Jail and in Botany Bay strike modern eyes as odd. We are accustomed to the total isolation of penitentiary-style imprisonment. But despite the absence of the prison bars in New South Wales, what the Kables like so many of their fellow convicts throughout the period most wanted was their 'freedom', by which they meant the termination of their convict status and all the consequences that went with it.

Some of this may appear too obvious to say. But characterisations of early New South Wales can too easily proceed on the common misconception that convicts had no rights. When it is pointed out that they did have some rights and that they could move around more freely than contemporary prisoners do, the effect of the revelation leads people to conclude that New South Wales was not such a bad place after all. By comparison to slaves, who had no rights, so the argument goes, convicts were much better off. But it is also a misconception to think that slaves had no rights.[5]

Comparisons between convicts and slaves are a good way to approach the question about the character of early New South Wales. But, of course, the comparisons must be well based. Similarly, comparisons between bonded labour (like convicts and slaves) and free workers assist in the task of saying what sort of society New South Wales was at its beginnings and what it later became. But such comparisons are not straightforward. Pro-slavery campaigners argued that the formal legal status of slaves should be put to one side, because in substance the position of the slave was equal to or better than that of free workers in England. The Marxist critique of liberalism makes the cognate point that formal freedom is an empty deception if material conditions preclude meaningful exercise of that freedom. To make the comparisons, we need to study both the form and the substance of the different conditions, convict, slave and free. From that point we can proceed to talk about the sort of society that existed in early New South Wales and the practical effects of that mode of social ordering.

New South Wales was 'an outrage [to] Law, Justice and Humanity', according to the great philosopher and penal reformer, Jeremy Bentham. Sir Samuel Romilly, the politician responsible for sweeping changes to the criminal law, wrote that New South Wales was 'a community of thieves and outlaws under the control of their military guards', New South Wales and Tasmania must 'chiefly be considered as receptacles for offenders', Colonial Secretary Earl Bathurst instructed Commissioner Bigge in 1819, reminding his commissioner prior to departure that the government viewed the settlements as places for punishment and reformation. Although there was the possibility that they might become free at some point, his Lordship was concerned that some people in England did not view New South Wales with sufficient terror. None of these men ever set foot in New South Wales. But some of those who did had similarly unflattering opinions about the character of the place. Convicts John Grant and George Loveless added the slavery analogy to the list of terms used to capture the character of early New South Wales; indeed Chief Justice Francis Forbes, born into West Indian slave society, thought New South Wales was worse than his birthplace. Tougher men, like the ship's surgeon, Peter Cunningham, described it as a penal colony, but too soft.[6]

Historians have generally agreed with the assessments of these contemporary observers. A police state say Geoffrey Blainey and Lloyd Robson, fastening on the dossiers kept on every convict. Or they would join with Hancock and Ward and think of it as 'Britain's Biggest Gaol', an open prison. Fletcher calls it a penal society and Manning Clark says it was a jail at first, and then by 1819, a colony. John Ritchie sees 1823 as the crucial point of transition from jail to colony; 'a convict colony in the same way as the West Indies were slave colonies' but one which would become a free society. Michael Sturma agrees with Clark's idea of a transition but he locates the change much later, in the 1840s, when the convict part of the population was swamped by free immigrants. Hainsworth, by contrast, sees the transition as the result of a dialogue between the Sydney traders and the governors, with the English government striving unsuccessfully to force its penal purposes on an unwilling colony. Most recently, Robert Hughes has suggested that New South Wales can be thought of as a precursor of the gulag and the Nazi concentration camps.[7]

Against the weight of this opinion, John Hirst has recently argued that New South Wales was a free society from the outset. The novelty of his proposition has probed the rival classifications which, it must be said, mostly assume the self-evident nature of their assessment without much argument. But the characterisations are not self-evident and they have important consequences. As Bathurst's instruction to Bigge shows, characterisation of the colony had practical policy consequences: it was to be a 'receptacle for offenders' and Bigge should cast his recommendations in that light.

The characterisation of New South Wales also had important

legal consequences. As will be seen in chapter 4, the assertion of judicial independence by the colonial judges can be seen as appropriate or not according to the character of the colony. Legal historians have disagreed about whether New South Wales should be seen as a settled colony or a conquest. The legal consequences for the Aborigines, among others, differed sharply according to which classification operated. This was not finally resolved, as we have seen, until 1836. The correct classification also determined the governor's legislative power in the colony and was the subject of confrontations between the governors, their judges and their subjects. The character of the colony was also used to justify measures like the *Bushranging Act* in the 1830s, agreed by everyone to be repugnant to English practices.[8]

New South Wales was a peculiar society. As the nineteenth-century colonial officer and scholar Merivale wrote in 1861, '[t]he penal colonies [i.e. New South Wales and Tasmania] provide the first instance (a very necessary one, no doubt) of settlements founded by Englishmen without any constitution whatsoever. . . . This is a remarkable novelty in British policy.' In 1786 England knew little more about Botany Bay than Cook and Banks had reported in 1770. Its remoteness and bizarre fauna made it almost literally a world turned upside down.[9] The government had transported convicts beyond the seas, before, but this was to pre-existing colonies in America controlled by free settlers.[10] In this colony convicts and their jailers would be the settlers. In England's other colonies, legislatures, courts, and juries roughly approximated the 'balance' of the English constitution. In New South Wales there was a governor, but no legislature, no trial by jury and a bastardised court structure. The governor had more power than any other colonial governor, and more power in New South Wales than any king in England since at least the time of James I. This was a framework consistent with England's major purpose for the colony, the punishment of prisoners.

At the outset, New South Wales was a penal colony. But it did not stay that way. Settlers in New South Wales developed different conceptions about what the colony was and might become. They differed among themselves about whether it was a sink of infamy or a land of opportunity for the emancipated convict. And they argued with the colonial power which saw it simply as a place of punishment. In the following fifty years people in the colony began to fight to change conditions there. By stages they were successful in transforming it into a free society. To appreciate the changes and their significance, we have to establish the bench-marks: that New South Wales was a penal colony to start with and a free society at the end.

Detailed accounts of daily life and for convicts, especially in their work, upset the traditional stereotypes of convicts as powerless tools at the mercy of brutal masters. Recent histories have replaced the caricatures with a three-dimensional picture of life in the colony, which captures the reciprocal power relationship between convicts and masters, details the achievements of a considerable public works program requiring both skilled and unskilled labour, and shows the skilled trades such as printing and journalism, nursing, baking, timber milling, dress-making, agriculture and so on, practised by convicts in the colony. Our hero, Henry Kable, for example, was in partnership building ships and importing merchandise within the first decade or so. The lash, while useful in coercing unskilled work, is more limited for skilled work. Necessity dictated that convict workers be given a measure of control over the work they did and their movement around the settlement to perform that work. They did not live in a prison. Until the Hyde Park Barracks was built in 1819, most convicts lived in private accommodation.[11] But once the stereotypes are exploded, what can be said to characterise this strange place where the colonists were convicts? Clearly the notion of a colony involves greater autonomy than a prison. But what did these arrangements have to do with penality? Was this after all a free society?

Let us examine these questions by way of some comparisons. First, let us compare New South Wales with a free society of the time, England. Let us make the assumption that England in the early nineteenth century was a free society, even though its unreformed parliament, disrupted social conditions, laws against trade unions and political associations and censorship of the press test this assumption sorely. But perhaps we can conclude that for England, control of the king by parliament, the right to petition, the rule of law and trial by jury gave the unenfranchised security consistent with the idea of a free society.[12] Even if we allow that England was a free society, New South Wales differed at least as much from England as it did from slave societies and prisons. Aside from the institutional differences, its population was predominantly composed of convicts for the first 50 years of its life. In that time New South Wales received some 80,000 convicts who constituted between 81 per cent and 30 per cent of the white population, roughly averaging 40 per cent over the transportation period. At the end of that period, emancipists, convicts and their offspring comprised 63 per cent of the population.[13] The Kables were surrounded by other convicts. Four out of every ten people you could meet in New South Wales had not come there freely, were not free to order their daily lives 'as they list', ran the risk of severe punishments for minor, vaguely-defined offences, and were not free to leave the colony. They lived in a society whose social, economic, legal and political arrangements turned on the presence of this large proportion of convicts. It was not a free society.

Was it a slave society? Opponents of the convict system both in England and the Antipodes certainly used that label. Historians have had an easy time knocking this Aunt Sally over. Ultimately, it is a misleading way of thinking about New South Wales. But eagerness to join the sport should not be allowed to rob us of the rich insights which can be gained from comparisons of the two forms of bonded labour.

Slavery has appeared in a bewildering number of guises from the Greek and Roman forms, to African, American, West Indian and so on.[14] Many images of slavery present the slave simply as the extension of the will of the master. Indeed the ideology of slavery in the American South proclaimed just that view.[15] In this picture ('the simple account'), the slave was little different from a beast of burden, possessing no rights, fed and housed miserably, infinitely pliable at the whim of corrupt and tyrannical masters, and subject to fearful whipping for the least infraction. Anti-slavery campaigners depicted slavery in this way.

The reality of slavery ('the complex account'), as recent historians of slavery have been at pains to stress, was quite different.[16] Slaves were not mere implements in their masters' hands, powerless to resist. The revisionist histories of New South Wales make the same point in relation to convicts. Slave resistance took a variety of forms, forms often similar to those employed by convicts. The humanity of slaves confounded the ideology which categorised them with inanimate objects and frustrated attempts to formulate a dual jurisprudence for the legal systems of American slave states.[17] The notion that slaves had no rights – a point on which many comparisons with convictism slip[18] – is contradicted by legal injunctions which deny the basic premise of chattel slavery: it was murder to kill a slave; excessive punishment (broadly defined to be sure) was a crime; slaves were held responsible for crimes they committed. Slave rights extended the contradiction further. Slaves charged with serious crimes (murder, rape) had the legal right to jury trial, representation and appeal before the same courts as whites. There were separate slave courts for minor offences. Extra-legally slaves could establish customary rights to limited hours of work, task work rather than gang labour, leisure time, ownership and inheritance of property, garden plots etc. Moreover, the supposed pliability of slaves must be offset against a variety of strategems for resistance brought to bear on masters by their slaves.[19] Just as convicts were employed in skilled jobs and in employment as liveried household servants, slaves in the United States also held these 'elite' jobs and enjoyed the perks associated with them. Like the convicts, slaves moved about the countryside lawfully and unlawfully in their own time and at night, and did so for work and social interaction of various kinds. While, as some critics have argued, the revisionist work on slavery may have painted too rosy a picture of slavery, the *simple* account of slavery or of convictism is no longer tenable.[20]

To make valid comparisons between slaves and convicts, like must be bracketed with like, the complex account of slavery with the complex account of convictism. Even then the differences in the conditions of slavery compound the problem. The legal codes in the West Indies offered slaves more protections than those of the American South but the law seems to have masked a converse reality: actual conditions in the American South were much better for slaves than those in the West Indies.[21] What begins by looking like a two-term comparison, slave versus convict, turns out to be hydra-headed, particularly when comparisons with the conditions of free workers in England are thrown in for good measure. But despite important dissimilarities, when the *complex* account of slavery is contrasted with the *complex* account of convicts, the distinction between convicts and slaves fades dramatically. Let us pursue those comparisons in a little more detail.

Slavery in the United States and the West Indies was the model under attack from those who were also opposed to assigned convict labour in New South Wales. It was the form of slavery best known to people in England and the colony, as well as to modern readers. It provides the most useful source of suitable comparisons.

Valid distinctions can be made between convicts' conditions in New South Wales and those of slaves. First, skin colour permanently marked the slaves off from white society in an external way not experienced by the convicts; in New South Wales the law distinguished bond from free, but physical marks such as branding or distinctive clothing for the most part were not used. Hirst illustrates this well with an example of a magistrate who had to ask a group of workers to divide into bond and free so that he could distinguish between them.[22] Race also allowed the master-class a set of rationalisations about the inferiority of slaves unavailable to the masters of convicts who were white, free-born and British (though slurs on the large percentage of Irish convicts should not be forgotten). The permanent and hereditary nature of slavery also distinguished slaves from the convicts, who, even if they were sentenced to life terms, could expect to be free within the colony after about fourteen years.[23] Even this 'permanent' view of slavery should be qualified slightly by the possibility of manumission.[24]

Next, of course, masters owned their slaves and could buy and sell them. Property in the services of convicts remained with the governor who regulated the convict system. The master had a licence at little or no fee to use the convict for a limited period of years. The governor could revoke the licence for good cause if the master mistreated the convict (e.g., by illegal punishment, failure to provide proper rations, and so on) and the master could send an unsatisfactory convict back to the government.[25] Finally, convicts were transported *as punishment* for a criminal offence. Slave status did not depend on this criterion of personal fault but on skin colour plus capture or birth into slavery. These characteristics, rather than the day-to-day conditions of work, are the major differentiators between slaves and convicts. Day-to-day conditions also differed but not always, and often not in ways favouring the lot of the convict.

In discussions of convict work conditions, historians sometimes point to the limitations on coercion as a means of getting work done and the vulnerability of a master to tactics such as the go-slow, passive resistance and sabotage. This is thought to distinguish slaves from convicts. Yet these exact problems of coercion confronted slave holders. For example in his discussion, 'flogging and work', Hirst tells us that plantation labour was more amenable to whipping than the dispersed convict labour system. But a range of factors militated against flogging slaves and they improvised methods to exercise a degree of control over their conditions of work.[26]

Convict masters were prohibited from flogging their assigned servants, a prohibition not imposed on slave holders. But the stereotyped image of the slave driver must be balanced against the legal and practical constraints on whipping slaves. There were legal restrictions on cruelty to slaves and cases in both America and the West Indies in which they were enforced.[27] It should also be added, as a relative measure of contemporary standards, that when Southern courts came to order floggings for slaves, they were considerably more humane than their counterparts in New South Wales! In 1830, the legal maximum for slaves was thirty-nine lashes, compared to 100 in New South Wales for convicts. Indeed some West Indian planters felt that the punishments they could hold out to convicted slaves were so ineffectual that they proposed to a parliamentary committee the need for a place of transportation such as Botany Bay which would instill real terror![28] The 'lash nexus' thesis of both the convict and the slave stereotypes – that the relationship of authority was one of simple and brutal physical coercion – misrepresents the position.

Of course one should look at the practical limitations on coercion of convicts *and* slaves. In one important respect they differ. Slaves were worth a lot of money. Values of $500–$1200 for slaves occur regularly in the literature.[29] Even if sale were not an immediate concern, slave holders were in long-term relationships with their slaves and had to ensure that they reproduced. They had to take care of their 'investments'. Masters of convicts, on the other hand, did not have the same stake in their assigned convicts: they did not own them, could only expect to have them for a few years and notwithstanding shortages, could rely on a continuing supply from England.

Self-interest, however, is not the whole story. Historians of slavery speak of a culture of paternalism and the Southern 'code of honour' which ameliorated the physical conditions of slavery. Southern planters learned to exercise power over slaves, discussed proper treatment and looked after 'their negroes'. They felt themselves bound by the Biblical limit of 39 lashes. Planters in the West Indies, influenced to some extent by the anti-slavery movement, claimed that use of the lash was falling into disfavour by the 1830s. Those of a more sanguinary disposition had been forced by threat of a slave rebellion to abandon proposals to introduce the cat-o'-nine-tails, the instrument used in the navy and New South Wales.[30] These constraints did not operate in New South Wales. Convict masters were not educated about power, nor were their convicts learned in subordination.[31] Despite the absence of a legal prohibition on slave holders whipping their slaves, the balance on flogging favours slaves rather than convicts.

Finally, both slaves and convicts had their food provided by their masters. Regulations about the amount, type and quality of food gave convicts a form of protest which shielded them from reprisals for insubordination. They could legitimately complain if one type of food were substituted for the prescribed ration. This meant, for example, that masters had to go to additional trouble and expense to supply the wheaten flour preferred to other cereals by convicts. Not only did this give the convicts more power over masters than the stereotypes would suggest, but it also shows that on an important measure of human well-being, food, convicts were better off than many free people, a point often made by contemporaries, such as

Commissioner Bigge. But food formed a point of resistance for slaves too. For example, the customary right of slaves to a plot of their masters' land for growing vegetables was even upheld in a Southern court. Anti-slavery campaigners were confronted by slave holders like the West Indian planter Sir Rose Price (father of the infamous commandant of Norfolk Island, John Price), who protested what was the fact, that slaves ate better than free workers in England. In these matters convicts and slaves had much in common.[32]

This discussion could be pursued but the general point is that emphasis on the day-to-day living conditions distinguishes slaves and convicts more from free workers than from one another. The labour of slaves and convicts was coerced and both were subject to severe corporal punishment. Paradoxically, however, for daily necessities such as food, both groups were at least as well or better off than the labouring poor of England. What substance can there be then, in the objections either to slavery or the transportation system?

The answer can be found in a re-creation of the drawing-room of anti-slavery and anti-transportation campaigner, Lord John Russell. As John Hirst recounts, his lordship could return home from Whitehall and expect to find his fires lit, dinner cooked and respectful, efficient servants ready to attend his needs – much more than convict masters in New South Wales could expect. The power to dismiss an English servant without a reference ensured long hours of dutiful service at the lowest pay the market would bear. Who was better off, the slave, the convict or the free servant?[33]

Notice the emphasis on physical conditions in these comparisons. They were the features that pro-slavery and pro-transportation advocates stressed. The features they most wanted to omit were the psychological factors: feelings, emotions, dignity, social, cultural and family ties, love of place and so on. One of the witnesses to the Molesworth Committee claimed that exile caused the greatest pain for the convicts. Convicts could express themselves poignantly on this:

> ... If I was for any time in prison I would try and content myself but to be sent from my Native Country perhaps never to see it again distresses me beyond comprehension and will Terminate with my life. . .[T]o part with my dear Wife & Child, Parents and Friends, to be no more, cut off in the Bloom of my Youth without doing the least wrong to any person on earth – O hard my fate, may God have mercy on me ... Your affec. Husband until Death

> We hears that we shall get our freedom in that Country, but if I gets my freedom even so i am shure I shall Never be happy except I can have the

pleshur of ending my days with you and my dear Children, for I don't think a man ever loved a woman so well as I love you.[34]

Portraying slaves as inferior beings and convicts as brutalised and devoid of these feelings assisted the argument. More abstract considerations such as the degradation of slave and convict status, difficult enough to insert into the political process at any time, fade out of the argument. Yet, at the risk of cliché, people do not live by bread alone; humanity has its claims.

Domination of people comes in a variety of forms and degrees. Slaves in the American South enjoyed better food than their contemporary workers in England but they suffered under a variant and more extreme form of domination than English people. The ideology of slavery fixed their position in society quite differently from the ideology of freedom. Convicts did not suffer such an extreme form of oppression as slaves. Like the slaves, however, their position in the productive relations of the society was fixed by law, the criminal law in the convicts' case. Moreover, it was fixed at a point 12,000 miles away from their native place and designated as a degrading punishment. That status meant that a convict could be further degraded by a flogging for a trivial offence where a free person could not, a feature that made a significant difference in the power relations between dominant and subordinate. The magistrate whom we met earlier in this chapter – the one who was unable at first to distinguish bond from free – illustrates this point. Once he had separated the group into bond and free, the magistrate could exercise his greater power over the convicts (for example, he could order a flogging for insubordination), which, of course, was the point of his exercise.

Free labourers in England were oppressed too but in a different and less extreme form than slaves or convicts. Even if they were victims of false consciousness, the fact of working people's perceptions about their dignity and freedom cannot be left out of the account. If we had given one of Lord John Russell's well-informed servants the choice of exchanging places with a well-fed slave or a convict in New South Wales, can there be any doubt that the offer would have been declined? Would the generality of ex-convict smallholders have wished to return to servitude and better food? The account of trade union organiser and Tolpuddle Martyr, George Loveless, transported to Tasmania in the 1830s is suffused by the degradation of convict life and leaves no doubt that his choice would have been to remain in England.[35] Psychoanalyst, Bruno Bettelheim, crystallises this point in the case of concentration camp victims:

Whether or not a societal organization is experienced as tyranny seems to depend mainly on whether its members are assured relative free choices and a part in decision making about issues that for them are the sum of their consciousness of freedom. One might then think that the more important areas of life to enter this consciousness, the greater the progress a society has made. But, alas, which are important areas, and which unimportant? What may be experienced by one man in society as tyranny, may seem only an inconvenience to others or a silly issue to again others. Still this is only true within limits. While it varies with men as to which are important areas of freedom in decision making, a sense of autonomy depends everywhere on the conviction that one can make important decisions, and can do it where it counts most.[36]

The ideology of freedom has been a powerful force in the making of modern capitalist economies and has profound effects on day-to-day life.[37] Criticisms of anti-slavery, anti-transportation campaigners which focus narrowly on the physical conditions of the two forms of bondage miss a critical dimension of social life: how people make sense of their position in the scheme of things, and how this affects the things they can and cannot do. It is surely right to say that there has often been a yawning gap between the ideology of freedom and the actuality. But failure to see that ideology structures social practice in crucial ways is a desperate error.[38] Bond labour – slave and convict – *was* anathema to the liberal ideas of the abolitionists. But they were not the only ones to subscribe to those ideas. The hope that you might strike it lucky one day, might have a say in government and might exercise some control over day-to-day life has fuelled millions of people, in addition to the abolitionists. Slaves and convicts had to postpone such hopes. Misguided though the hopes of the millions may have been, the ideology of freedom did make sense of their place in the world in a way that it did not for convicts or slaves. The position of slaves and convicts was fixed in contra-distinction to freedom; in the one case by the ideology of slavery and in the other by the ideology of the criminal law.[39] For all their distortions, the anti-slavery campaigners understood this. Such arguments are not easy to make in public forums, so they resorted to the tactics of the advocate: rhetoric and hyperbole. But exaggeration operates on a central core of truth. At its core, the analogy between convicts and slaves made sense and this meant that it was not rejected as far-fetched or inapposite.

As to the extent of the central core of truth, we would be wise not to minimise the severity of conditions in New South Wales by dismissing the anti-transportation campaigners as arm-chair theorists.

If the need for a first-hand comparison of slave society and New South Wales be felt, then we have one from Francis Forbes, Chief Justice of New South Wales during the 1820s. Forbes was a liberal and to some extent his views are predictable, but presumably not to be dismissed on that ground alone. He had the decided advantage of first-hand experience of the more brutal of the slave societies we have been considering, the West Indies, where he was born and raised. In an extensive commentary on New South Wales, he writes:

> These gentlemen [the free settlers] regard convicts in precisely the same way as a planter in the West Indies regards his slaves – I am you know a West Indian, and I can truly say that the assigned convicts appear to me to be considered, and treated by the generality of settlers in precisely the same way that slaves are considered and treated in the West Indies...it [NSW] is not the el dorado which it has been insidiously represented, to the great diminution of its terror as a place of punishment, and even temptation to crime in England – it is a place of privation, labor and suffering and the place where by far the greater number of offenders who have been sent here, have found a life without hope and a premature death. The Terrys and Lords [wealthy emancipists] *et hoc genus omne*, who from the beginning comprehend about one hundred persons, are artfully held up to public view – while thousands of nameless wretches who have lingered out the remains of a burdensome life, are as forgotten as their graves[40]

And in some respects, Forbes considered the convicts worse off than the slaves. He recommended that the new legislation on summary punishments by magistrates include a provision 'to prevent the *master* from punishing in that way, his *own* servant, as a necessary restraint, which is interposed even in the case of slaves in the West Indies.'[41]

Convict transportation and slavery can be differentiated on a range of criteria but they share this crucial feature: both supplied legally degraded, coerced labour to systems heavily dependent on their input. The dynamics of extracting that labour from bonded workforces which were already supplied with the basic necessities of life (food, clothes, shelter) sharply differentiate convicts and slaves from the free workers of England. Masters in the penal colony might complain about the difficulties of obtaining willing workers, but they did not want to pay the price of the most obvious solution: free the convicts and pay them full wages! They wanted unpaid labour.

Similar points can be made about the prison analogy often invoked in relation to New South Wales. Again the distinctions between prisons and New South Wales have to be acknowledged. A range of criteria sharply differentiates New South Wales from the modern prison, especially the single cell penitentiary of Bentham's model: the walled-in isolation from the society in which the prison is located, its long-term detention, surveillance of every phase of the prisoner's life, and the detailed disciplinary regime. New South Wales was much more like the relatively open, less isolated prisons of the eighteenth century than the 'total institutions' described by the modern literature.[42]

But these obvious differences should not obscure the significant similarities between conditions in prisons and in New South Wales, similarities which bring out the extent to which the character of the colony was – like prisons – penal. One of the biggest problems which confronted prison administrators was the maintenance of order. Prisoners, like transportees, retain many of their legal rights, including rights about additional punishment. This foreclosed one control option – at least formally – use of unchecked physical coercion.[43] Indeed as far as floggings are concerned, prisoners at one nineteenth-century prison found guilty of disciplinary offences fared better again than slaves, who as we have already seen, probably did better than convicts: ten lashes was considered a severe punishment in the Massachusetts State Prison in 1830,[44] compared with an average of 44 lashes per male convict in New South Wales during the 1830s.[45] This limitation led to the need for prison administrators to develop alternative strategies for orderly behaviour such as shortening of sentences, indulgences, the trusty system, etc.[46] Even the payment of wages for work done in the prisoner's 'own time', also a feature of convict life, was well known in nineteenth-century prisons in the United States as 'overstint', although the work had to be done within the prison walls.[47]

However, a fundamental problem centered on the notion that prisons constitute a society at all, besets the analogy. Insofar as society is a geographic concept, prisons form part of, are located in and are marginal to a larger society. Indeed, if we accept the arguments of Bentham and Foucault, this feature performs an important function in disciplining the society in which the prison is located by its ever-present example. Prisons are institutions within the margins of the larger society, and their inmates constitute a tiny percentage of the population of that larger society. The point is tellingly made by the celebrated historian of American slavery, Eugene Genovese, when he rebuts an analogy between prisons in nineteenth-century

Massachusetts and plantations in South Carolina. Many of his points apply directly to New South Wales:

> He [the author] does not mention that slavery determined much of the relevant tradition and social and economic development of South Carolina and cannot, therefore, be isolated in a set of parallel variables. By contrast the dissimilarities that he mentions include such trifles as the difference between a labor system that subjected its laborers to physical constraints and a system that removed from the labor force those regarded as antisocial, the difference between a labor system that provided the basic social relation for society as a whole and a system that touched only marginal elements, the difference between a system of organized production and a system of selective punishment, the difference between a society based on the ownership of labor itself and a society based on the reduction of labor power to a commodity.[48]

As the designation colony suggests, and unlike the prison, New South Wales was geographically separate from the parent society: a twelve thousand mile journey taking about four to six months by sailing ship in the early nineteenth century.[49] Although the colony was ultimately controlled by England, distance meant that governors of New South Wales had far more autonomy than any prison governor in England itself.[50] And the fact that it was a *colony*, a colony which was supposed to become self-supporting set up an entirely different penal dynamic from prisons in London, Dover or Liverpool. Distance and autonomy allowed the potential for people to resist and frustrate the coloniser, and to transform the society if they so desired. England represented an ultimate check on the directions of the colony, so long as its inhabitants submitted to British control. For day-to-day matters – and eventually for more far-reaching changes – distance, among other conditions, meant the potential for change existed.

Convicts comprised the major part of the population but they eventually became free and largely stayed in the colony. There were also the native born and people who came free. The groups mixed freely on a day-to-day basis for much of the time; no walls separated bond from free in the early colony. The ocean, mountains, unfamiliar bush, Aborigines and the convicts' fears and ignorance provided the outer boundaries of their captivity. Magistrates, constables, overseers, free settlers, soldiers and other convicts policed the area within these boundaries. Very formidable barriers delimited the convicts' movement within the colony, but they set generous limits by comparison to prison walls and prison cells.

In many other ways, the regime in New South Wales compared favourably with the inhumanity of the prison. The false god of reformation in the penitentiary system was doomed for just the reasons cited by the contemporary observers in New South Wales: 'the exclusion of convicts from all society but their own, and of their keepers,...divests them of all virtuous habits and sympathies and renders them, year by year, less fitted for returning to that community from which they have been entirely estranged';[51] the brutality of prison life; the unreality of the finely tuned pleasure/pain calculus; and the diversion of attention from the social and economic factors at work in the production of crime.

If for all these reasons and more, we see New South Wales as different from and in some ways more humane than the prison, well and good. But making these distinctions does not show that New South Wales was a free society. New South Wales should be seen as a separate society, a colony, but it still remains to be seen whether this peculiar settlement colony deserved its most frequent designation: penal colony.

One major, intractable fact about New South Wales deeply colours any attempt to understand the nature of the place: its purpose was criminal punishment. Forty per cent of the white population was there *as* punishment.[52] Add to this those officials and military officers whose presence was directly attributable to the convict system and some idea of the degree to which the society rested on a penal base emerges. Emancipists, children of convicts and free settlers defined themselves in distinction to convicts. Employers and workers acted in a labour market structured by the presence of convicts. The anxieties of a 'dependent culture' turned on the perception that the people 'at home' (i.e. in England) thought of New South Wales as a convict society.[53] Let us explore some of these points in slightly more detail.

The economy of New South Wales depended on convicts. Convict labour built the infrastructure of roads, bridges and public buildings, as well as providing the minor functionaries of public administration (clerks, overseers, constables, and so on). In the productive sector too, convicts did the lion's share of the labouring tasks. Private employers played their part in the convict system by receiving assigned convicts and obtained their labour in return. Like the slave states in the American south, where slaves comprised a similar percentage of the population, the economic system was articulated on the premise of convicts' labour. Unless one wants to insist that slavery or punishment has to be the *exclusive* rather than the dominant activity – the activity which 'determined much of the relevant tradition and social and economic development', to quote Genovese again – of the society in question, it seems perverse to withhold the title of penal colony from New South Wales, and slave society from places like South Carolina in the United States.[54]

Yet socio-economic criteria such as these only partially determine the issue. We must add to the mosaic of life in New South Wales a panel which depicts the mental world that obtained there. And in particular, we must gauge the effect of the punitive purposes that underlay the foundation of the colony on the mentality of the colony. To say that Britain's penal purposes in establishing the colony were in tension with the social and economic dynamics of the colony does not entitle us to write punishment out of the account.

Penal philosophy and practice underwent major changes in the late eighteenth and early nineteenth century, as we have seen in chapter 1. Writers on modern prisons, from Bentham to Foucault, have pointed to a re-orientation of punishment from the body to the mind of the prisoner. This is epitomised in the movement away from heavy dependence on the death penalty and other forms of corporal punishment to the aptly named penitentiary, whose gloomy stone walls were intended to generate repentance in the minds of the condemned and reflection in the minds of those outside the walls. Foucault has persuasively argued that in fact the prison represents a change in a whole set of social institutions, ranged along a disciplinary continuum which includes the school, the factory, the asylum and the prison.[55] We may agree with him but add, along with philosophers of punishment, that what marks the prison off from the other institutions on this continuum is the punitive purpose. Unlike the school, the factory and the asylum, the population of the prison undergoes that pain because they have committed an offence for which the State prescribes punishment.[56] This punitive purpose colours the behaviour of social actors in a variety of ways ranging from the legal status of the prisoner to social interactions of day-to-day life. In other words, apparently similar physical situations can have radically different social meanings, or as one judicial wit put it, even a dog knows the difference between being kicked and being tripped over.[57]

Punishment stamped the *mentalité* of New South Wales. For all the 'freedoms' enjoyed by convicts in New South Wales (freedom from prison walls, no convict uniform, some legal rights, better food than English workers, etc.), there was one fact that everyone in the colony knew, both convict and free: convicts were sent there *as a punishment*. That meant precisely that they were *not* free in many significant ways: not free to stay in England, not free to go back there for a given period, not free to employ themselves like other workers, not free to make the life choices open to other people in England and New South Wales. Their consciousness, to invoke Bettelheim again, was of a lack of freedom consequent on their conviction. What happened to them *was* punishment, meant and experienced as such. Precisely these considerations made the lash and the system of incentives necessary. Escape was difficult and dangerous. Convicts knew they were not free. When historians tell us, for example, that masters sought ticket-of-leave men as workers because they could exercise more control over them, we learn how much the convicts valued their freedom (cf. freedoms). Contemporaries tell us the same thing. The political leader W. C. Wentworth focused his proposals to tighten convict control on just this point:

> It is well-known that there is no object which the prisoners, to a man, are so intent upon, as what they term their liberty . . .that liberty which, as I have before said, is their chief aspiration.[58]

To say that no 'local ideology of oppression' developed in New South Wales, to claim that masters did not see their task as punishment, to say that masters referred to convicts as assigned servants rather than convicts, to point out that the convicts did not challenge the legitimacy of their convictions, and to describe the range of everyday matters in which the convict status did not arise, does not save the case of those who would argue that New South Wales was not a penal colony.[59] In fact, these points cut the other way. Day-to-day social interaction could be less status conscious *because* the powerful, coherent ideology of the criminal law, taken over from England, ensured the subordinate position of convicts. Convict status only needed to be invoked to assert power over the insubordinate. Why belabour that status? The rationale for the existence of coerced labourers in New South Wales was punishment and the fact that this did not have to be constantly stressed should not obscure its fundamental importance in shaping the tone and character of the society.

For all the everyday matters where the convict distinction did not arise, in many other ways it did. Further punishment in the colony figures importantly and is a factor that the revisionists are inclined to downplay. This argument turns partly on the character of the convicts, partly on the nature of the offences for which they were transported, and partly on the nature of the further punishments themselves. If it can be shown that the convicts were hardened characters who committed serious offences, we are less likely to think of their punishments as brutal or excessive. And, if this is so, we are less likely to think of New South Wales as a penal colony; even a free society might be driven to severity in order to deal with hardened criminals. This is a crucial and subtle point, one that cannot go unexamined.

Crime and criminals call forth our deepest and most intensely felt beliefs about right and wrong. Nuances of language can subtly but profoundly alter the course of the debate.[60] Whether the convicts were working-class heroes or professional criminals has been one of the big debates in Australian historiography. The work of Clark, Robson and Shaw is generally taken to have disposed of the contention that the convicts were political criminals or victims of circumstances. Certainly their crimes were mundane enough but there is reason to remain unconvinced about their rejection of the 'victims of circumstances' thesis. The remarkable 'reformation' of so many of these 'criminals' and their pristine offspring, remarked on by so many authors, would not seem so remarkable if the transportees were viewed as victims of circumstances and, when given the opportunity of an 'honest' living in New South Wales, took advantage of it. There is an 'inherently criminal' theory just below a good deal of this writing, especially in the surprise at the wholesomeness of the offspring. References to the convicts as 'professional thieves' and 'professional criminals' flow rather too easily from the pens of some authors.[61] The meaning and connotations of the term 'professional criminal' go unexamined. On a plain reading, the term means someone who earns their living exclusively from crime. This could equally be serious or trivial crime, but usually we understand it to involve serious crime. What evidence is there to show that convicts sent to New South Wales were professional criminals?

Hirst presents little evidence of his own on this, choosing to rely on the work of Robson and Shaw.[62] One immediate problem is their lack of support for the point. The closest Robson comes to 'professional criminals' is to describe the infamous 'dangerous class' of youthful convicts 'who were persistent, if not habitual criminals, living a hand-to-mouth existence.'[63]

But caveats have to be entered before one can reason from Robson's sample and his comments on the London 'dangerous classes', to the character of the convicts who arrived in New South Wales. In the first place, only seventeen per cent of Robson's sample comes from London.[64] Second, he tells us that the more serious offenders were sent to Tasmania rather than New South Wales;[65] only seventeen per cent of the sample of convicts sent to New South Wales have one or more prior convictions, compared to 56 per cent for Tasmania.[66] On the other hand, Irish offenders who were less likely to have committed serious offences (or what we would think of as criminal offences at all), were more likely to be sent to New South Wales.[67] Third, the overwhelming percentage of convicts, 90 per cent, report an occupational status.[68] (The balance, ten per cent, fall in the 'not recorded' category.) A record keeper's statement gives us pause here with his queries to his master: 'When I ask what their trades are, all I get from three fourths of them is "a thief, a thief"; shall I put them down as labourers, sir?'[69] But it should only be a momentary pause. An intensive study of the occupational skills of convicts transported to New South Wales between 1817 and 1840 puts paid to the notion that the trades claimed by convicts were bogus. The occupations listed in the records fit the backgrounds of the convicts and jobs they were assigned to in the colony. They were a cross-section of the English working class whose employment often gave them the opportunity to commit the crime for which they were transported, theft.[70] Finally, note that overwhelmingly the offence for which these people were transported was simple larceny, i.e. not for violent or aggravated forms of theft like robbery or burglary or the other violent crimes we associate with professional criminals.[71]

The other principal historian of the convicts' background, Shaw, reaches similar conclusions from a study of *all* the convicts: '. . . most of the convicts were not the "atrocious villains" so often spoken of, though some of them were; but most were ne'er do-wells, stimulated to crime by low wages, a bad poor law, bad living conditions, periodical unemployment, lack of education and non-existent family life, though often "polished, artful and vicious",. . .'[72] Even then, both Shaw's and Robson's conclusions should be treated with some measure of caution. Their descriptive material comes from middle and upper class reformers. The reformers had reasons to distort the crime problem and the biases and ignorance of their class towards the people they described.[73] Recent studies of crime in nineteenth-century England, such as David Philips' study of the Black Country, reject the notion of a criminal class and shows that those convicted were in some form of employment and that their crimes were opportunistic. Whatever the case in England, the evidence about those transported to New South Wales suggests that they were ordinary working-class people who, whether for reasons of economic pressure or simple greed, stole small items.[74]

Even those who probably do fall in the class 'professional criminal', the juveniles from London,[75] do not fit the modern popular associations of the term professional criminal. Half the crime in England was committed by males under twenty-one.[76] The Artful Dodger probably comes nearer to the true picture than the image conjured up by the term 'professional criminal'. The modern day shoplifter, a daily player in the magistrates' courts of large cities, often with several prior convictions, may provide another image. Whether one thinks of the convicts as professional criminals or Artful Dodgers or shoplifters affects one's perception of the punishment they received. Transportation does not seem so bad for 'professional criminals', but for teenage boys the perception differs.

Nor should we forget that treatment in New South Wales did not differentiate between professional, habitual or first offenders. A first offender, blazing with the injustice of his treatment, was probably more likely to get 'a red shirt' (an expression for a flogging) for insubordination than a seasoned denizen of the street. Modern readers probably do not associate even the Artful Dodger with the sinister and impersonal term, 'professional criminal', but he is close to the profile Robson and Shaw develop. Records of gruesome floggings of such young boys in New South Wales may counterbalance the scales tipped in the other direction by repeated references to professional criminals.[77]

The other part of the argument that New South Wales was a penal colony focuses on the nature of the secondary punishments themselves. Some have claimed that the prominence and severity of punishments – particularly flogging – have been exaggerated, especially by the contemporary standards which countenanced corporal punishment for crimes, for military and, not long since, family discipline. Flogging stories can set the imagination racing. From 1820 floggings were not carried out in public; flogging could only be ordered by a magistrate, not by private master; floggings were usually administered by a convict flogger, leaving open the possibility for laxity and bribery, and variation in the types of whip used.[78] But, even so, the rate of floggings and number of lashes was enormous. On average, one out of every four convicts was flogged in 1835, although this would have to be discounted for repeat floggings; the average number of lashes per flogging was 46. Magistrates ordered 7,103 floggings that year to a population of 27,340 male convicts (female convicts were not flogged). By way of a rough comparison with a contemporary free society, there was an average of 234 court-ordered floggings per year over the period of 1811-27 in England.[79]

There were legal protections against flogging in the colony which mitigated the incidence of this form of punishment. However, these protections should not be overstated. In 1832, for the first time, Bourke's *Summary Punishments* legislation specified the offences for which flogging could be inflicted, and even these were very vague offences like 'insubordination'. Moreover, the legislation set high maximum numbers of lashes, 50 for a first offence and 100 for a second, substantially higher than contemporary limits in slave societies or prisons. These limits were easily avoided by 'splitting' offences, or disregarded, as repeated evidence of magistrates ordering illegal punishments from the earliest days testifies.[80] As we will see in chapter 5, most magistrates were masters of convicts themselves. While the requirement that flogging be administered only on the order of a magistrate imposed limitations on what masters in New South Wales might otherwise have done, masters knew that if they took their convicts before a magistrate, a member of their class and an employer of convict labour, they were pretty well assured of support. Evidence for this comes from a wide range of contemporaries on both sides of the debate. In New South Wales, courts offered some protection, but much less than formal statements of legal protections would suggest.[81]

But what of the severity of these floggings? The severity of flogging cannot be measured by the number of strokes alone; type of instrument and vigour of application also make a difference rendering comparisons based simply on the number of lashes doubtful. Hirst points out that floggings by convict floggers unsupervised by magistrates allowed for bribery. But floggings *were* supervised by district constables, so two bribes rather than one would be necessary. Convict John Fletcher, already under a sentence of 50 lashes, deposed that when he told the Chief Constable at Queanbeyan that he was unable to supply any further evidence against another prisoner, the Chief Constable said, 'Take the damned scoundrel down to the tree'. He got the full 50 lashes while the man sentenced with him got only half his punishment. Fletcher's master testified that Fletcher was unable to work for many days and when he did, the discharge from his back came through his shirt.[82] Moreover, constables, and especially floggers, were hated and ostracised by the convicts. So there is equal reason to suspect severity in flogging, especially if a bribe was expected but not forthcoming or the convict was foolhardy enough to remark on the flogger's lack of class solidarity. Some of those who left accounts of floggings – people familiar with the use of corporal punishment in other contemporary contexts – left no doubt about their horror of what they saw in the colony. Father Ullathorne and convict author Alexander Harris left gruesome accounts. James Wright, a flogging magistrate of 'Lanyon' (near present day Canberra) in the late 1830s, showed that there were means of checking to see that the flogger had done his work properly: his convicts grumbled that he would sometimes examine the back of his convicts when they returned from work. In mitigtion, the witness who gave this evidence at an inquiry told the magistrates that this only occurred because the convict was complaining that the effects of the punishment prevented him from working. We are not told if Mr Wright was satisfied.[83]

Type of instrument also affects the calculation. The cat-o'-nine-tails, each tail knotted, wounded the buttocks and backs of convicts much more than the hide paddles designed by slave holders to avoid scarring the back.[84] A 'good' flogger would draw blood at the fourth or fifth stroke, according to the Catholic priest Ullathorne, more quickly if the back were freshly scarred from a recent flogging.[85] Crowley cites two cases of boys being flogged twenty-five lashes each on the breach for feigning sickness. Blood flowed from fresh scars from the first stroke.[86] An eyewitness tells the contemporary chronicler, Harris, how as he passed a triangle at Bathurst, he 'saw a man with the blood that had run from his lacerated flesh squashing out of his shoes at every step he took. A dog was licking blood off the triangles, and ants were carrying away great pieces of human flesh that the lash had scattered about ...they had a pair of scourgers, who gave one another spell and spell about; and they were bespattered with blood like a couple of butchers'.[87] Convicts at the Hyde Park Barracks in Sydney were mustered to watch the floggings there. The Quaker, James Backhouse, tells of a prisoner who claimed to have seen a thousand men flogged in his fifteen months there.[88] Flogging in New South Wales compared unfavourably with the slave societies we have been considering and with places like the Massachusetts State Prison.

Nor should the psychological effects of flogging be left out of the account, though they are also difficult to gauge. At the very least it was degrading and probably much feared by those who were clean-skins, and brutalizing to those who underwent it. Its deterrent effect, like deterrence generally, can only be guessed at; but if repeated usage is any guide, masters and magistrates in New South Wales had a great deal of faith in the lash. While flogging may not have been an everyday spectacle for people in New South Wales, the class of people to whom it was directed, the convicts, were not spared the pleasure. Paradoxically, its deterrent effect on those people who had not actually seen or experienced a flogging but had heard the stories, may have been heightened. Flogging was the symbol of the system for contemporaries and for us. But symbols are not empty. In New South Wales, the flogging triangle signified how directly the hierarchy of power depended on physical coercion. As Hirst explains, '... the lash had to do the work of the walls, the wardens and the punishment cells'.[89] In other words, stone walls a prison doth not make. But free societies do not need this sort of substitute for the normal trappings of prisons; penal colonies do.

The lash did not have to do all the work. New South Wales was a system of Chinese boxes where those not persuaded by the 'three sisters' (i.e. the lash) could be dealt with by increasingly severe measures. Assigned convicts who misbehaved could be sent back to the government to work in gangs on public works. Convicts could also be sentenced to work at the treadmill, on road gangs with or without chains, to one of the convict barracks or internal penal settlements, or to Norfolk Island. Conditions in the gangs could be appalling. Crowley describes a road gang working in the Blue Mountains in the 1830s. Freezing weather, frozen tools, inadequate clothing, one blanket at night, accommodation too cramped for everyone to lie down, corrupt overseers who fiddled the food rations and victimised complainers set the scene. Apart from the overseers, desperate conditions meant that fellow convicts posed a continual threat, not only in the gangs but generally. Contrary to accounts of convict solidarity, a great deal of evidence points to convicts stealing from one another, homosexual rape, setting up others for punishment as revenge, and informing to obtain rewards offered by the system, such as remissions.[90]

Other penal settlements provided another option. Norfolk Island with its isolation and modern prison-like conditions, combined with even more brutality, was the most severe of the penal settlements, another step up in the graduated scale. Norfolk so etched itself on the consciousness of the convicts that some men would rather be hanged than be sent there; the antagonism of the authorities in Sydney, to say nothing of those in London itself, to the humane reforms of Maconochie testify eloquently to their assessment of its importance in the intimidatory array.[91]

And of course, all this says nothing of executions, and here New

South Wales has an unenviable record too. Aside from two lean years, 1832 and 1837, 'the Minister for Public Instruction', in Marcus Clarke's grim reference to the gallows, carried off as many as 50 victims per year. The population of male convicts hovered around 26,000 for this period. This is approximately 200 times higher than the contemporary English execution rate![92] Terror was a principal ingredient in eighteenth-century English criminal practice but the threat rather than the actuality took greater prominence there.[93] Flogging, hanging, chain gangs and penal settlements in New South Wales held out terrible consequences to the recalcitrant and potentially recalcitrant. The nature and extent of punishments in New South Wales reflect its character: it was a penal colony.

Conditions for free people (i.e. emancipists, those born in the colony and free settlers) were also profoundly affected by its status as a penal colony. First, as has already been noted, the presence of convicts dominated the labour market whether one was an employer or an employee. Free workers complained that employers had become too used to convict labour. Certainly the ambiguities surrounding the applicability of master and servant legislation allowed maltreatment of free workers, especially in the earlier part of the period. Second, the presence of convicts dominated social relations. Society split into the respectable and non-respectable classes. The convict taint provided the basis of disqualification for emancipists whose wealth would otherwise have qualified them as respectable. As we have seen, social position was jealously guarded in this peculiar colony. The confrontation between Governor Macquarie and the Chief Justice of the Supreme Court over the latter's refusal to allow ex-convict attorneys to continue in practice as barristers, a gentleman's profession, led to the Court remaining closed for more than two years and the eventual recall of the judge.[94] A few years later the refusal of another judge to allow an emancipist to bring an action because of the suitor's former convict status promised to bring the emancipist-dominated commerce of the colony to a standstill. It jeopardised the legal capacity of the colony's wealthiest merchants to carry out civil litigation and hence to protect their property and their transactions. The respectable avoided social practices which had convict associations: getting a sun tan, or serving fresh fish, or salt meat, or dancing at the same end of the room if emancipists were present. Thus they would avoid the convict taint.[95]

Freedom of movement and freedom from police interference also proved casualties of the convict system for free people, as we will see.

Disregarding private informants, New South Wales had a very high police to population ratio: 1:144 in Sydney and 1:96 for the colony overall in 1828 (cf. the authorisation of not more than 1:1000 for English rural areas at the time).[96] Moreover at various times up to five different forces with overlapping jurisdictions policed the colony. The Superintendent for Sydney boasted with reference to Sydney convicts: 'There is scarcely one with whom we are not well-acquainted'.[97] Travellers' tales of harassment by police under the *Bushranging Act*, an Act justified by the special circumstances of the colony, also testify to a level of surveillance more akin to a penal colony than the society they knew in England.[98] Police powers irked the elite too. Hannibal Macarthur complained bitterly about the encroachments of 'Convict Constables' on his British liberty.[99]

The nature of the colony also told on the question of who was to exercise State power. The considerable local power exercised by magistrates, open to a few emancipists during Governor Macquarie's time, was denied to them from 1820.[100] Criminal procedure, the greatest threat to individual liberty by the State, was a caricature of the English system. The absence of a grand jury meant that the judge-advocate received the complaints, drew up the indictments, and decided if there was sufficient evidence for trial. He then presided over the trial, not with a jury but with a panel of military officers, conducted the prosecution, ruled on the evidence, voted on guilt or innocence and sentenced. A right of appeal on sentence lay to the governor who, like the judge-advocates until 1808, had no legal training.[101] These were not merely theoretical difficulties, as Judge-Advocate Ellis Bent forcefully complained to the Secretary of State in 1811. Tasks which British law split between several legal officers to ensure that one person was not judge, jury and executioner were all part of the judge-advocate's duties in New South Wales.[102]

Of these disabilities, the absence of trial by jury was the most galling, as we will see in chapter 7. Emblematic of the rights of all true-born Britons and guaranteed by the Magna Carta, trial by jury and the right of emancipists to serve on juries became the banner under which the Emancipists grouped in their struggle to prevent their exclusion from political power in the colony. Despite calls for trial by jury from the earliest years of the colony, the British government repeatedly refused, citing the penal nature of the colony and the composition of the population.[103] Complaints about the additional irregularity of the Criminal Court, presided over by a judge with a military judicial commission and six military officers in uniform, evoked little sympathy from England. In 1814, Earl Bathurst responded bluntly to the complaints of the judge-advocate (who was by now a legally qualified judge), about the un-British, military character of the court. The British Government considered that the character of the colony necessitated the continued show of military force in the courts.[104]

The jury issue later became the linchpin of Emancipist claims to civic status and was not finally resolved in their favour until the late 1830s. Because of its symbolic importance, jury trial and especially the right of emancipists to sit on juries, became inextricably linked with that other hallmark of free societies, elected legislatures. Exclusives, who had also been able to have emancipists excluded from the magistracy, opposed jury trial bitterly.[105]

On both issues Emancipist campaigners from 1819 onwards repeatedly invoked the terms of the British constitution. Emancipist leader, Edward Eagar, bitterly protested their *unfree* condition:

> [E]very Island in the West Indies, the white population of the greater part of which does not in most instances amount to the one tenth or the one twentieth of the population of this colony, has each its House of Assembling, Legislative Council and Governor or Deputy Governor – what just reason can exist for denying to us the same invaluable, and I would say rightful privilege.... It is true we have another description of people, namely prisoners, it is equally true, that the immense majority of the population of every island in the West Indies is composed of equally corrupt and far more dangerous individuals, slaves, and if the one should be considered as a sufficient reason, why the free British Colonists of New South Wales should be denied the benefits of the British constitution, so ought it to have been as sufficient to have denied it to the British Planter in the West Indies ... until some very sufficient reason is produced sufficient to justify the depriving the free British Inhabitants of New South Wales of their Birthright ... that which is enjoyed by every petty island in the West Indies – I trust the British Legislature will be influenced by the Justice as well as the policy of our Claims, to grant us such a form of Government.[106]

But many years were to pass before Eagar's *cri de coeur* was answered. The Exclusives won the battle over emancipist magistrates but eventually lost over trial by jury and the companion issue, the right to vote for elected representatives. In the event, the attempt to saddle the Emancipists with an hereditary disability failed, but there was no inevitability about this. The Exclusivist leader, James Macarthur, confessed in the late 1840s that their bitter campaign against jury trial had largely been based on the fear of Emancipist dominance. That fear only evaporated with the decision in 1838 to end transportation of convicts to New South Wales.[107]

Convictism cut deeply into the social fabric of New South Wales. As we come to see that some of the stereotypes about the convict experience skew the picture – that convicts could exercise some power over their conditions, that they were not powerless victims at the wrong end of the master's whip, that other people suffered similar forms of oppression – the temptation is to forget the reason they were there in the first place: as punishment for crime. If we succumb to that temptation, we will misunderstand how people in New South Wales understood their world, we will misunderstand the extent to which the convicts and emancipists felt their lack of freedom, and we will misunderstand the struggles and changes that did take place there.

This book is about those struggles, and in particular how people used rule of law ideas to change a penal colony into a free society. Part of that story is to see exactly what sort of society early New South Wales was and what it became. The comparisons with other social formations – free societies, slave societies and prisons – provide a conceptual frame for understanding the social ordering of New South Wales. The other part of the story is to explain the meaning and significance of the rule of law to the colonists and to see how they brought it to bear in their crusade to transform that society.

New South Wales was a penal colony for the first fifty years of white settlement. And while in many respects conditions there were different from prison and slave conditions, there were important similarities. Some features of life in Botany Bay seem rather free, but it was not a free society. To paraphrase a famous statement on class, men and women experienced their convict status as they lived their lives in the colony: in their relations with other people (convicts, their masters, overseers, constables, the military, free people and the convict administration), in the conditions of their work, in the experience of further punishments, in the desire for emancipation, in the provision of shelter and food and in the legal and political situation of the colony.[108]

When convicts regained their individual liberty, in the sense that their sentence expired, they did not live in a free society. They lived in a society whose purpose and conditions of existence centred on punishment, a penal colony. Their lack of respectability, the presence of so many convicts and the penal purpose were used to maintain a system of political power that excluded them from participation.

They knew that they lived in a penal colony and so did their colonial masters.[109]

And because they deplored their status and the conditions of a penal colony, some of the colonists, in particular the Emancipists, strove to transform New South Wales into something they – and we – could recognise as a free society. But what are the characteristics of a free society? Some of the criteria have been implicit in the discussion so far but let us make them explicit.

A representative legislature is a key characteristic of a free society. Its absence was sorely felt in New South Wales, as Eagar complained, the more so because even Britain's slave colonies had their 'House of Assembling' and 'Legislative Council'. The ability to participate in the legislative process which touches on so many aspects of daily life – as free workers came to see when, for example, they complained of the colonial master and servant legislation – is fundamental to the notion of a free society.

A second feature of a free society is the protection from the exercise of arbitrary power afforded by the rule of law. The rule of law framework, which in its English form included things like *Habeas Corpus* and trial by jury, offers protections against arbitrary interference from other citizens and from government. As we will see, the rule of law operated only in a very attenuated form in New South Wales in the early decades of white settlement, a pale shade of the complex set of ideas and institutions understood by 'free-born Britons' as their birthright and guarantee of liberty.[110]

Two other characteristics should be noted. If a large proportion of a society's population – either by legal status or economic factors – is precluded from making important life choices (e.g. about where to live, family ties, employment, etc.), it will be impossible to describe that society as free.[111] Certainly societies in which 30 to 40 per cent of the population is not free to make such choices, as was the case in New South Wales, fail the test. Finally, we must take account of the important ideologies at work within a society. Freedom in England, slavery in South Carolina, and punishment in New South Wales made sense of social and institutional arrangements in ways which fundamentally affected the character of those societies.

These criteria supply the essential conceptual framework for the comparisons we have been dealing with in this chapter. Applied to New South Wales, they show that it was a penal colony at the outset but by degrees it became a free society. Many factors contributed to the process by which the society became free: the arrival of free people, the emancipation of convicts, the birth of free children, economic growth, changing ideas about bondage and punishment in England, and most importantly for this story, the struggles of the political actors in New South Wales. The transition was not merely a result of the effluxion of time, the birth rate and the influx of immigrants. The impersonal nature of these processes starves the story of the struggles, the achievements of those who waged those battles and the contingency of it all. The outcome was not a foregone conclusion even in the late 1830s. The convicts still formed a very large percentage of the population when the decision to end transportation was taken. The Molesworth Committee heard strong testimony in favour of continuing transportation. Contingency and struggle figure strongly in this story, a story which centres on the use of limited institutions of freedom that were available in the colony. The barriers to the freedom of the society lay in the *absence* of those institutions – like trial by jury and a legislative assembly – which the colonists associated with free societies and which were opposed in England on the basis that they were not appropriate for a *penal* colony.

So when did New South Wales become a free society? Some, like the eccentric convict, John Grant, took up the cause of British freedom almost immediately; the Kables' case was an important first step in establishing the rule of law. But if one had to nominate the one point at which the transition from penal colony to free society was complete, the grant of a part-elected legislature in 1842 would be the date to choose. This achievement crowned the political struggles of the 1820s and 1830s. Other points on the continuum had been the growth of the Emancipist group, the *New South Wales Act* of 1823 granting a nominated council, the development of a free press in the 1820s, the battles over the jury issue, the growth in the number of free immigrants in the 1830s, and the decision to cease transportation in 1838 thus ending convictism as the defining feature of social and political life in the colony.

But to say that New South Wales had become a free society is not to say that paradise had been achieved in the South Pacific. Free societies vary enormously in quality and we must guard against the tendency to elide free and good. Free societies are preferable to unfree ones – that was the point of the Emancipists' struggle over the status of New South Wales – but they are not immune from the most serious criticisms. For example, the dispossession of the Aborigines, the minimal recognition of their legal rights and their exclusion from political status constituted a most serious criticism of that society.

As the percentage of convicts in the colony declined and thousands of free immigrants swamped the convict proportion of the population at the end of the 1830s, the presence of convicts as the defining feature of social and political life receded and eventually disappeared. With that came the acceptance that New South Wales was a fit place for the institutions which were emblematic of British freedom, trial by jury and representative legislatures. New South Wales remained a colony of England, but as a free society not a penal colony.

Mounted Police escorting prisoners for trial, from country districts to metropolitan gaol. From a drawing by S. T. Gill, 1855, Mitchell Library, State Library of New South Wales.

CHAPTER 3

The Rule of Law

It was this great and universal esteem he [i.e. Sir Mathew Hale] was then in, that made Cromwell so desirous to have him for one of his judges, which offer he would willingly have declined. Being pressed by Cromwell to have his reason he at last plainly told him, that he was not satisfied with the lawfulness of his authority, and therefore scrupled at accepting any commission under it, to which Cromwell replied, that since he had got possession of the government he was resolved to keep it, and would not be argued out of it; that however it was his desire to rule according to the laws of the land, for which purpose he had picht upon him as a proper person to be employed in the administration of justice, yet if they would not permit him to govern by red gowns, he was resolved to govern by red coats.

Sollom Emlyn, 1678[1]

>   Ye Captains to a Monarch lov'd rever'd
>   Draw on his head and yours disgrace Down!
>   The 'Magna Charta' our forefather's rear'd
>   *That* brightest *jewel* in the British *Crown*
>   Ye trample *on* *! – Tho' Britons rule the Waves
>   Great George's subjects (Britons!) here are Slaves.
>   O country beauteous! Climate healthful! mild!
>   O George belov'd (Unlike some *Kings*) abus'd!
>   O People into Slavery beguil'd!
>   O Rulers guilty of a power misus'd
>   When shall *All* cry 'Britannia rules the Waves
>   And Free-born Britons are no longer Slaves'?

John Grant, convict, 1805[2]

So how did people in New South Wales go about the task of transforming New South Wales from a penal colony to a free society? What shape would politics take in a newly-formed penal colony? As foreshadowed in the introductory chapter, legal ideas and institutions played a major role in the politics of the Botany Bay settlement. Indeed a cluster of ideas known as the rule of law provided the major institutions, arguments, vocabulary and symbols with which the colonists forged the transformation. The rule of law served as a fund of English ideas about political ordering, as the instrument with which to accommodate these traditions to the unlikely circumstances of the penal colony of New South Wales, and as a means of incorporating the newer democratic ideas of the nineteenth century. Like all new societies, New South Wales confronted the problem of political authority. Who is entitled to give orders and how are conflicts about those orders resolved? Cromwell faced the same problem after the English Civil War. As the quotation above illustrates, he knew the limitations of force and sought to legitimate his government through the forms of law. Like the other seventeenth-century judicial colossus, Sir Edward Coke, Hale saw the rule of law as the touchstone in English politics, even in the face of monarchs and quasi-monarchs. The bloody instruction of the mid-seventeenth century left a deep impression about the importance of the rule of law. It was an impression that travelled to Botany Bay along with those who sailed there. John Grant was simply one of the more eccentric examples of the strength of this ideology but the same sentiments saturate political discourse in the colony. In the battles between the colony's judges and governors, for example, themes familiar to Coke and Hale play again and again in the unlikely setting of a penal colony two centuries and 12,000 miles away.

Politics and law mixed to a far greater extent in New South Wales than existing accounts of the colony suggest. To many modern minds – especially in countries like England and Australia, where the doctrine of the separation of powers has produced sharp mental borders between law and politics, and legal positivism has taught people to think of law as a technical and value-free science – there appears to be a natural separation between law and politics. The effects of this way of thinking can be found in many spheres, and one of them is the way in which people have written about early New South Wales. The historiography pays little heed to the importance of the rule of law in the political and day-to-day life of the colony. On the one hand, general historians have either failed to notice it at all or, like Clark, Shaw and Ellis, have reduced it to the pedantic or politically motivated interference of various judges with the prerogatives of the governor. On the other, the self-conceptions of legal and constitutional historians tend to treat law and constitutional history as discrete fields of enquiry with politics at the margin or left out altogether. Despite Evatt's pioneering insight about the political role of the courts, the general histories and the legal histories have proceeded in parallel.[3] Even in the most recent of the general histories, Hughes makes only a passing reference to the political role of the courts, and even this is misunderstood. He claims that convicts' rights counted for little prior to 1810. His bibliography makes no reference to the legal and constitutional histories.[4]

But law, to borrow Edward Thompson's phrase, was 'deeply imbricated' at all levels and in all aspects of the colony's life. Evatt's argument about the importance of the courts up to the Rum Rebellion in 1808 only partly captures this. The courts occupied a central political role in the colony throughout the transportation period, not just in the period to 1808.[5] Courts provided a physical and institutional site for a rich tradition of political and legal concepts referred to in modern parlance, though not so commonly at the time, as the rule of law.[6]

But the focus on the courts is too narrow; the rule of law concept encompasses a great deal more than courts. The law supplied the basis for the transportation of the majority of the population; it also set the length and terms of sentences. When convicts became free, master and servant law fixed the parameters of their employment. Law supplied the framework for property holding and the contractual basis on which people traded. Police and magistrates – with varying degrees of fidelity – gave practical effect to the law throughout the colony. Newspaper editors went to the limits of laws setting press freedom, and sometimes beyond. Governors and their subordinates had to worry whether the actions of the executive conformed to law lest they find themselves before the courts in New South Wales or England. To be sure, there was some play in all of this, as Henry and Susannah's case shows. English law did not allow felons to sue. But sue they did and so did others like them. That flexibility and the fund of tradition incorporated in the rule of law, proved to be a great boon to those in the colony who sought political change; their opponents found it hard to counter arguments couched in terms of the Magna Carta and the birthrights of all true Britons.

To fathom this, we need to cast ourselves into the cultural background of the settlers. Seventeenth- and eighteenth-century English politics laid heavy stress on the rule of law. Hay and Thompson claim that the rule of law underpinned political authority in England.[7] They are joined in that assessment, as will be seen, by an impressive list of contemporary seventeenth- and eighteenth-century authorities and by historians.[8] The rule of law occupied a central role in the struggles and settlements of the seventeenth century and their consolidation in the eighteenth century. What they all mean by the phrase, how importantly they regarded it, requires careful examination. This examination forms essential background for understanding the importance of the same ideology in fashioning a new order in the penal colony.

Discussions about the rule of law take place in a twentieth-century context, where the phrase has importantly different connotations from those which it had for seventeenth- and eighteenth-century English people. Whereas a twentieth-century commentator like Hayek concerns himself with legal certainty in the context of the dangers he sees in the discretions exercised in the welfare state,[9] seventeenth- and eighteenth-century concerns focused on battles between king and parliament, the royal prerogative, the independence of the judiciary and the rights of free-born Britons, guaranteed by the British constitution.[10] The older debate takes up the rule of law in a political configuration very different from that of the twentieth century. At the beginning of the seventeenth century, the monarch was still powerful and exerted extensive control over both the parliament and the courts. The conflict centred on the relative powers of these three. While at bottom many of the same issues run through both debates – individual liberty in particular, constraints on authority, and the idea of rule by rational principles rather than the wishes of some individual or group – different historical conjunctions throw up importantly different settings for the operation of the rule of law. For English settlers in New South Wales, conflicts over the extent of the governor's powers – a governor who stood in the place of the king in the colony but wielded more power than any king since James I – conjured up seventeenth-century demons about royal tyranny.

But aside from the differences generated by different historical contexts, additional problems arise from the widely divergent political viewpoints of the various commentators who invoke the phrase, the rule of law. While its rhetorical force has sounded loud and long in the halls of conservative and liberal political thought, recently it has also been taken up and hotly debated among Marxist historians.[11] Can they all be talking about the same thing?

Both time and political viewpoint affect the *meaning* of the rule of law. But its *importance* varies too. For example, according to Hay, the rule of law weighed more heavily in the political life of seventeenth- and eighteenth-century England than it did in the nineteenth or twentieth centuries. Vivid memories of the turmoil of the Civil War and its aftermath produced an almost ridiculous scrupulousness for legal form in the 1688 revolution.[12] The seventeenth-century reliance on the 'ancient constitution' and on the rule of law as the protectors of English liberty – underlined not only by the *Bill of Rights* but also by the *Act of Settlement* of 1701, which protected the independence of the courts by granting life tenure to judges – left a powerful legacy to the Whig consolidators of the eighteenth century.[13] It was a legacy which allowed England to be governed by the gentry without a standing army or a professional police force.[14] The changes of the nineteenth century (e.g. the dominance of the laissez-faire ideology, the growth of a capitalist industrial structure, the advance of police forces and prisons, and changes in the electoral franchise) and the rise of the welfare state in the twentieth have meant that the rule of law occupies a different and arguably less central place in the legitimation of political authority. But what would the rule of law mean in a penal colony? The answer to that question begins in understanding the meaning and salience attached to the rule of law by people in late eighteenth-century England.

At the most general level, people distinguish between the rule of law and rule of men. Properly understood, the opposition means to suggest that government operates on the basis of general rules laid down in advance – the first element of the rule of law conception – rather than *ex-tempore* decisions by the ruler. The antithesis is somewhat misleading in that it suggests that law is self-executing; it conceals the inescapable discretion involved in the application by human beings of general rules laid down in advance of specific situations. The tension between the requirement of generality and the vagaries of individual cases is accommodated by a second element implicit in the rule of law: the requirement that the rules be applied rationally. Properly understood, the idea that we are ruled by law, not by men, signifies the restrictions imposed by the rule of law on rulers, not the reign of an impersonal order of rules. 'The laws ensure that reasons rule and not particular passions, but they are invented and maintained by men and can prevail only when men are guided by reason to the public good and not by passion to private ends.'[15]

The power of the rulers is subjected to constraints against arbitrariness. What they do must be justifiable in terms of the pre-existing general rules. Societies where the rulers' power rests predominantly on physical force (e.g. reliance on the army, hit squads, terror and secret police) do not operate on the basis of the rule of law. I do not mean to suggest here that governments which do adhere to the rule of law in theory and in practice do not rely on physical force. The monopoly on the use of legitimate physical force is a fundamental claim of modern political authority. But to say that the state can and does resort to physical force in the ultimate case is a very different thing from saying its power depends predominantly or in large measure on physical force. Legitimate power makes normative claims on the obedience of its subordinates based on reasons of religious or secular principles. This differs from obedience based predominantly on fear of physical coercion. The rule of law is a way of organising power, not the opposite of power. It is, however, the opposite of *arbitrary* power.[16]

If reasons rule, the notion of reasons is wider than the general legal rules of the society, such as thou shalt not kill or thou shalt not steal. Does Shylock's contract entitle him to his pound of flesh? Does the law of attainder prevent Henry and Susannah Kable from suing in New South Wales? How are the general rules elaborated to bridge the gap between them and the particularities of the case to be adjudicated? We have already seen that the general legal rules have to be applied rationally but the notion of rationality at work here is of a specialised kind. Legal rationality superimposes a specialised process of argumentation on the general conception of rationality. Cases, as Coke said, are not to be decided by natural reason 'but by the artificial reason and judgment of the law'. Law has special traditions, forms and styles of argument, judgments about appropriate analogies, hierarchies of authority, references to precedent and so on. Only a certain sort of rationality will be admitted in legal argument from general rules to particular cases.[17]

Although most of these points logically apply to anyone in society, the rule of law theme usually plays on the relationship between governors and governed. Thus, while the first strand in the rule of law concept emphasises that the governors may only act pursuant to pre-existing rules, the obverse is that the governors are also *bound* by the rules. But there is still more to it than this.

Sometimes stated as equality before the law, and sometimes that nobody is above the law, the rule of law framework does not allow irrelevant exemptions – on account of wealth, position, ability to pay a bribe, etc. – where the rules otherwise apply. The principle does allow classification of people to whom particular rules apply, within limits of generality; once these are established they apply equally to all those affected.[18] But the important part of this principle, established in the seventeenth-century struggles between the Stuart kings and their parliaments, is that everyone, including the king, is bound by the rule of law. More importantly, it meant – and still means – that executive government may only do what has been authorised in the form of law by Parliament. In New South Wales – and this became a vital point – it meant that colonial governors and their officials could be sued in the courts if their actions were not backed by law.

The third element of the rule of law concept is the courts. The rule of law connotes more than the rational application of general rules, at least in the case of complex societies, and certainly in English usage of the term. A king who sat and adjudicated personally, applying the general rules according to the dictates of legal rationality, would be described either as practising only a very attenuated form of the rule of law, or as overlooking an essential aspect of the rule of law, a differentiated legal system. As understood in England, and systems deriving from the English system, the rule of law involves courts, judges and a legal profession independent of the executive. The courts provide the mechanism through which executive actions can be examined against the standard of the general rules applicable to the society. Theoretically a king, a governor or officials could assess their own actions in terms of the laws. If law was the mechanical process that it is sometimes supposed to be, this might work. But people intuitively mistrust those who are judges in their own cause, an intuition which correctly identifies the flexible nature of legal rules. Fidelity to the rule of law requires independent forums for adjudication, a key part of the modern understanding of the separation of powers.[19] It places the courts between citizens and governments.

To this point we have established that the rule of law has at least three elements: general rules laid down in advance, rational argument from those principles to particular cases, and, at least in a developed form, a legal system independent of the executive for adjudication of disputes involving the general rules.

It is important to see what this promises, and what it does not. First, the rule of law is compatible with the existence of morally bad general rules. If, for example, the general rules are racist, such as those of the American South during slavery or in South Africa today, then the operation of courts applying those rules in a rational way will still signify the existence of the rule of law. Stalin's terror, Nazi Germany and other examples are often cited in connection with this point either to deny that these cases are examples of the rule of law because of the fundamental immorality of the rules,[20] or to deny Thompson's claim that the rule of law is a 'unqualified human good'.[21] This is not the place to rehearse the long debate over whether fundamentally immoral rules count as law.[22] For present purposes, I simply want to declare my legal positivist stance on this point and say that fundamentally immoral rules can count as laws. So, to take the South African case, I would regard the apartheid laws as morally repugnant but laws just the same.[23]

What follows from this is that in such systems, the rule of law exists and enforces morally repugnant laws. It also follows that in such situations the claim that the rule of law is an unqualified good may not amount to much. But it does amount to a constraint on arbitrary power, a not inconsiderable advantage over death-squads, disappearances, and mass executions, to nominate some current examples of arbitrary power. Regimes, which in fact rely on the rule of law, do accept limitations on what they might otherwise do. In this limited sense, the rule of law does seem to be a unqualified human good.

But the rule of law has to be practised, not just preached. The examples noted above can only dubiously claim to operate under the rule of law. To be valid the claim to adhere to the rule of law must correspond reasonably closely with the actual practice of government in that society. Ideals which exist only in political rhetoric or in a constitutional document do not equate with the rule of law. The essentially executive flavour of the phrase should suggest that the practice must show fidelity to the ideal. If, at a minimum, the rule of law requires known principles laid down in advance but the practice is that the rules are not 'public' or are invented *ex post facto*, then this is not the rule of law but a fraud.[24] Arbitrary power is impatient of such standards, valuable as against power because of the demands they make for justification. Insofar as a regime such as that of South Africa in practice conforms to the procedural canons of legality, then that society is governed by the rule of law, notwithstanding the repugnant nature of its apartheid legislation.[25] Fuller's attempt to avoid this conclusion by reliance on a requirement of certainty – that the apartheid laws are so vague in some cases as to make it impossible to determine whether a particular citizen is bound by them – is not convincing.[26] Determination of a person's racial category is no more and no less certain than a host of other laws that no one thinks to question, be they tax laws or the penal code. For example, the law respecting self-defence and provocation in murder, the most serious crime and hence the one where the highest degree of certainty should be expected, depends on very fine judgments about the reasonableness of the action, the immediacy of the threat, the degree of the provocation, etc. Similarly, thousands of disputes about the application of tax laws do not yield the conclusion that their uncertainty nullifies their status as laws. Other examples from all branches of the law would show the point over and again. Some degree of uncertainty is inherent in the application of general rules to particular cases. There is a limit on the degree of uncertainty but it is sufficient here simply to say that these limits allow enough room for the application of immoral rules. Seen this way, the rule of law offers a certain structure of power, in which the executive government has to justify its actions in terms of the general rules and legal argumentation to an independent legal system. This will not protect the governed from immoral general rules but will protect them from arbitrary interference by government.

Finally, and this point follows from the preceding points, the rule of law does not promise absolute certainty or 'right' answers, at least in the sense of a right answer in arithmetic.[27] As already seen, the nature of general rules laid down in advance means that a particular instance will require reasons and arguments to act as a bridge from the general rule to the particular situation. The variety of circumstances to which the general rules may be applied means that very often the outcome will not be clear in advance of adjudication. The very fact that two well advised litigants are prepared to spend large amounts of money to take their case to court, that learned judges at a variety of levels in the court system, from trial court to appeal court (or appeal courts in some cases) differ, should be enough to demonstrate this point.

Legal logic does not have mechanical precision. It is closer to moral or political decision-making than it is to reasoning in the 'hard' sciences.[28] It draws on rules, principles and policies which have a great deal more play in them than arithmetical logic. Words and devices like 'reasonable,' 'necessary' and 'insofar as the circumstances of the colony permit', allow rational people – and judges – to differ without being arbitrary. In the end, the right decision is determined structurally rather than by reference to 'absolute truth'. Decision rules based on judicial majorities and court hierarchy determine what is the 'right answer'. Hence, when historians assert that Chief Justice Forbes was wrong in his decision about the Governor's power to revoke assigned convicts from private service, they may mean something different than that the judge did his sums wrongly.[29] It might be that the judge did make a methodological error, for example, if he overlooked a relevant case or statute. But that is not so in the case about the governor's power to revoke the assignment of a convict; that controversy concerned the *interpretation* of a statute. In fact, in terms of narrow legal decision rules, Forbes was right, since he formed the majority in the highest court to take up the case. It is not to the point that the governor, or James Stephen who drew up the statute at the Colonial Office, or the historian disagrees with the interpretation. That is a commonplace among disappointed litigants and frustrated legal drafters. It might be suggested that Forbes was improperly substituting his views for the clear provisions of the statute. However, that would be a difficult case to establish, especially where ambiguities in the statute or constitutional provisions (such as 'insofar as the circumstances of the colony permit') require fine judgements about the application or meaning of the rule in a particular factual setting and the appropriateness of that interpretation of the rule in an unusual and changing society.

To summarise the main point, the rule of law does not promise absolute or even nearly absolute certainty but decision-making within a specific type of procedural framework. And within this framework of general rules, legal argumentation and personnel indeedendent of government, there will be considerable room for different people to arrive at different results while still being faithful to legality. Although a great deal of the legitimating rhetoric surrounding the law suggests something more mechanical, legal reasoning is more art than science.

The structural elements of the rule of law may be found in many different societies. But in English eyes, especially in the eighteenth century, the rule of law had much fuller meaning, a meaning which was the legacy of English history. While it is possible to separate the rule of law into two aspects – one structural and one cultural – as various writers have suggested,[30] the people with whom we are concerned saw the rule of law as an integrated entity which underpinned the British polity. To understand the rule of law through the eyes of the New South Wales colonists, we must appreciate not only its key structural elements but also its centrality in their political ideology.

The window to that appreciation opens onto England in the seventeenth and eighteenth centuries. That is the primary source of the cultural inheritance which the settlers brought with them to the new colony. Many of the constitutional problems of England in the seventeenth century – as well as the radical ideas and actions of the American and French revolutions – found their analogues in the small penal colony on the other side of the world. The importance the colonists attached to the rule of law – their rights as free born and English, their reverence for the Magna Carta, Habeas Corpus, the Bill of Rights, their concern about the independence of the judiciary, trial by jury, and their opposition to paid police forces, all encapsulated for them by Blackstone in the second half of the eighteenth century – was rooted firmly in the politics of the seventeenth and eighteenth centuries. These features of British politics were central to their conceptions about the shape of the new colony in a way not at all captured by the phrase civil liberties, suggested by some as a substitute for the rule of law[31] and by others to describe the campaign for trial by jury in New South Wales.[32]

Under the tutelage of J.G.A. Pocock, historians of seventeenth-century England have stressed the overwhelming importance of the 'ancient constitution' in the political struggles of that epoch. The relative powers of the king, parliament and the courts occupy the centre stage. Argument about these issues takes its referents not from theories of a social contract but from England's 'ancient constitution', lost in the mists of time, which set the pattern of the relationship between king, parliament and courts, over a very powerful subtext about English birthrights. As one historian summarised it, 'the Revolution Settlement was first and foremost the Rule of Law. It was the triumph of the common law and lawyers over the king, who had tried to put prerogative over the law.'[33]

The drama opens at the beginning of the seventeenth century with Sir Edward Coke, judge of the King's Bench and the foremost legal figure of his day, at the feet of his monarch telling him that even the king is subject to the law. The details of the story are better told elsewhere,[34] but here is the stuff of powerful icons, coming from a judge appointed and dismissible by the king. The idea of the separation of powers was not even a speck in Montesquieu's eye at this point,[35] and life tenure for judges, a product of the experiences of the seventeenth century, still almost one hundred years away.[36] Coke's legacy for the purposes of this story lies in his assertion that no person, including the king, is above the law. Even then the sense of this had to be qualified by reference to the king's prerogative, which clearly was part of the law, a prerogative that would be whittled away in the course of the century. Confinement of this prerogative, so that the king could then neither make laws by proclamation nor offer dispensations from the parliament's legislation, made it clear that the king could not make laws. This was a legacy the early settlers of New South Wales and their governors were to remember almost two centuries later.

But this was by no means Coke's only legacy. In the course of the seventeenth century he and his brother judges were able to extend that bridgehead by establishing not only that nobody was above the law but also that the only interpreters of that law were professional judges, educated in the arcane mysteries of the law. By the end of the century both houses of parliament and the prerogative courts had yielded their jurisdiction over legal disputes.[37]

But probably the greatest legacy of the seventeenth century lay in the stress on the rights of free-born Britons, resurrection of the Magna Carta and the embodiment of English political principles in the Bill of Rights. The political actors were careful to invoke the precedent of the English constitution and to pay punctilious attention to legal detail while executing Charles I, forcing James II into exile and tricking the line of royal succession to suit the needs of the day. Their precedent established the essential role of parliament for legislation, confined the prerogatives of the Crown and established the independence of the judiciary. The balanced constitution they produced – king, lords and commons, underwritten by the rule of law – guaranteed true liberty. Indeed for them true liberty meant government under law.[38] But this constitutional system also contained other features, most importantly the right to trial by jury, sourced to the Magna Carta and held by John Maynard to be the 'subject's right yea his birthright and inheritance as his lands are'. Hallowed by Blackstone, a thorn to the executive, and one of the triggers of the American Revolution, the eighteenth century valued it no less than the seventeenth.[39]

Other issues, such as royal taxation to maintain standing armies, raised constitutional questions about the legislative power which would also remain a powerful legacy to the eighteenth century and become an issue in New South Wales when governors sought to raise revenue by port duties and road tolls.[40] The depredations of the army under the Commonwealth and the appointment of Catholic officers by James II made standing armies anathema to the Whiggish ideology of the eighteenth century. The involvement of the army in civil government was seen as a detestable encroachment, as late-eighteenth-century debates on unsuccessful proposals to establish standing armies or paid police forces showed.[41]

However, if these were the contours of the rule of law for English people of the seventeenth century, its salience for them is also a very important consideration. Part of Coke's difficulty in convincing James I that the 'artificial reason' of the law had to be left to professional lawyers lay in the fact that some training in law was thought essential to an English gentleman's education. What need of judges did the king have when he could deduce the proper legal outcome for himself? But the more important dimension of this was that the gentry was accustomed to a legal measure in all aspects of life. Their private affairs, especially land and marriage arrangements were set up in extremely complex legal arrangements, while their duties in parliament and as justices of the peace required a working knowledge of the law. As Christopher Hill tells us, 'Most gentlemen had a legal education of some sort, and thought of politics in legal terms.'[42] This habit of thought and action is reflected in the way the great political issues of the day were framed in legal terms. A recent historian of the period has put it this way:

> The one element of constitutional continuity in seventeenth-century England was the acceptance by king and parliament of a political rule of law. Law was the touchstone of politics. No matter how men might differ over what the law said or what it might be made to mean, all were committed to a legal standard in the conduct of their political affairs... the common law provided a constant conceptual framework for political action...virtually every important controversy was formulated, and every position justified, in legal language and common law paradigms.[43]

The Whig inheritors of the 1689 settlement elevated the rule of law to a central place in their political ideology.[44] 'The rhetoric of eighteenth-century England is saturated with the notion of law'[45] for a variety of good reasons. In the first place, as the pacific nature of the 1688 revolution and its emphasis on legal form suggests, the violence of the Civil War and the ensuing upheavals had quenched the country's inclination towards violent solutions. Hence we hear the leading spokesmen of the age blunting the revolutionary justifications offered by the seventeenth-century precedents and by Locke's *Two Treatises of Government*. Blackstone stressed the perfection of English laws and institutions. The balanced constitution of king, lords and commons combined the best aspects of the possible forms of government, thus inviting the conclusion that the circumstances which would justify a revolution must be very rare. Stability was the order of the day.[46]

A second reason for the importance of law in the ideology of the eighteenth century can be found not so much in the strength of legal ideas as in the absence of a plausible alternative. As has been noticed by a number of historians, religion had undergone a marked decline as a legitimating force by the eighteenth century, leaving the role of secular priest to the assize judge and the rituals of law.[47] Another unavailable option, a standing army or what amounted in their eyes to the same thing, a paid police force, supplied a third reason for the pre-eminence of the rule of law in the eighteenth century. Despite Jacobite threats, outbreaks of rioting and disorder throughout the century, and the deep fears engendered among the rulers by the French Revolution, neither a standing army nor a paid police force could be countenanced. The memories of the seventeenth century bulked large here and raised a panoply of gentry fears. First, paid police and standing armies conjured up the violence they sought to avoid. Second, they posed a threat to English liberty by raising the spectre of the French spy system. Third, paid forces threatened the balance of the constitution, because they were inconsistent with the existence of the county militia and – unlike the militia which was controlled by the local gentry – paid forces were open to control by central, executive government. Fourth, the gentry would be taxed to pay for these expensive innovations or forced to billet troops as they had been during Cromwell's time. For all these reasons, the gentry chose to rely on the rule of law and their own resources rather than resort to a standing army or a paid police force.[48]

Their solution to the problem of how to govern, as a growing body of literature shows, was to base their authority on the rule of law, in particular, the criminal law rather than the force of arms.[49] The theatre of criminal justice most vividly illustrated this theory of legitimacy, a theory which can be found powerfully in conservatives like Blackstone,[50] as well as in radicals like John Wilkes, whose strategy actually depended on the adherence of his opponents to a rule of law model.[51] Whether this system was actually fair is for present purposes, beside the point.[52] What is important, is the significance attached to the rule of law:

> In seventeenth and eighteenth-century England the law was a remarkably potent force. It was the chief means of exercizing authority, the main vehicle of state power, an important way of resolving disputes and, because of the extraordinarily wide acceptance of the notion of the rule of law, a vital means of legitimizing private initiatives...The fiction of the rule of law commanded remarkable support and was the framework within which most conflict occurred.[53]

Although Whigs took these principles more seriously than Tories,

Tories also subscribed to them even if, as we will see, they sometimes strayed from virtue. The rule of law occupied a central place in the political ideology of late eighteenth-century England. It was from this political culture, then, that the white settlement of Australia was launched.

The author of the poem quoted at the start of this chapter, John Grant, was a convict. He wrote the poem on the way to Norfolk Island where he was being transported for irritating Governor King beyond endurance. Grant was an eccentric and a gentleman, not representative of the convicts in general. His eccentricity was, in part, that he took the Magna Carta too seriously. By pushing the claims too far, he enabled a no doubt exasperated Governor King – with whatever nagging doubts in case Grant had a legal point – to put him beyond the pale.

Grant's fellow 'settlers' all had direct personal experience of the rule of law. Fragments suggest a sort of wry, mocking humour among the convicts about the legal system : 'Farewell to the well-known Old Bailey, where I once used to cut such a swell' go the words of the song 'Botany Bay'. Surgeon, Peter Cunningham, describes convicts staging full-dress satires of their trials on the decks of the transport ships; convict slang for the sharks they saw off the sides of the ships was 'sea lawyer'.[54] But the humour does not run to wholesale rejection of the English legal system. If anything, the evidence suggests a cautious appreciation of its possibilities. Grant wholeheartedly embraced English rule of law principles and was astonished that King George could have allowed the travesties of New South Wales. Bentham's *A Plea for a Constitution* proceeds along a similar line of argument. Others like the Kables and the officers of the New South Wales Corps were more pragmatic. They had as keen an appreciation of the power reposed in the legal system as any of the combatants in the constitutional struggles of the seventeenth century. People in New South Wales saw the potential of the colonial legal system and used it to pursue their political and other objectives. If indeed the British government had intended to establish a purely military system of command at Sydney Cove, the provision of civil courts was a fatal mistake. The Kables proved that within the first six months. Henry and his business partners, emancipists Lord and Underwood, used the civil courts to their business advantage repeatedly in the ensuing years. Commentators express their surprise at the amount of litigation in the colony. Some convicts were prepared to make their complaints to magistrates, as indeed they were encouraged to do by

Governor Macquarie. They were even prepared to complain about the merciful magistrate who departed from the legal forms; they could pick a counterfeit.[55] Indeed, their willingness to employ the legal system in the colony, their ability to mount criticisms of the colony's hybrid institutions based on their own close observation of the English system, and their predisposition to cast their claims in terms of their constitutional inheritance showed an acceptance of authority which ultimately yielded a radical rather than a revolutionary political stance.

In short, the convicts, like the other settlers – from officials, to army personnel, to free settlers – bore with them a strong conception of what the rule of law meant, the uses to which it could be put, and its importance in English political life. While new and unusual circumstances called for some reorientation of the rule of law model, they drew on this heritage when confronted by the problems of establishing a new political order. Like their seventeenth-century forebears, they summoned up the ancient constitution, their birthright and inheritance, rather than adopting the revolutionary road and philosophical schemes of the French or American revolutions.[56] Although Tom Paine's ideas and Jacobinism had a group of highly educated and articulate proponents in New South Wales from the 1790s onwards, plus rebellious Irish convicts, their impact was at best indirect compared to the prominence of ideas drawn from the English rule of law model.[57]

The rule of law in colonial New South Wales meant from the outset, that the pressures against arbitrary rule were considerable. The presence of courts meant convicts could claim the benefits of the laws of England in criminal and civil matters. It also meant that settlers and convicts could be tried only for offences known to the law; in the superior courts after 1810, trials were conducted by judges who were legally qualified. The liability of officials to be sued in the colony for exceeding their powers – and of the governor to be sued on return to England – was well known.[58] On several occasions this principle necessitated indemnity legislation either for the governors or the magistrates, and ultimately provided sufficient leverage to make them conform to the law. When the marines under Major Ross reminded Governor Phillip that they need only obey his *lawful* orders;[59] when Governor Hunter reminded the military that 'no man within this colony can be put out of the power or lose the protection of the law under which we live, from the meanest of his Majesty's subjects up to the Commander in Chief [i.e. himself] or first Magistrate, we are all equally amenable to and protected by the laws';[60]

when Mr Justice Jeffery Bent refused to pay at the toll gate on the basis that the Governor lacked the *legislative* power to exact it;[61] when others made similar arguments, they were re-asserting the principles of the rule of law, established in the seventeenth century and venerated in the eighteenth as the English inheritance from time out of mind.

Both their actions and their words reflect the meaning and emphasis on the rule of law described in this chapter. John Grant's poem, quoted at the beginning of this chapter, is indicative of the language used in the politics of the colony. There were many in the colony prepared to brandish the Magna Carta and Blackstone at would-be autocrats. Free settlers, convicts, emancipists, governors and judges objected, as we will see, to the un-British nature of their institutions. They were referring to the absence of trial by jury, to the fact that the officers who made up the Criminal Court all sat in their uniforms, to the governor's power and to their lack of a colonial assembly. When the Emancipists came to assert their political claims, they did not plead the rights of man. Rather they pleaded that the terms of their pardons restored them to all their British rights and liberties, and the Magna Carta's guarantee of trial by jury. Throughout the 1820s, the colony's three main newspapers were filled with this rule of law rhetoric. The Emancipist leader, lawyer and journalist, W.C. Wentworth, flamboyantly argued the Emancipist cause in the colony's courts and then broadcast virtual transcripts of the proceedings via his newspaper, the *Australian*. The newspapers took on the de facto role of law reporting; editorials and letters could read like law journal articles. Points and authorities on the availability of the writ of mandamus were not beyond the popular press. The colony's third newspaper, the *Monitor*, edited by the radical E.S. Hall, campaigned ceaselessly for the legal rights of convicts. As the number of judges and lawyers in the colony grew, especially from about 1820, the rule of law ideology found more eloquent and authoritative exponents. Chief Justice Francis Forbes assessed his own role with a great sense of the history described above:

> The people of this country look with the most intense anxiety at every act, every opinion of the Judge; without trial by jury, without the corrective power of an assembly, without one single popular right, they naturally regard the Supreme Court as their only protection against absolute power; their rulers may be the best possible, but they will not probably be better than the rulers at home, and why have the people of England imposed all those checks and balances, but upon the assumption that they are necessary; and if they are necessary there, why should they be less so in

New South Wales?...I have strained hard to preserve its [i.e. the Supreme Court's] independence...a far greater protection to the government, than in the seeming acquiescence of a pliant judge, than in all the subserviency of the most obsequious bench.[62]

But of course, these Botany Bay Whigs did not have it all their own way. 'Damn the Law! My will is the Law!', Governor Bligh expostulated with a fine disregard for the rule of law tradition. He was not the last of the military and naval governors of New South Wales to become impatient of the checks placed on his authority. Justice Jeffery Bent scorned Governor Macquarie's principle of government described by the judge as, '*quod gubernatori placet, legis habet vigorem.*'[63] Similarly, Chief Justice Forbes said apprehensively of Governor Darling that there was 'Law in his voice, and fortune in his law.'[64] It is not difficult to hear the echoes of the seventeenth century in these utterances.

On the other side of the argument, governors, and the Exclusives, chafed at the idea that felons had rights. Yet even they were sensible of the demands of the rule of law. John Macarthur and his faction skilfully used the courts in the lead up to the Rum Rebellion to achieve their objectives. Only when that strategy failed did they resort to armed force. After the Rebellion they sought to cloak their actions in legality.[65] Macquarie, at his wits' end and driven to ill-considered actions by the recalcitrance of his judges, pleads for an indemnity from the government for 'unwitting' illegalities.[66] After a brief flirtation with rights for convicts, Governor Darling thought it absurdly pretentious of the Emancipists – as the quotation opening chapter 2 shows – to assert rights that he considered forfeited by those, bond and free alike, who had settled in a penal colony.[67] Exclusives' spokesman of the 1830s, James Macarthur, complained to the Molesworth Committee about the Supreme Court's harassment of the gentry magistrates with 'legal' technicalities.[68] From the Bench in 1834, the Tory Judge Burton's famous charge to the jury railed against the Emancipist campaign for trial by jury.[69] James Mudie ridiculed the claims of 'the felonry of New South Wales'.[70]

For the original inhabitants of the colony, the Aborigines, the rule of law provided cold comfort. For the white free settlers, convicts and emancipists, it provided a measure of protection against power from the top, and eventually was the instrument through which their claim to political status was realised; for the Aborigines, its authority stood behind their forceful dispossession, its protections proved largely illusory, its courts were closed to Aboriginal testimony, and its principles denied the existence of their own laws. As we have seen in chapter 1 – and will see again in relation to policing – legal rules, even for murder could mean little without the mechanisms and the will to realise the protections promised by the rule of law. At times this could descend to savage parody. In 1826, for example, Attorney-General Saxe-Bannister protested to Governor Darling about the illegality of an army reprisal patrol against Aborigines in the Hunter River area:

> I have formed the opinion that the indiscriminate slaughter of offenders, except in the heat of immediate pursuit, or other similar circumstances, required preliminary solemn Acts – and that to order soldiers to punish any outrage whatever in their way is against the law, which is powerful enough to guard the Public Peace from any permanent aggression.[71]

As the governor pointed out to London, the attorney-general's solution to the problem was mad: a declaration of martial law and the attorney at the head of the troops.[72] Official enquiries into such raids raised the ire of land-hungry white settlers and antagonised the governor's only agents for the imposition of the rule of law at the frontier, the military and the police.[73] Aborigines were excluded from the protections of the rule of law just as surely as they were from their land.

Two cases in the 1830s clarified the status of the Aborigines. In the first, Jack Congo Murrell was tried for murder of another black. Defence arguments that the British law did not protect the blacks, that they did not understand the white law, and evidence that they had their own code of laws all failed.[74] Two years later seven whites were tried for the murder of some 28 Aboriginal captives. It was dubbed the Myall Creek Massacre. At the first trial they were acquitted. The attorney-general filed a new presentment for murder of victims, including some children, not named in the first indictment. This time the jury convicted and seven defendants were hanged. White campaigners for the defendants berated the attorney-general; the Grand Jury system – a casualty of the colonial situation in New South Wales – would not have issued an indictment, they claimed. Since one of the organisers of the campaign was a magistrate and therefore likely to have been on any Grand Jury, this was almost certainly true. The gentry regarded the attorney-general's role as a dangerous innovation and a threat to their freedom.

The Myall Creek murderers were civilians, and those who hanged were convicts or emancipists. A large part of the protest on their behalf turned on the injustice of selecting them for prosecution and punishment, despite the occurrence of many previous similar incidents. The number of blacks killed, the cold-blooded nature of the killings and the fact that those tried were all convicts or emancipists probably explained the selection. But the argument reveals how little protection the rule of law offered Aborigines.[75] An inquiry in the following year was unable to find conclusive evidence against a combined party of soldiers and the Mounted Police led by Major Nunn. Governor Gipps had to yield the day against them and the British government resigned itself to anarchy and the extermination of the Aborigines beyond the frontier. It was not willing to pay the price required to enforce the rule of law at and beyond the frontier.[76]

The rule of law had a strong hold within white society because whites had access to the courts. The blacks had to rely on whites to activate the processes of law for whatever protections it offered them. Despite the ruling in *Murrell's* case, as a practical matter, the Aborigines stood outside the protection of the rule of law. While the whites carried on their own battles within the rule of law framework, it was put to one side in their dealings with the blacks

The transition of New South Wales from penal colony to free society owes a great deal to the English conception of the rule of law. Although the claims of convicts on emancipation owe something to the 'rights of man', they owe more to arguments based on the terms of their pardon which purported to restore them to all the rights and liberties of English people. Through the legal system, as will be seen in the following chapters, they explored those rights and had them symbolically confirmed, for example, by testing their standing to sue in the courts, paradoxically a right not allowed to people in England convicted of a felony unless in receipt of a royal pardon. Their complaints about the constitution of the Criminal Court in the colony, staffed by a judge-advocate and uniformed officers, echo the themes of English history for the two previous centuries: they objected to the involvement of military officers in civilian tasks; they objected to being tried by any means other than a British jury, a vital aspect of their liberty; they objected, with good reason, to the partiality of the military juries in the early years. They saw these departures from English models as deprivations of the rights guaranteed to them by the Magna Carta which, as Blackstone assured, accompanied them wherever English people planted colonies.

The growth in wealth and influence of the Emancipist group by about 1820 meant that the ambiguities of their position and that of the colony, somewhere between a penal colony and a free society took on new importance. The increasing numbers of free former convicts, in addition to the handful of wealthy free settlers meant that pressures built up to realign relationships not only between the free settlers and the emancipated convicts, but also between those groups and the autocratic power of the colonial governors. The issue had been developing in earnest since Governor Macquarie's arrival in 1810. He attempted to enlist the symbolic force of the legal system to pursue his pro-emancipist policy. His attempts to establish a place for emancipists in the magistracy and to force the courts to continue to allow ex-convict attorneys to practise before them met tenacious opposition from the Exclusives.[77]

This conflict intensified opposition between Emancipists and Exclusives. Moreover, by 1819 it was becoming clear that some devolution of political power was on the agenda. The legal status of emancipists became a politically crucial issue. If they were indeed returned to all the rights and privileges of free-born English people, then their wealth and greater numbers guaranteed them a large share in such power. On the other hand, if they could be fixed with some disability pertaining to their former status, power would be left to the Exclusives. As their name suggests, the Exclusives did try to use former convict status as a disqualifying factor over and above property qualification, the traditional criterion of civic status in English politics. They fought out this battle within a legal rubric in which from 1819, trial by jury became the central issue of contention.[78]

Parallel to this struggle, two others ran on at the same time. The first centred on the power of the governors. Successive governors found themselves in conflict with the opponents of the particular group they favoured. The second concerned the position of the courts in the configuration of power. Their relationship to the governor and to the contending groups was crucial because so many of the disputed issues either fell to the courts for decision or, because of the limited options for political action in the colony, were forced into legal form and directed to the courts as a strategy in the political conflict. The usefulness of the courts in this strategy depended on their relationship to the governor; they would be of little use to the contenders if they were simply subordinate to the governor on issues touching government policy.

As we will see in chapters 4 and 5, the issue of the independence of the courts, both at the level of the Supreme Court and the magistrates' courts, was a persistent one throughout the transportation period. For the first two decades, the judge-advocates (with one brief exception) had no legal training. In a colony where the government was small, any finding of executive illegality would be one untrained person's opinion as judge against that of his governor. Moreover, the ruling was more than likely to touch on an issue in which the governor was directly involved, and hence to constitute a very public blow to the governor's authority.

With the arrival of the first of the professional judges in 1810, and the growth of a legal profession which could claim expertise in legal matters (convict attorneys in the colony prior to 1808 had advised the governor and assisted the courts), the potential for these conflicts increased. The judges, without exception, found themselves caught up in the politics of the colony on one side or the other, pro-governor or pro-monopolist, pro-Emancipist or pro-Exclusive, radical or conservative. The arrival of Wentworth and Wardell in the early 1820s – men skilled as both barristers and journalists enlivened these conflicts with their radical ideas. Not content with the political forum offered by the courts, they used their own newspaper, the pro-Emancipist *Australian*, to broadcast their courtroom arguments and rule of law rhetoric. Attempts by the conservative Governor Darling to silence these press critics only gave rise to further conflicts, which were played out in the Supreme Court. In a very direct sense, the judges and the lawyers were the culture bearers who engraved the detail on colonial politics using the rule of law as their cutting stone.

At another level of the legal system, the magistracy offered another site from which to fight the colony's political battles, a site colonised by the Exclusives. Governors were forced to rely on justices of the peace to administer the convict system as well as to run the summary courts and administer the police at local level. Yet the traditions of the office, as well as the independence offered them by the rule of law in their judicial capacity, meant not only that the magistrates could enjoy a good deal of freedom from the governor's supervision, but also that the position could be used to oppose the governor's policy, harass political opponents and enhance the claims to prestige of the office holder. And this is to say nothing of the personal power and advantages offered by the magistracy at local level over the convict and the free population.

As we will see in chapter 5, after a few emancipist appointees, magisterial appointments fell to the Exclusives. With the exception of stipendiary magistrates, whose loyalties were somewhat divided, control of local government and those everyday enforcers of the rule of law, the police, fell to the Exclusives. In the end, however, they missed their opportunity to maintain this power by their failure to move into the squatting districts beyond the frontiers of the settlement. Policing of this territory fell by default to forces controlled by central government.

The concept of the rule of law in a penal colony may appear incongruous. We might have expected something more akin to martial law or prison discipline administered by the governor, as some in England had envisaged.[79] However, courts were provided and politics in the penal colony soon took on an English form which stressed the rule of law as the measure of legitimacy. Ideas which were already prominent in English politics took on heightened importance in a penal colony where there were so few other means of political expression.

Sir Francis Forbes. From a portrait by an unknown artist, no date, Mitchell Library, State Library of New South Wales.

CHAPTER 4

The Courts

One security for liberty is that all judges hold their offices for life and are entirely independent of the King. Everyone therefore is tried by a free and independent judge, who are (sic) also accountable for their conduct. Nothing therefore, will influence them to act unfairly to the subject, and endanger the loss of a profitable office and their reputation also, nothing the king could bestow would be an equivalent. The judge and the jury have no dependence on the crown.

Adam Smith[1]

I have reason to believe that the Governor considered that I was bound to support him...but assuredly it was my duty to preserve the irreproachability of the judgment seat. The people of this country look with the most intense anxiety at every act, every opinion of the judge; without trial by Jury, without the corrective power of an assembly, without one single popular right, they naturally regard the Supreme Court as their only protection against absolute power; their rulers may be the best possible, but they will not probably be better than the rulers at home; and why have the people of England imposed all those checks and balances, but upon the assumption that they are necessary; and, if they are necessary there, why should they be less so in New South Wales? . . . it has been my incessant endeavour, ever since I have been in this Colony, to raise the character of the Supreme Court in the opinion and confidence of the Colonists; that I have strained hard to preserve its independence, and prevent its being supposed to be capable of being influenced;...it will require some extraordinary power of persuasion to induce me to believe that, in a Court firm in the confidence of the people, there is not a safeguard of the public peace, stronger than in the force of armed men;

that in a just, and vigorous because just, execution of the laws, there is not a far greater protection to the Government, than in the seeming acquiescence of a compliant judge.

Chief Justice, Francis Forbes[2]

The classic theme which opposes the rule of law to the rule of men found a fertile field in New South Wales. And courts found themselves confronted by familiar problems made strange in the setting of a penal colony. By what authority did the governor issue orders and how far did his warrant run? Was he like England's early seventeenth-century kings with power to make legislation for the colony, or was he bound by the terms of the revolution settlement and dependent on parliament for legislative authorisation on matters touching the rights of subjects? What were the rights of those subjects – the bond and the free – in the strange circumstances of a penal colony? And what of the role of the colonial courts? Could they legitimately say what the governor may and may not do?

Forbes' answers to those questions are the familiar ones of seventeenth-century constitutionalism and the rule of law. Protection from 'absolute power' would best be secured through the courts. Echoing Cromwell, he too saw in the courts a source of legitimacy 'stronger than the force of armed men'. Perhaps Forbes overstepped if he saw himself as playing Coke to Governor Darling's James I, but his analysis has a great deal of force and picked up a resounding theme in the politics of his age.

The core components of the rule of law model – general laws, legal forms of argument and courts – gained a foothold in the colony along with the colonists; they were soon put to use, as we have seen. The courts, in particular, established a crucial bridgehead for the development of a fully-fledged version of the rule of law and for the transformation of the penal colony.

Evatt's point that the courts in New South Wales took on heightened political significance because of the absence of other political forums needs to be re-stated here. But other significant peculiarities also worked to similar effect. The first is that while the rule of law model is so strongly linked with liberty and a free society, New South Wales was a penal colony. That contradiction set up a powerful dynamic in the colony. It created important ambiguities which could be raised in the courts and exploited by groups and individuals struggling over the colonial configuration of power. The courts provided the central forum for this conflict.

But the structural position of the courts in New South Wales meant that they occupied a heightened political role quite independently of the absence of the usual political forums. Some in England had suggested that the ancient but unwritten constitution of England constituted a fundamental or higher law which could not be altered by parliament. If it attempted to do so, the courts could declare the legislation invalid. The idea did not take root in England.[3] In New South Wales, however, local legislative and quasi-legislative Acts clearly were subjected to a higher law, namely that of England. Local courts could declare colonial laws invalid on the basis that they were repugnant to English law in the way that, say, the Australian High Court or the United States Supreme Court can declare legislation unconstitutional. English courts have never had such a power. More than that, the colonial courts could and did modify English law where the circumstances of the colony demanded. English law applied only so far as the circumstances of the particular colony permitted. For example, although it is not given as the rationale, the Kables may have been allowed to sue because the circumstances of the penal colony demanded it; as felons, they would not have been allowed to do so in England. Similar considerations apply to the acceptance of convicted felons' testimony in the courts. The 'local circumstances' provision was well known in the colony at the outset and cited by contemporaries in justification of local practices.[4] This power was made even more extensive in the *New South Wales Act* 1823 which formally required the Chief Justice to certify that legislation from the new Legislative Council was not repugnant to English law (cf. the previous situation where the repugnancy arguments required someone to raise them in court).[5] These powers gave the colonial courts a far more political role than their English counterparts. They had the power to nullify government policy on the basis of their interpretation of colonial circumstances.

But would the colonial courts be independent? The special position of the courts in New South Wales would come to little if they were simply subordinated to the governor. The opening quotes from both Adam Smith and Chief Justice Forbes stress the importance of judicial independence from the Crown as a protection for individual liberty. In fact, an independent judiciary signified a cluster of ideas which might better be caught by substituting 'court system' for judiciary. This would emphasise the important point that power has to be rationally justified to an independent *system* of which judges form only a part, albeit a very significant one. The focus on courts, rather than on judges alone, permits an examination of the different elements of the courts (lawyers, juries, etc.), as well as the relationship of the courts to other parts of the legal and political system (e.g. the governors and the magistrates).

The independence of the judiciary – to concentrate just on the judges at first – meant that judges in England had life tenure. The *Act of Settlement* in 1701 put an end to the power of the king to dismiss judges who displeased him. The appointment of judges only from the ranks of practising barristers – also a product of the seventeenth century – further emphasised the notion of independence: only those with technical expertise and long experience in the specialised knowledge of the law could determine the outcome of a case based on the apolitical logic of the law. Recruitment of judges from a professional group, barristers, whose training, practice and prestige depended on adherence to the logic of the law, seemed to guarantee the rule of law, not of men.[6] The ideology required that judges decide cases by reference to legal rules rather than the dictates of the sovereign, personal whim or political expediency.

Judges in New South Wales did not enjoy life tenure; they could be – and were – dismissed at will by the British government. Moreover, the early judges had no formal legal training and they were subordinate in rank to the governor; the same subordination applied to the first professionally-qualified judges when they arrived in 1810. Their power relative to the governor would prove to be a major issue in shaping political power and in imposing checks against the 'absolute power' that the governor had over the lives and liberty of the colonists, especially those serving sentences.

The superior courts occupied a central place in the grid of power relations in New South Wales and held the key to the development of the rule of law in the colony. The judges and the legal profession served as the traditional bearers of the full-blown rule of law conception, as well as the possessors of the technical expertise and prestige necessary to make the model work. In early New South Wales, where litigation was often politics carried on under another name, the courts, judges and lawyers played a major part in the transition from penal colony to free society.

It may seem strange that the British government decided to establish courts in a penal colony at all. It certainly seemed strange to some of those involved in the planning and does not seem to have been a foregone conclusion even at cabinet level. Evan Nepean, Under-Secretary at the Home Office, wrote to Lord Sydney about his meeting with Lord Howe from the Admiralty:

I told him that a Dy (sic i.e. Deputy) Judge Advocate would be wanted and that it was probable that he would be appointed also to controul the Criminal Courts for the trial of matters which might pass between the Convicts, and from what his Lordship says I do think that Capt. Collins will answer the purpose. When I mentioned a Civil and Criminal Court His Lordship seemed rather surprised as he had understood that the whole was to have been under Military Law *Convicts* as well as *Soldiers*, and though I attempted to convince his Lordship that the former were not amenable to Military discipline, he did not appeared (sic) satisfied, but seemed to think perhaps without considering well the importance of the subject that they should be punished according to the discretion and judgment of the Governor even in a capital part. How far his Lordship's opinion may be proper to be adopted I will not pretend to say, but I should think that such a discretion would occasion infinite clamour at home. However the matter will be talked over when the Cabinet next meet and I suppose something conclusive will be done.[7]

Lord Howe's opinion did not prevail. Legislation established a Criminal Court to try and punish 'all such outrages and misbehaviours as, if committed within this realm, would be deemed and taken, according to the laws of the realm, to be treason or misprision thereof, felony or misdemeanour...'[8] Although the Act permitted the court 'to proceed in a more summary way than is used within this realm', much of the traditional criminal procedure was adopted. The legislation required the court to proceed by:

> calling such offenders respectively before that Court, and causing the charge against him, her, or them respectively to be read over, which charge shall always be reduced into writing, and shall be exhibited to the said court by the Judge Advocate, and by examining witnesses upon oath, to be administered by such Court, as well for as against such offenders respectively, and afterwards adjudging by the major part of the members composing such Court, that the party accused is or is not (as the case shall appear to them) guilty of the charge, and by pronouncing judgment therein (as upon conviction by verdict) of death, if the offence be capital, or of such corporal punishment not extending to capital punishment, as to the said court shall seem meet: and in cases not capital, by pronouncing judgment of such corporal punishment, not extending to life or limb, as to the said Court shall seem meet.[9]

Thus, the legislation provided convicts and free settlers alike with due process of law in serious criminal cases similar to the English system. Minor or summary offences were to be dealt with by magistrates. There were, however, some serious differences. First was the absence of a grand jury (usually 20 freeholders, in England) to determine whether there was sufficient evidence to warrant laying an indictment. Second, indictments were drawn by the judge-advocate, a judicial member of the court, rather than an independent prosecutor. Third, the court was composed not of a judge and trial jury of twelve, but by a judge-advocate appointed by the British government, and a panel of six military officers. The judge-advocate's position was novel. Unlike the position in a court-martial where he would only move the prosecuting documents and advise the panel on points of law, he was also a member of the bench. Unlike judges in English trial courts, where he would only direct a jury on the law, he also voted on guilt or innocence. Fourth, decisions were taken by majority rather than unanimous verdict, although in the case of a death sentence, either a majority of five was needed, or four plus approval from London. The governor's warrant was needed before the sentence of execution could take place; he also exercised the royal prerogative of mercy.[10] Fifth, even where the judge-advocate was a lawyer, his opinion on the law counted no more than the that of any other member of the court. All members of the panel had a vote on questions both of law and fact. When professional judges arrived, they made a practice of summarising the law for the panel, as if charging a jury, but the voting system was not changed until the *New South Wales Act* was passed in 1823.[11]

The British government also provided the penal colony with a civil court, established by charter, not by legislation.[12] This court, called the Court of Civil Jurisdiction, was composed of the judge-advocate and two 'fit and proper persons' to be appointed by the governor.[13] It had jurisdiction over all pleas 'concerning Lands, Houses, Tenements and Hereditaments, and all manner of interests therein, and all pleas of Debt, Account or other Contracts, Trespasses and all manner of other personal pleas whatsoever. And We do further Will and Ordain and Grant to the said Court full power and Authority to grant probates of Wills and Administration of the personal Estates of Intestates dying within the place or Settlement aforesaid.' Appeals from this court could be taken to the governor and, if the case involved more than three hundred pounds, a further appeal could be taken to the Privy Council in London.[14] The presence of free people in the colony gave this court a rationale but the court was also resorted to by convicts, as we have seen.[15]

These courts established important institutions of civil government in the penal colony. Although separate provision was made for breaches of penal and military discipline, prisoners, soldiers and free settlers alike were subject to the general law of England for criminal and civil cases, and provided with courts in the colony to operate that law. Neither the imperatives of a penal colony nor those of a military outpost had displaced the principle that English people, even convicts, carried with them such of their rights as were not forfeited. Hence, New South Wales experienced the paradox of the rule of law in a penal colony. However, in the Antipodes, where strange creatures abounded, one having fur like an animal but a bill like a duck, paradox was plentiful. The colony was an amalgam of civil, military and penal elements. In the case of conflict between these three elements, which would prevail?

The superior courts played a very large role in answering this question. In the day-to-day life of the colony, their authority, their structural position, and the distance of the colony from England meant they had no equal as brokers of legitimate power. But for all that, their position was by no means clear-cut, nor uncontested. In order to see this, we first have to look at the structural position of the courts in relation to the governor, a position astutely exploited by the main political actors in the colony. Ultimately, the imperial power decided the direction and pace of change. But issues could be highlighted and shaped in the courts long before they reached the Colonial Office. So, for example, the issue of whether emancipists could serve on juries – an issue which will be taken up in chapter 7 – had been extensively litigated in the colony in the early 1820s before it went back to England for final resolution. Even then, the litigation and controversy surrounding it had put considerable pressure on the British government. And the same issue showed how the colonial courts and the rule of law traditions they embodied exerted powerful normative claims both locally and at the metropolitan level.

The legal theory underlying Britain's acquisition of the Eastern coast of Australia was by discovery and settlement. Some of the consequences of this have already been discussed. The consequence of the doctrine for the Aborigines was that English law applied to them; they were regarded as lacking laws of their own. For the British settlers, as the Charter of Justice confirmed, the law to be applied was the common law of England 'as nearly as may be, considering and allowing for the Circumstances and Situation of the place and Settlement aforesaid and the Inhabitants thereof.'[16]

Two important points arise from this in relation to the courts. First, settlers in the colony could invoke the protection of the courts against *executive* actions that breached any of their accompanying English legal rights, unless such action could be justified from the circumstances of the colony. As will be seen, these rights were quite vigorously asserted in the colonial courts against, for example, magistrates, court officers, and police. The governor, who was immune from civil suit in the colony, was liable to be sued for damages on return to England for illegal acts done in the colony.[17] One of the disaffected judges of the Civil Court, for example, mused malevolently about the number of suits awaiting Governor Macquarie as soon as he set foot back in England.[18]

Second, the courts could be used to contest the exercise of legislative power. Prior to 1823, the governor lacked legislative power, although he could make day-to-day regulations not amounting to legislation. Just where the difference between legislation and regulation lay was a fine point and one of the ambiguities of the colonial arrangements which led to serious confrontations between the governors and the judges, and exposed the governors' authority to serious challenge.[19] After 1823, the power to refer to a higher law, namely that of England, put the courts in New South Wales in a position where they could contradict the governor and the legislative council by declaring colonial legislation invalid on the basis that it was repugnant to the law of England. The fact that English courts had no such power over parliament may partly explain the confused responses of the Colonial Office when the power was exercised by the colonial courts. The Supreme Court could even override the operation of English laws by reference to the nostrum that English laws only applied 'so far as the circumstances of the said Colony will admit'. These powers required courts to make political judgments in circumstances often fraught with tension between bitterly opposed factions.

While the power of the courts to declare legislation invalid offered extensive potential power to the colonial courts, other factors imposed checks on its realisation. All the judges of the colony, as has been seen, were appointed by the British government and held office at the British government's pleasure; unlike English judges, they did not have life tenure.[20] Like the governors, colonial judges were vulnerable to detractors in England.[21] A dearth of lawyers, the status and non-guaranteed tenure of the judges, the political outlooks of the judges and lawyers, and their access to legal information all qualified heavily the actual operation of the rule of law in the penal colony.

With the exception of Phillip, all the early governors complained about the courts. The manipulation of the courts by the rum monopolists prompted complaints from Hunter, King and Bligh. Hunter said the bias of the Criminal Court was obvious to anyone and called for a chief justice, other judges, lawyers and law books. For appeals, he complained, the governor lacked the advice of even the judge-advocate whose position was prejudiced by the fact that he had tried the case.[22] King lamented that he was forced to turn to a convict, Crossley, for legal advice.[23] Bligh told the Colonial Secretary that, 'The Benches of Magistrates and Courts of Justice are mockeries of what they represent . . .'[24] A petition to Bligh from 800 settlers in 1808 had called for changes in court structure. 'The colony is so far improved,' Bligh wrote, 'that the superior people now look with concern on the Civil and Criminal Courts as established by the Patent, and are particularly desirous that the military may have nothing to do in the jurisprudence of the country either as magistrates or jurors. ... The semblance also to Courts Martial is become irksome.'[25] In England, the 1812 Committee on Transportation thought it quite natural that the colonists would view the substitution of military officers for juries as distasteful and recommended the introduction of trial by jury. The surgeon and magistrate, William Balmain, also commented on the lack of impartiality of the courts.[26]

The composition of the courts lay at the heart of these complaints. But the relationship between the judge-advocates and the governors also cut across the notion of judicial independence. The judicial commission of the judge-advocates was military in form and ordered them 'to observe and follow such Orders and Directions from Time to Time as you shall receive from our Governor of Our said Settlements or any other your Superior Officer.'[27] Commissions of the first three judge-advocates had the added explicitly military formulation, 'according to the Rules and Discipline of War'.[28]

Lack of formal legal training compounded the problem and breached another of the rule of law tenets that we have been discussing, that only those learned in the 'artificial reason' of the law would sit in the judgement seat. Collins and Atkins, who between them held the post of judge-advocate for 18 of the first 22 years, had no legal training.[29] Consequently, their legal interpretations had no better claim to validity than any of the other six naval or military officers who sat on the Criminal Courts, nor, for that matter, than that of the governor himself, who was also their 'superior officer'. In these circumstances the independence of the judiciary was a shadow of its English self. Worse, the involvement of the military in a civilian court breached one of the sacred taboos of British political culture, a legacy of the Civil War. Even people of such opposing views as Commissioner Bigge and Emancipist leader Edward Eagar could agree that the military appearance of the courts was repugnant to the feelings of British subjects.[30]

These issues came to a head during the tenure of Judge-Advocate Ellis Bent (1810–1815). Significantly, and unlike his predecessors, Bent was a barrister of eminence on appointment.[31] As might have been expected, he objected strenuously and often to his subordination to the governor and to the military trappings of the court.[32] Numerous incidents illustrate the ways in which these arrangements could be exploited. In his *Rum Rebellion*, for example, Evatt details the manipulation of the court system to frustrate attempts by early governors to control the activities of John Macarthur and the rum monopolists.[33] The governor's attempts to have illegal rum stills seized provoked civil suits against his officers. Macarthur attempted to forestall the installation of the most suitable successor to Judge-Advocate Collins by suing him for criminal libel. Intimidation of a civil magistrate investigating an assault by members of the New South Wales Corps, and prosecutions against Macarthur himself make up some of the list of examples.[34] Indeed, Evatt argues that only when it appeared that Bligh had finally legally cornered Macarthur, did Macarthur adopt the tactics of Fletcher Christian and have Bligh deposed by main force.[35]

Evatt points out that these early experiences taught the colonists about the political uses of the colony's courts. The events of seventeenth-century England and the example of the Wilkites in the eighteenth had shown the same thing. Throughout the period the colony's courts were the site of crucial political struggles. Example after example could be chosen to demonstrate the point. Perhaps one or two examples from before, and a couple from after the *New South Wales Act* of 1823 – an Act which made significant changes to the political constitution of the colony – will show the importance of the courts in the politics of the colony not only up to the Rum Rebellion in 1808, but throughout the transportation period.

In 1814, Governor Macquarie proposed regulations for the port of Sydney. The regulations imposed duties on ships coming into the port and provided heavy penalties for breaches. From the outset governors had published what were called Government and General Orders regulating the colony's affairs. It was clear that the governor did have power to make such regulations, so long as they were not legislative in character. The governor derived his power from the king; since the king could not legislate, neither could he delegate the power to legislate. This lack of legislative power was not well known in the early days of the colony and caused some surprise to Governor King when pointed out to him by John Macarthur.[36] The defect had been part of Bentham's attack on New South Wales in his pamphlet, *A Plea for a Constitution*. Bentham's correspondence indicates that the point was not well-known in England either.[37] The problem, however, was to determine whether any given Government and General Order was legislative or regulatory in character. Clearly enough, any Government and General Order which contradicted an English law, deprived a citizen of a right or was in the nature of a tax, would fall foul of the principle. The exception for local circumstances, itself of uncertain scope, allowed the governor more leeway to argue that the circumstances of the colony necessitated a departure from English law.[38]

By 1814 the harmonious relationship that had existed between Governor Macquarie and Judge Advocate Bent since their arrival in the colony in 1810, had been sorely strained. Ellis Bent, a product of the London bar and its rule of law traditions, chafed at the military associations and subordination of his position. The soldier in Macquarie rejected the judge's claim to equal status. The conflict between the two men had taken place on a symbolic level up to the time of the port regulations dispute. The governor had refused to allocate a building for the Court consistent with the prestige due to it, at least on the judge-advocate's view. There had also been conflict over directions by the governor to the Sydney bench of magistrates respecting liquor licences. The judge-advocate broke with local convention and withdrew from the bench, arguing that the governor's action conflicted with the judicial independence of the magistrates. Matters descended to their lowest level when the governor objected to London that the judge-advocate did not observe the custom of standing when he entered church for service.[39]

The ill-feeling between Governor Macquarie and Ellis Bent came to a head over the proposed regulations for the port of Sydney. In late 1814, Macquarie sent Bent a draft of the part regulations and asked Bent to put them in legal form. Macquarie was forced to consult the judge-advocate because of the absence of government law officers or qualified non-convict lawyers in the colony. Bent had obliged the governor on previous occasions, but now he objected that the task was a slight to his judicial status. More than this, he thought a number of the regulations amounted to legislative action and exceeded the governor's power. For example, some of the provisions involved imposing penalties of 500 pounds or three years hard labour on free British subjects. The judge-advocate perused the draft regulations and informed Macquarie, citing the relevant Acts, that in his opinion that they were inconsistent with English trade legislation.

Macquarie, without referring to these points and authorities, told Bent that local circumstances justified his policy and required Bent to draw up the regulations. Bent was incredulous:

> I hope that I am not presuming too much when I express a humble confidence that it never could be intended that so vast a power should be placed in the hands of any one man without the smallest provision against its abuse; a power which, as far as this Colony is concerned, and under the bare pretence of local circumstances, I will be bold to say, sets the Governor of New South Wales above the Legislature of Great Britain, and at once resolves the rule of action here into the mere will of the Governor, a will not subjected to any previous advice or control.[40]

The conflict had now begun to assume epic dimensions, talking about 'vast power' in the hands of one man who would put himself above parliament, substituting his unchecked will for the law. These are classic rule of law references.

In response to this impasse Macquarie called for a direction from the Colonial Office.[41] Lord Bathurst supported the governor. His reasoning, however, reveals the depth of the tensions between the penal/military nature of the colony and the notion of the rule of law. Bathurst thought of New South Wales as a penal colony, not long over an armed rebellion and still in need of a prominent military presence. He had already made this plain in refusing to accede to Ellis Bent's requests to remove the military trappings of the Criminal Court. Now he warned the judge of the dangers of dissension:

> I must content myself therefore with impressing on you, in the strongest manner the Necessity of maintaining a right Understanding with the Governor, and affording him on all occasions your ready and cordial Cooperation. Filling as you do the Situation of Judge Advocate in the Colony, it is more particularly incumbent on you to uphold the Governor's Authority and to set an Example of due obedience to it: for there could not exist a greater Misfortune to a Settlement, of so peculiar a description as New South Wales, than a spirit of Resistance, or anything more calculated to produce such a Calamity than an Appearance of Misunderstanding between the Governor and yourself, or a Suspicion that you were disposed to question or disobey his Orders.[42]

Of course, the notion that a judge should set an example of obedience was wildly at odds with Bent's conception of the requirements of the rule of law, even in such a society. Bent's difficulty in continuing under such radically opposed understandings eventually led Bathurst to dismiss him.[43] But in the dismssal, the contradiction in Bathurst's own position becomes painfully evident. In his censure of Macquarie's conduct in a closely connected case, Bathurst tells

Macquarie that the port regulations could not be justified by the circumstances of the colony. Worse was to come for Maquarie. Piqued by the Bents and other enemies, Maquarie plainly exceeded his authority in several incidents and earned himself a stinging rebuke from Bathurst:

> I have now only to lament that you should in a moment of irritation, have been betrayed into an act which, at the same time which it exposes you to considerable risk, cannot fail to diminish your influence among the more respectable part of the community *who justly look upon the law as the only true foundation of authority.*[44] (Emphasis added.)

Macquarie complains about the censure only to have Bathurst reiterate the point:

> I am sure that you cannot but admit that the presumable guilt of any individual affords no justification for adopting towards him any course of proceeding other than what the law prescribes. I feel confident also that you will allow that violations of the laws, whatever be their object, can never add strength to a Government or increase its influence.[45]

Bathurst has changed his view here. Whereas he was originally prepared to persist with a military/penal approach to the problems of New South Wales, the admonishment of Macquarie reminds the viceroy that the basis of political authority in the English system is law. Whatever his foibles and motivations, with his legal training and respectability, Ellis Bent served as a potent tradition bearer for ideas which could not stand beside Macquarie's autocracy. Bathurst dismissed Bent and his brother in 1816. But they had planted seeds that would cause Bathurst to send Commissioner Bigge to investigate this 'penal' colony, and to make fundamental changes in its legal and political framework.

Apart from sorting out the relationship between the governor and the governed, the courts were also an important site for determining issues of status and power among the colonists themselves. Sometimes, for example, when the governor's policies promoted the interests of a group such as the Emancipists, litigation could work at both levels. In the early years the rum monopolists systematically employed the civil process of the court both to frustrate attempts by the governors to interdict their trade and to seize land pledged to them as security by smallholders. Indeed, our friend Henry Kable also seems to have found the colony's courts useful in this way. Bligh complained: '... By the leading People of this Class, whose names are Lord, Kable and Underwood, several Masters of Ships have been ruined, and Merchants at home defrauded to a serious amount, and the mercantile interest almost destroyed. With constant litigation and infamous prosecutions in the Courts they have been accustomed to be gratified.'[46] The economically dominant groups used the law against both the governors and the smallholders in the colony.

The small settlers in the period before the Rum Rebellion doubted the impartiality of the courts, but they lacked imaginative legal advice which might have turned the tables against the monopolists in the courts. This situation generated the disaffection which prompted the petition to Bligh, referred to above.[47] As we will see, the arrival in the colony in the early 1820s of two clever barristers who were able to enlist the law on behalf of the Emancipist cause made a considerable difference to these politics. But until the arrival of Macquarie in 1810, the role of the small settlers on the Hawkesbury River and the growing group of emancipated convicts – groups which became politically associated by dint of their opposition to the 'respectable' members of society – was politically marginal.

Respectability was a major line of cleavage in the colony.[48] Acute concern about status required a kind of double life for many of the would-be genteel sort, since many of the officers lived with convict mistresses and breached the taboos of gentility by their involvement in mercantile pursuits. They overcame the contradictions by a tacit social agreement not to notice what was more than obvious in a small society. Hence, an officer could live with his convict mistress, but would never take her into 'society'. Some of these women acted as fronts for their common law officer husbands, running their trading activities. This social prohibition on gentlemen engaging in trade also provided an entrée for emancipists who started in business as go-between for the officers, and then struck out on their own account.[49] While gentlemen might do daily business with emancipist merchants, social protocol dictated that they should not dine with them or invite them to their houses or the officers' mess. So formidable was this tacit social agreement that those who did point to it, such as Governor Macquarie, showed their lack of appreciation of what it meant to be a gentleman.[50]

The issue of the status of former convicts came up sharply for the first time in Governor Macquarie's time. Soon after arrival in 1810, Macquarie instituted his pro-emancipist policy. The policy was central to his administration and envisaged that on pardon or expiry of sentence, a well-behaved convict would be returned to the rank of society forfeited on conviction.[51] Macquarie envisaged New South

Wales primarily as a society where, upon emancipation, former convicts could make a fresh start, unimpeded by their former status. As the numbers and, importantly, the wealth of the emancipists grew, the issue of their social and political status sharpened.

Macquarie's policy included making room in the upper echelons of colonial society for emancipists. By the time of Macquarie's arrival, there were already emancipists qualified by wealth to occupy positions of prestige. For example, the merchant Simeon Lord was among the most wealthy people in the colony. But Lord and his fellows certainly were not acceptable in polite circles. Macquarie's initiatives to introduce emancipists into 'society', to invite them to dine at Government House, and to offer them official positions, most notably in the magistracy, provoked intense opposition. The officers in Macquarie's own regiment, which had accompanied him to the colony to replace the New South Wales Corps, accepted the policy with some difficulty. But the officers in their replacement regiment, which arrived in the colony in 1814, were outraged by the policy. The policy provoked hostility on a number of fronts, but most notably in the courts.[52]

This sets the stage for the way in which the explosive issue of status first came into the colony's courts. It also shows how the legal system became the forum for the fundamental political struggle of the transportation period. The principal contest between Exclusives and Emancipists was fought over civic status: whether political power would be exercised solely by an oligarchy based on respectability and non-convict associations, or whether emancipation restored a person to all the rights of a free-born Briton. Whether the issue was the right of emancipists to become magistrates, to have standing to sue, to be able to serve on juries, to be able to practise as lawyers, or eventually to vote for colonial assemblies, the underlying issue was the same : civic status and the exercise of the political power consequent on that status. Emancipists and Exclusives fought these battles bitterly through the colonial courts.

New South Wales had lacked qualified lawyers from the outset. There were three convicts who had been lawyers in England or Ireland. The most prominent of them was George Crossley who had arrived in the colony in 1799. The absence of free lawyers, and indeed the lack of legal training of even Judge-Advocate Atkins, forced Governor King and Governor Bligh, as well as the judge-advocate, to rely on Crossley for legal advice.[53] The situation changed little with the arrival in 1810 of the legally-qualified Judge-

Advocate, Ellis Bent. For the sake of expediency, he reluctantly allowed Crossley and two other emancipist attorneys by then in the colony (George Chartres, and a man who figures prominently in this story on the Emancipist side, Edward Eagar) to practise in the courts as agents pending the arrival in the colony of qualified lawyers. The expediency arose, on Bent's own testimony, from an extra burden thrown on him: having to advise unrepresented litigants and having to take more time in dealing with people unfamiliar with court procedure. Indeed in the absence of legal practitioners familiar with them, the usual forms and legal procedures did not prove to be of much use to the courts.[54] Nevertheless the situation did clash with Bent's conceptions of the status of barristers as gentlemen, and professional canons about the unsullied reputations of legal practitioners. Bent thought the situation insulting to:

> the respectability of the Court, my own feelings as a barrister and as head of the Court, the interest and the feelings of Mr. Garling and Mr. Moore [the free lawyers] and the claim they have upon the attention of the Government in consequence of their having left their country and the exercise of their profession in England to come here, ...

He pointed out that even those magistrates who supported the convict lawyers and Crossley's application would not have him to their dinner table.[55] Certainly their convictions for dishonesty in the course of their professional lives would have disqualified the emancipist attorneys from practice in England. The issue at stake, however, was how far this would take effect in the circumstances of the colony, especially in view of Macquarie's emancipist policy.

Macquarie's position on the emancipist issue was made abundantly clear almost from the outset by his appointment of three emancipists to the magistracy. The governor always appointed magistrates to fill the positions of the 'two fit and proper persons' who sat with the judge-advocate (or the Chief Justice after 1814) on the Civil Court. The appointment of these emancipists to the magistracy meant that they also satisfied the requirements to sit on the Civil Court. Macquarie did in fact appoint an emancipist magistrate to the court in 1817, a few years after the events I am about to describe.[56] If emancipists could be magistrates and members of the Civil Court, then *a fortiori*, they could practise as lawyers in the colony, or so the logic ran.

The issue of Macquarie's emancipist policy, which had been smouldering in the colony, burst into flame with the arrival of the Second Charter of Justice in 1814 and the colony's second qualified judge, Judge-Advocate Ellis Bent's brother, Jeffery. The new Charter did not alter the Criminal Court but it did reorganise the civil jurisdiction into two new courts. The Supreme Court would hear civil cases where the amount in dispute exceeded fifty pounds. Its composition differed from the previous Civil Court by substituting the new judge for the judge-advocate, but it retained the system of using two lay members to sit with the judge; but now they had to be magistrates, not just 'fit and proper persons'. The Governor 'with the Assistance of the Judge Advocate' could hear appeals from the Supreme Court. In cases exceeding 3,000 pounds, either party could take a further appeal to the Privy Council in London. Cases involving not more than fifty pounds could be heard in a new minor civil court, the Governor's Court. The judge-advocate and 'two fit and proper persons' sat in that court.[57]

In response to persistent complaints about the lack of qualified lawyers in the colony, the Colonial Office agreed to subsidise two English solicitors to practise in the colony under the new Charter of Justice. For the first time, the colony would have a group of qualified lawyers both on the bench and at the bar table. The implications of this were far-reaching. Apart from their technical skills and qualifications, they brought with them the possibility of second opinions, professional advice for both parties to litigation, and the capacity to understand and use the rules of court. And they brought their law books – in 1824 Chief Justice Forbes brought a personal library of 500 volumes.[58] All this made a significant difference to what was, on many accounts, a very litigious colony; not long after his arrival, Bent reported that he had issued between 350 and 400 writs for amounts up to 20,000 pounds. On arrival, he faced a backlog of some 250 cases, including legally and politically difficult cases arising from the Rum Rebellion. In long letters to his brother Jeffery in England, he complains of the arduousness of his tasks, the illegalities that had been practised, the lack of organisation, the lack of other lawyers to advise him, the fact that the litigants themselves were ignorant of legal procedures and needed his advice, and the fact that the Governor himself sought his advice on a daily basis.[59] The advent of the lawyers also marked the arrival of a second professional group in the colony – the first being military officers – a group deeply versed in the rule of law ideology and imbued with the professional and political traditions of their calling. Macquarie was to find, 'When an aristocracy [or in his case, an autocracy] closes its ranks against the lawyers, it finds them to be enemies all the more dangerous, because although beneath it in wealth and power, their work makes them independent of it and they feel that their enlightenment raises them to its level.'[60] By 1819, five solicitors practised in the colony. Had it not been the Bents, other lawyers would have invoked rule of law principles against Macquarie's autocracy. As it happened, however, it was the judges who forced the issue.

The arrival of qualified lawyers had immediate consequences for the practising rights of the emancipist lawyers. These rights were conditional on the absence of qualified lawyers. When the new Supreme Court met on 1 May 1815, it had before it petitions for the right to practise from the emancipist attorneys Crossley, Eagar and Chartres.[61] Eagar's petition was rejected because of improper form but he was allowed to re-draft it. After calling for argument from the other two applicants, the court adjourned until 11 May to consider the applications. Apparently in anticipation of a refusal, the emancipist attorneys had approached the Governor to enlist his support. Mr Justice Jeffery Bent discussed the matter with Macquarie who later sent the judge a letter supporting the applications 'in a manner almost to preclude denial,' according to the Judge.[62] Bent was nettled by Macquarie's disregard of the points cited against the applicants and wrote back reiterating his arguments for refusal. His disquiet was heightened by public discussion of the issue and statements allegedly made by Crossley that, 'as the Governor was on his side, he did not care for the Judges'.[63]

On 9 May, the members of the court met in the judge's chambers and he outlined his reasons for refusal. The two assessors, Broughton and Riley, both indicated their support for the applications. Both were free settlers but, according to Bent, very much in the Governor's debt.[64] The members of the court met again in chambers before the court sat on 11 May. They again disagreed. The court convened and admitted W.H. Moore, one of the qualified lawyers from England. The other lawyer had not arrived in the colony. When Crossley rose to address the court, Mr Justice Bent ruled that he would not hear him further, but he was contradicted by Broughton and Riley. Bent was again contradicted when he said he would refuse to admit 'him or persons in his circumstances to practise in that Court'.[65]

Outnumbered and exasperated by the fact that the legal opinions of the assessors carried the same weight as his own, Bent adjourned the court.[66] The magistrates then told him they would not sit with him again. The court was further adjourned until 28 May when, because the governor would not accept the magistrates'withdrawal, they agreed to sit. By that stage the situation was extremely highly charged. Broughton and Riley took their seats on the bench but Bent refused to enter and sent his clerk to adjourn the court. The magistrates threatened to jail the clerk for contempt but in the event relented.

In the meantime a request for a public meeting censuring the judge's conduct failed to attract sufficient signatures for the governor to allow it. Macquarie wrote to Bent demanding a report of proceedings. The call for the report only further inflamed Bent who immediately invoked classic rule of law tenets:

> I have felt it my Duty to resist all interference on the part of the Governor with the Courts of Justice in any manner not authorized by His Majesty's Charter; For His Excellency's Tone and Language I must refer to the letter itself; But had his Excellency expressed a wish to mediate and conciliate, and not to encourage so gross an outrage on my character and Feelings, I should have been ready and happy to have given him every Information ...he has evidently expressed a wish to assume a jurisdiction where he had none, and wished to inculcate the Principle, that, if he should be pleased to order such Persons to be admitted, it would be my Duty to Obey.
>
> The Rule and Principle of action of Governor Macquarie has been that *Quod Gubernatori placet, legis habet vigorem*, and it has been carried out in this Colony to the greatest Extent; ...[67]

From that date on the Supreme Court remained closed until two qualified lawyers were available to practise in the court; this turned out to be October 1816, over two years after Jeffery Bent's arrival in the colony. Further skirmishes between Bent and the governor aggravated the situation. Believing it an illegal tax, the judge refused to pay his fee on the toll road. He was summoned to the magistrates' court but refused to attend, denying the court's jurisdiction over him, an odd position for one who so vigorously asserted that no one was above the law in other contexts.[68] In another clash, a writ issued by Bent to have Broughton arrested for contempt of court, arising out of a dispute over an assigned convict, was countermanded by Macquarie's warrant. The Sydney Bench of Magistrates found Bent had no basis for his action.[69]

Exasperated, Macquarie finally wrote to the Colonial Office calling for removal of the Bents or acceptance of his own resignation. Lord Bathurst sacked both judges; Jeffery Bent was censured by

Bathurst who considered the issue of 'whether the convicts be or be not authorised to practise . . . a question of little importance, when compared with the consequences arising out of its agitation, the closing of the Supreme Court of the colony for at least twelve months . . . I cannot find any apology for your refusal to accede to the qualified admission, recommended by Governor Macquarie'.[70]

Wittingly or not, Bent had fixed on an issue – the eligibilty of emancipists to hold positions of status and importance in the colony – which would be hard-fought for the remainder of the transportation period. Like the right of emancipists to serve on juries and in the magistracy, the admission of emancipist attorneys followed a pattern in which important legal offices became the touchstone of civic status. The conflict over that status was then largely played out in the courts. This forum gave the protagonists the opportunity to couch their arguments about power and status in terms of principle. So, while Bent had cast his opposition in terms of the fundamental principle of judicial independence under the rule of law – a value he no doubt sincerely adhered to – the force which animated him was resistance to the governor's attempts to upset the proper social order.

Bathurst did not see the status issue but he did give support to the principle of judicial independence in his dispatch to Macquarie, informing him of the removal of the judges. It was not that the judges were not entitled to voice their legal objections, but the way in which they effected them, he wrote. They should have cooperated with the Governor as far as possible and lodged their dissent with the Colonial Office, according to Bathurst.[71]

But this advice only partially met the problem of what was to be done in the colony. The turnaround time on any issue was well over a year: a six- to eight-month journey in either direction plus time for the Colonial Office to deliberate on the issue. Major problems in the colony could not be suspended for such long periods while the Colonial Office made up its mind, as Bathurst's criticism of the closure of the Supreme Court made clear. Indeed another controversial case, involving an illegal court-martial, came up before Jeffery Bent had even left the colony. This time Macquarie received no support for his illegal action from Bathurst. Squarely basing himself on the principles of the rule of law, the Colonial Secretary firmly reminded Macquarie, as quoted above, that he regarded 'law as the only true foundation of authority'. Although the Bents had lost the battles – and, given the particular issues and their personalities, it is difficult to sympathise with them – the rule of law principles they advocated would win the war.

The autocratic power exercised by Macquarie was meeting determined opposition through the courts in the colony and this was raising doubts in the metropolitan seat of power. As the colony grew in wealth and in numbers of free and freed people, Macquarie's broad powers – consistent with a small penal outpost but not a colony of the size and type that New South Wales had become – met increased opposition. Those opposed to him, as the Bents had shown, had genuine issues to raise. And although they were the prime movers in some of the issues, as lawyers and judges they were also a magnet for other disaffected colonists. The Bents and the other lawyers could cast their grievances into a form that neither Macquarie nor the government could ignore. On the Exclusives' side, the Bents' invocation of the rule of law further dented both the governor's autocratic power and, for the time being, the Emancipist claims. Ironically, in view of Macquarie's advocacy of their cause, the Emancipists too would oppose his style of rule, a style which relied much on paternalism and military models of governance, and not on the rights of British people, guaranteed to them by the ancient constitution.

The year 1818 marks a transition in this story, a transition to which the events described so far had contributed. In that year, the British government appointed John Thomas Bigge to conduct an inquiry reassessing British policy in New South Wales. The prospect of change and the increasing wealth, population and complexity of the colony threw up a new set of political issues. As we will see, the courts continued to play a prominent role in shaping these forces.

The turbulence of the Macquarie years was assiduously chronicled in Commissioner Bigge's reports to the British government in 1822 and 1823. The Reports formed the basis for a re-assessment of British policy towards the colony, especially in its constitutional and legal arrangements. These found new form in the *New South Wales Act* of 1823.[72] In both his first general report and in the second, *On the Judicial Establishments*, Bigge writes at great length about Governor Macquarie's collision with the legal system. Macquarie's clashes with the magistracy, as we will see in the next chapter, followed the themes of his clashes with the superior courts. Bigge was a judge himself, former Chief Justice of Trinidad, and as such could be expected to be sympathetic to arguments cast in the language of the rule of law. His sympathies with the Exclusive faction explain many of his recommendations, but they also show the marks of his training. He treats the independence of the judiciary as a self-evident truth, for example, in his support for the Bents on the admission of the emancipist lawyers. Despite his lack of sympathy for them, he found for the Emancipists on the issue of their right to bring suit in the courts, though he could not bring himself to support their claims to trial by jury, at times appearing to advance arguments which he must have known to be spurious.[73]

The *New South Wales Act* of 1823, drafted on the basis of Bigge's reports, concerned itself with the legal problems that had bedevilled Macquarie's administration. First and foremost, it cured the lack of legislative power that had exposed Macquarie's authority to attack in the courts on the port regulations issue. The Act provided that the Governor, 'with advice of the Council [of between 5 and 7 Crown nominees] to be appointed as aforesaid, or the major part of them, shall have the Power and Authority to make Laws and Ordinances for the Peace, Welfare and good Government of the said Colony, such Laws and Ordinances not being repugnant to this Act, or to any Charter or Letters Patent or Order in Council which may be issued in pursuance hereof, or to the Laws of *England*, but consistent with such Laws, so far as the Circumstances of the said Colony will admit ...'[74] Hence, save for emergencies, the autocratic power of the governor was checked by the Legislative Council. More important, for present purposes, the chief justice of the new Supreme Court was given a veto power over proposed legislation. He could refuse to certify that a piece of legislation met the conditions established by the *New South Wales Act* (i.e. consistency with English law so far as the circumstances of the colony permitted).[75] This provision left the chief justice still in a position where resort to the higher law of England was possible, and where assessments of the circumstances of the colony would be necessary, even without the issue going to court. The position of the chief justice on the new legislative council made his position even more politically central and problematic since, as judge, he would have to rule on legislation that he had had a hand in enacting.[76]

The 1823 Act abolished all the old courts and replaced them with a new superior court, and some inferior courts.[77] The superior court, the Supreme Court of New South Wales, was comprised of a chief justice who, like his predecessor judges, did not have life tenure but was liable to recall at the will of the British government. The number of superior court judges was thus cut back to one, but the legislation provided for additional judges should the need arise.[78] The new court combined not only the criminal and civil jurisdictions of the previous courts, but also the combined powers of the English courts of King's

Bench, Exchequer and Common Pleas, as well as Oyer and Terminer and General Gaol Delivery.[79] Other sections added admiralty, equity and ecclesiastical jurisdiction.[80] For the trial of serious criminal cases the old method of the judge plus military officers (now seven, not six), nominated by the governor was retained.[81] However, the initiation of criminal process was placed in the hands of an attorney-general, not the judge-advocate as had been the case.[82] Unlike the previous situations where the judge-advocate merely had a vote along with the other members of the court on issues of law and issues of fact, under the new system, the judge decided matters of law and the military panel decided only questions of fact. This replicated the division of functions between judge and jury in England. The Act also provided the right to challenge members of the panel, unlike the previous situation.[83]

The civil jurisdiction followed the old formula of using two lay assessors sitting with the judge. The governor nominated the assessors from among the magistrates, although they were subject to challenge by the litigants. The major innovation in the civil jurisdiction was the allowance of jury trial where both parties requested it.[84] (The Act also ratified introduction of jury trial for the future by executive action in London.[85]) In cases involving more than five hundred pounds, the parties could appeal as of right to the Court of Appeals. Where the amount involved was less than that, the judge could authorise an appeal. The Court of Appeals consisted of the governor, a continuation of the old system, except now the governor was authorised to seek advice from the chief justice. Echoing Coke's remarks about the artificial reason of the law, Forbes pointed out that 'people here will never be satisfied with any judgment of a Governor upon matters of law ...' A further appeal lay to the Privy Council in London.[86]

The Act also created two inferior courts. Courts of quarter sessions were established for the trial of less serious criminal cases, conformable to the practice in England. It also had summary jurisdiction over non-capital offences including breaches of penal discipline committed by transported convicts.[87] Three or more magistrates tried cases in these courts. The Act was silent on courts of petty sessions (minor criminal cases tried by one magistrate), an omission which caused some inconvenience in the colony.[88] A lower court of civil jurisdiction, the Court of Requests, was given the power to determine claims not exceeding ten pounds. A salaried commissioner appointed by the governor presided over the Court of Requests.[89]

Conflict over the governor's power and the status of emancipists continued in the post-Macquarie era. As the Emancipists became a more identifiable group – especially after their public meeting and petition to the king in 1819 – and the prospect of representative political institutions drew nearer, conflict between governors, the Exclusives and the Emancipists over their relative powers intensified. The role of the new Supreme Court in mediating became correspondingly more important. There were some differences in alignments from the Macquarie period. Governor Darling was a conservative military officer and his sympathies lay with the Exclusives. The new Chief Justice, Francis Forbes, was an experienced judge, a liberal and disposed towards the Emancipists. This was a neat reversal of the Maquarie–Bent relationship. Macquarie's attempts to install emancipists in the magistracy failed, leaving an important office in the hands of the Exclusives. In the mid-1820s, the Emancipists – particularly through the barristers William Wentworth and Robert Wardell – used the Supreme Court to offset the power of the Exclusivist magistracy and to subject it to the rule of law. Governor Darling became embroiled in these disputes both indirectly, through his support for the magistracy, and directly through his attempts to silence his critics in the press. As a counter-attack against the Exclusives and the governor, the Emancipists campaigned hard to establish jury trial and the right of emancipists to serve on juries. Wentworth led this campaign. He and Wardell conducted the litigation and then used their newspaper, the *Australian*, to amplify their court room oratory. By casting the great political struggles of the day in legal terms, they gained access to the forum of the courts and to the fund of ideas, arguments and rhetoric encapsulated in the rule of law. These battles over the shape of power in the colony marked significant points in its movement towards the status of a free society. Our focus will shift to the magistracy and jury trial in chapters 5 and 7. For now let it remain on the Supreme Court.

Unlike the 1814 Charter of Justice, the 1823 Act gave the Supreme Court the power to supervise the magistracy through the traditional administrative law remedies: the prerogative writs of *mandamus*, *certiorari* and *prohibition*, used to supervise the actions of government officials and inferior courts (e.g. by ordering them to do or refrain from doing a particular function). In addition, it could award damages against anyone, including a magistrate, who unlawfully interfered with a person or property. A magistrate who ordered an unlawful punishment, for example, might be sued for unlawful imprisonment or, in the case of a flogging, for the tort of assault. These powers gave the Supreme Court a powerful supervisory jurisdiction over the officers of the inferior courts, especially the magistrates.[90]

Tort actions had been available in the old Supreme Court, but the additional supervisory functions of the Supreme Court, and the increasing number of lawyers in the colony resulted in a much higher degree of effective supervision and conflict between the Supreme Court and the magistrates. The Exclusivist magistracy, which had effectively resisted attempts by governors to limit its authority, bitterly resented and resisted the Supreme Court's control. James Macarthur complained that the Supreme Court placed difficulties and 'legal technicalities' in the way of the magistrates.[91] Of course, one person's 'legal technicalities' could be another's rule of law. As we will see in the following chapter, the colony's magistrates had a long history of imposing illegal corporal punishments, including floggings to elicit confessions. Emancipist Alexander Harris thought the controls over the magistrates by the Supreme Court were salutary. But the governor's control of assigned convicts and the magistrates' support for him led to a serious confrontation between Governor Darling and the magistrates on the one side, and the Supreme Court on the other.

> Neither the Governor's Commission nor his instructions give him any power over the judges; such power is not within His Majesty's prerogative; the notion of control is inconsistent with the nature of a Supreme Court, which stands in the same relation to the King in New South Wales, as the Superior Courts at home stand in to the King in England. His Majesty may remove the Judges here, and so may the two Houses of Parliament at home; but the judicial office itself stands uncontrolled and independent, and bowing to no power but the supremacy of the law. This is a lawyer's view of the Supreme Court; but I rather suspect that the Governor looks upon it in the light of a court martial, the proceedings of which are subject to the revision of the Commander-in-Chief, and in so far as it recedes from that useful tribunal, it is a direct encroachment of his authority, as a representative of the King. This is in some degree the opinion of most military men, and is at once a very natural and excusable error; ... But power, power, who but the man that knows its use, and feels its responsibility, can withstand the temptations of all-seducing power.[92]

The theme of the quotation is by now familiar. Written just four years after the *New South Wales Act* of 1823, by the Chief Justice of the Supreme Court, Francis Forbes, it evidences the persistence of conflict between the courts and the governors. In the context of the wider politics of the colony, especially with the growth of the Emancipist cause after 1819, and the absence of representative political institutions, it is not surprising that the political lessons of the earlier period about the political uses of the courts would be taken to heart.

The early 1820s had seen several more pitched political battles in the colony's courts. Judge Advocate Wylde had called a meeting of the colony's magistrates in 1822 to invalidate Macquarie's 1818 proclamation that master and servant legislation operated in New South Wales.[93] The colony's commerce had been thrown into uproar when Justice Field disallowed a suit by the Emancipist Edward Eagar on the basis of his prior convict status.[94] The use of juries in quarter sessions and the right of emancipists to sit on them had been fought out in the Supreme Court.[95] The performance of the magistracy in several incidents – some of which came before the courts – immersed it in very public controversy.[96] Wentworth had threatened to have Governor Darling impeached over the death of a soldier undergoing a punishment meted out by the Governor.[97] In campaigns which would have delighted John Wilkes and his followers, the *Australian* and the *Monitor* energetically entered these frays.[98] Naively, Governor Darling played into opposition hands by attempting to prosecute the newspaper editors for seditious libel. Not only did this provide additional copy, but it landed General Darling on alien territory. His military conceptions of governance found little comfort in a court presided over by Forbes. Moreover, as Darling repeatedly complained, his callow law officers were no match for the skills of Wentworth and Wardell.[99] Attempts to thwart the press by draconian licence fees and censorship could not get past Forbes' certification powers.[100] Any of these incidents, and more through the 1830s, could be used to illustrate the extent to which rule of law ideas and the courts continued to dominate the colony's politics. But one incident in particular deserves some extended treatment because of the links it shows between major points of the colony's authority structure – the governor, the courts and the magistracy – and because of repeated misunderstanding of its significance in the colony's historiography.

Legislation controlling the assignment of convicts in New South Wales vested property in the services of those convicts in the governor. The governor was permitted to assign those services to settlers but the governor also had the power '... from time to time, as to them shall seem meet, to revoke any such assignments of offenders as may have been or shall hereafter be made in pursuance of the said Act and to grant any offender or offenders transported to the said

Colonies such temporary or partial remissions of their sentences as to such Governors may seem best adopted for reformation of such offenders, and such temporary or partial remissions from time to time to revoke or renew as occasion may require, . . .'[101]

Darling determined to silence his newspaper critics by depriving them of assigned convict workers. He did revoke Peter Tyler, assigned to the editor of the *Monitor*, Hall.[102] A short time earlier in 1829, the Supreme Court had ruled in another case that the revocation provision did not give the governor unfettered discretion. According to the ruling, revocation had to be connected to a proper purpose, such as the conferral of a partial or temporary remission of the convict's sentence. Upon revocation of Tyler, as we will see in the next chapter, the Sydney magistrates convicted Hall of illegally harbouring a convict. For the moment, however, we will concentrate on the confrontation between the governor and the Supreme Court which found that the revocation of Tyler was invalid, because it was done to spite Hall rather than for the convict's benefit.

The matter was referred back to England where the Colonial Secretary, Murray, and the Under-Secretary, Twiss, both rejected the Supreme Court's interpretation as baseless.[103] The section is badly drafted and its text is ambiguous; the interpretation depends on whether the second clause about the grant of remissions was a condition of revocation or a general power. Even if it were a general power, it could not legally be used for an improper purpose. In cases of ambiguity, standard techniques of legal interpretation allow the court to look at the purposes of legislation, appropriate legal analogies and public policy. The purpose of the legislation was to allow the Governor to grant indulgences and to protect convicts from abusive masters. But the techniques of interpretation confine themselves to determining the meaning of the statute from the text and do not extend to consulting the drafters of or advisers on the legislation. As a matter of formal statutory interpretation, the opinions of Murray and Twiss carry no weight. Disappointed legislators are an inevitable by-product of a system which commits the interpretation of statutes to courts rather than to the executive. Forbes used standard techniques: he analogised the rights of the master to whom the convict had been assigned to a property right which could not be arbitrarily withdrawn at the whim of the governor in order to ruin the assignee.[104] This was exactly what Darling had attempted to do to his critic, Hall. Conferral of remission or prevention of ill-treatment would have justified revocation, but not reprisals against the convict's master. When the Colonial Office subsequently discovered

Darling's purpose and the fact that he had made only two revocations – one from the *Australian* and one from the *Monitor* – it issued a stinging rebuke.[105]

Historians who have written about these events have misunderstood the political and legal culture at work here.[106] Clark thinks Forbes was an intellectual who took 'a basic delight in enmeshing a dunderhead in the nets of legal sophistry and pedantry'.[107] He slights the importance of the issues on which Forbes opposed Darling, reducing them to personal motivation and toadying to London. He does accept, however, that Darling's use of the re-assignment power was illegal and tyrannical. Not so John Hirst, who asserts that Forbes and his colleagues 'wilfully misconstrued the passage in the amending legislation', and when the law officers in London disapproved, the judges 'sheepishly' gave it up.[108] Hughes gets the position completely wrong when he has Darling on the side of convict rights and Forbes for the proposition that, like slave masters, masters of convicts had untrammelled rights in the services of their convicts, as had been the case with American convict masters.[109] Shaw, after citing Stephen's criticism of Forbes at length (Stephen complained that the judges had not given effect to the government's intention) goes on to say that 'the legal technicalities were as irritating to the non-legal mind, including that of the Governor, as they nearly always are'.[110] But, of course, 'legal technicality' became very important for the Colonial Office when it found out Darling's purposes and instructed him to exercise the power in exactly the way the Supreme Court had directed.[111] The restrictions posed by the rule of law irked Darling but it is a mistake to reduce this to 'legal technicalities'. As Hay has pointed out, eighteenth-century English law was extremely technical, especially where property was concerned.[112] And there were important historical and political reasons for this, as we have seen. The rule of law meant that governments would sometimes be defeated in the courts, but in the long run, as Forbes points out in the quotation opening this chapter, the stability of governments whose legitimacy depends on the rule of law must be bound by it. With the courts under such close scrutiny in the colony, Darling's clumsy abuses of his power could not be condoned. The corruption of the legal system by the officers of the Rum Corps already had caused dissension enough in the colony.

Personal ambition may have been at the base of Forbes' opposition to Darling, as the various historians suggest, although the evidence for this is slim. But the principles he espoused had a very solid grounding in English political and legal traditions. The fact that

Horace Twiss, who took the legislation through parliament, disagreed with the opinions of the Supreme Court judges counts for little in legal reasoning. Charles I also disagreed with his judges; at least Twiss was not beheaded!

Forbes saw the Supreme Court as a check on arbitrary authority in classic rule of law terms. The continued assertion by the court that powerful people in the colony would be held to a legal standard did impose a significant constraint on governors and magistrates who had been guilty of exercising their powers in an arbitrary way. At the same time as this power was constrained, the courts also provided the Emancipists with a means of harassing their opponents in the colony and increasing the pressure on the British government to grant them free institutions.

Classical Greek architecture in the Australian bush. Hartley Court House, in the Blue Mountains, NSW, building completed 1837. From a photograph ca. 1872, Holtermann Collection, Mitchell Library, State Library of New South Wales.

CHAPTER 5

The Magistracy

Hitherto such governance as our counties have had, has been government by the justices of the peace – government, that is, by country gentlemen appointed by the Lord Chancellor in the Queen's name, on the recommendation of the Lord Lieutenant, legally dissmissable at a moment's notice, but practically holding their offices for life. . .To deal with the vulgar affairs of the counties, to show what the laws made in Parliament, the liberties asserted in Parliament, really meant to the mass of the people. . .[A] history of the eighteenth century which does not place the justice of the peace in the very foreground will be known for what it is – a caricature.

F. W. Maitland[1]

Great families, by their being Magistrates and Civil Officers, form a strong chain of political power in this Colony. The faint, distant cry of these poor people [i.e. the small holders], if it should happen to penetrate to the Government House in Sydney (which is not very probable) will have to break through the clamour and misrepresentations of a host of wealthy, interested and greedy men. Of men who are on terms of friendship with the members of our close Council, who are the makers of those laws by which the poor of this Country are now being every day sacrificed to the rich ... Even the rich Settlers when they become inimical to the country justices and their head constables (the latter being generally the pound keepers, by which means our numerous grazier justices escape all impoundment of their own cattle), even the richer Settlers, I say, do not, happily for the poor, always escape the rigour of the new impounding law.

E. S. Hall[2]

The rule of law promises citizens that their rulers will exercise their power according to law. There must also be courts to ensure that the promise is kept. In New South Wales, as we have just seen, after a shaky beginning the Supreme Court played a significant role in curbing the power of the governor. But as the Maitland quotation emphasises, on a day-to-day basis, the exercise of power in conformity with law depended on the magistrates and their subordinates, the police. In England, the justices of the peace 'showed what the laws meant to the mass of the people'. But what would the magistrates of New South Wales make of these laws in a penal colony? The clashes between the magistracy and the Supreme Court referred to in chapter 4 and in the opening quotation from Hall suggest abuses. Would the dual power of men who were both magistrates and masters of convicts pose more of a threat to the rule of law than a means of ensuring it?

There was a great deal more to the magistracy in New South Wales than those familiar with twentieth-century magistrates might expect. The office of justice of the peace (or magistrate) offered prized symbolic, practical and strategic advantages to those in New South Wales who could secure it. As Maitland says, traditionally justices of the peace stood at the pinnacle of local authority in England. The office of justice of the peace was usually held by a local magnate whose income from landed wealth gave him the leisure to contemplate the common good. Justices of the peace were important political figures in rural England. Often the local Member of Parliament was also a justice of the peace. Central government relied on the local benches of magistrates to implement central government policies and to perform the functions of local government: roads, bridges, jails and police, for example, were all responsibilities of the local bench. Not only was the magistrates' court the forum for deciding less serious criminal cases, it was also the local council at a time when the role of central government was small. The legal and political powers of the justices of the peace – intermixed with their economic and social prestige – made them very powerful figures in English governance.[3]

People in the colony knew this pattern of power well. Most of them did not have the status to claim such an office in England but the patterns of power in the colony were relatively fluid; the office was open to the ambitious. Whoever could command the magistracy would win a considerable prize, through which they could augment their power and shape the colony. If the Exclusives were to establish an oligarchy in New South Wales, the magistracy would be a crucial part of the plan. Hall's comment in the opening quotation shows the extent to which the great families already exercised a quasi-oligarchic power through the nominated Legislative Council and the magistracy by 1829. But the power garnered by the magistracy in New South Wales had not been won easily; the magistracy proved to be consistently controversial. The crossover of political, judicial and administrative functions in the office, its traditional place in the configuration of British political power, and the dramatically different social and political conditions in New South Wales make the magistracy a rich source for exploring our theme about law and power. The magistracy posed a serious threat to the Emancipist cause. It also posed a serious threat of arbitrary power at the local level. If New South Wales was to become a free society, the magistrates were part of the problem and part of the cure. Here was another legal site for struggles between the governor, the Emancipists and the Exclusives over political power and authority in the colony.

Justices of the peace in New South Wales were given the same power as justices in England.[4] Originally established to maintain 'the king's peace' in the fourteenth century,[5] the accretion of powers to the office by the eighteenth century was enough to fill four thick volumes of Burn's manual for justices of the peace.[6] The local equivalent, by Plunkett, appeared in 1835. It was a weighty tome, intended be a guide to local legislation and to supplement and update the editions of Burn which were available in the colony. How extensively these books were used or understood by magistrates who, unlike superior court judges, had no legal training, remains a matter for speculation.[7]

In addition to their court duties, English justices of the peace supervised the police, maintained the roads, bridges and jails, set the price of bread, administered the poor laws, the law of master and servant and performed a host of other local government functions. Law, politics and administration were so intermixed in the magistrate's office that even in exercising their administrative functions, the justices used courts and legal forms such as the 'assize of bread' to fix the price of a loaf. All these duties were undertaken in an honorary capacity by men of a class based on landed income who had the time to perform at least some of them.[8]

Justices of the peace in New South Wales inherited all of these duties. They did not at first sit in quarter sessions but did sit as a bench to hear minor cases.[9] But they also had onerous responsibilities in the administration of the convict system including assignment, convict discipline, and the grant of tickets-of-leave (a prototype of parole). The administration of a wide range of general local ordinances added to the list of duties. Unlike their English counterparts, magistrates in the colony were not men of leisure but pioneers striving to establish themselves on the land, or men who held posts in the military or civil departments of the colony's administration, who often had considerable interests in land and commerce as well. (For example, the chaplain, Samuel Marsden was also a magistrate.) Hence frequent complaints about inattention to the duties of their magisterial office could have been expected. As early as 1802, the former Governor, Hunter, suggested that paid magistrates appointed from England (a comment on the choices available in the colony) would alleviate the problem. His suggestion fell on deaf ears.[10] Hunter's successors in the 1820s and 1830s responded to the problem by appointing stipendiary magistrates, but even that expedient met metropolitan and colonial criticism.

The relationship of the magistracy to political authority in the colony can be examined at two levels: as a mechanism for the transmission of the central authority of the governor, his councils and the Supreme Court; and at local level, as an office which conferred considerable state-backed authority on economically powerful figures. In some ways the two levels can be quite sharply separated but overlap occurred, for example, when someone from the local level complained to the central authority about the conduct of the magistrates. Distance, isolation, the absence of any other instrument of effecting government policy and problems of credibility, however, meant that there was a good deal of separation between the two levels of authority. But contrary to what might be expected, this degree of separation need not be fatal to the execution of central policy; as Ladurie has shown, the writ of the Inquisition ran even to the remote villages of the Pyrenees.[11] Indeed creation of the office of justice of the peace in England stemmed from a concern to *extend* central authority by means of officials resident at local level but dependent on the king for office and therefore loyal to him.[12] As we shall see, however, this theory of central control via the justices did not always succeed in New South Wales (or in England, for that matter). Pro-Emancipist governors time and again found themselves opposed by a magistracy dominated by Exclusives, who were able to use their office to oppose policies which affected their interests.

Implementation of central policy in New South Wales at the local level depended on a landed magistracy which had policies of its own to promote. The success of the magistrates in turn depended on their ability to establish and maintain their authority at the local level. This was no easy task. Even apparently subservient populations such as slaves have demonstrated their ability to limit the power of their masters.[13] Eighteenth-century England had a tradition of protest in which the local justice of the peace played a key role.[14] Despite the formidable array of devices for ensuring compliance available to justices in New South Wales (which ranged from the traditional authority attached to their office to brutal physical coercion), in various ways the local population managed to contest the attempts by the magistracy to establish themselves as a master class.[15]

The relationship between the magistracy in New South Wales and the central authority of the governor was conditioned by the fact that the governor virtually held the sole power of appointment and dismissal.[16] Appointment conferred considerable practical power on the recipient as well as the prestige traditionally associated with the office. From the point of view of the governor, it was a considerable item of patronage as well as a crucial means of promoting his policy. Because of the difficulties involved in controlling the day-to-day exercise of the magistrate's power, and because of the political significance of the office, appointments had to be carefully considered. Mistakes could provide opponents with a valuable position from which to oppose or frustrate the governor's policy and to launch criticisms. Moreover, the power over the appointment and dismissal of justices did not give the governor a free rein by any means. It became very much part of the local politics. The prospect of a new commission of the peace (the document by which justices were appointed and dismissed) could be made the subject of press speculation about who would be purged and who preferred.[17] Complaints about the exclusive power of the governor to make appointments came from several quarters, including two of the four judges to hold office under the governorship of the Macquarie (1810–1821).[18] The judges thought that they should have a say in who was appointed to the magistrates' bench; but Macquarie, jealous of his prerogative and justifiably suspicious of the motives of the judges, refused to concede any of his powers.[19] Macquarie had in fact used his power of appointment to the magistracy as the flag-bearer for his key policy of forwarding emancipated convicts. In 1810, as one of his first acts of office, he appointed two emancipists to the magistracy and a third in 1812.[20] The subsequent controversy over these appointments, discussed below, underlined the symbolic importance of the magistracy, the importance of the appointments power and the limitations on it.

Theoretically, the patronage of appointment and granting precedence in the magistracy should have had the effect of disciplining the upper classes in the colony. To this end, James Stephen, legal adviser to the Colonial Office, counselled:

> So soon as the division of the colonies into Counties can be carried into effect, it will probably be convenient that a Commission of the Peace should issue, as in England, for each particular County; and I would also submit to you that it might be convenient to follow the course, as in Jamaica, of investing in each County, some Magistrate with the office of 'Custos Rotulorum' [keeper of the rolls, i.e. head magistrate], selecting for that purpose the person in whom the local Government might place the greatest confidence.
>
> I need not observe on the value of distinctions of this nature, the influence of which is felt in all societies, and which have the effect of securing to the Government the cheapest and most effectual influence over the higher classes of society.[21]

Certainly the office was considered prestigious: 'The Committee must bear in mind, that in general estimation to be in the Commission of the Peace is considered a decisive test of belonging to the rank of a gentleman,' Mr Justice Therry told the Select Committee on the State of the Magistracy in New South Wales.[22] In fact precedence in the commission did become a controversial issue in 1820[23] and election for the chairman of Quarter Sessions in 1835 led to the resignation of Governor Bourke.[24] But contrary to the appearance of unfettered patronage in magisterial appointments, the Exclusives were able to tie up the office for their side of politics in a variety of ways.

One of these ways was the simple lack of people other than Exclusives suitable for appointment. And once appointed, controversy surrounded any attempt by a governor to dismiss a magistrate. Governor Bligh dismissed a magistrate for refusing to commit a member of the military for trial.[25] Governor Brisbane acted similarly towards magistrates politically opposed to him, who were using their positions as magistrates to carry on that opposition.[26] So did Governor Bourke.[27] Each sparked controversy. Probably the most celebrated case, however, involved Governor Macquarie's sacking of the Reverend Samuel Marsden from the Parramatta bench.[28] The ill-feeling between Macquarie and Marsden was of long standing, due to Marsden's opposition to the emancipist policy and to the severity of sentences passed at Parramatta by Marsden. The event which precipitated the dismissal was Macquarie's release of several prisoners from Parramatta Jail because of overcrowding; he acted after recommendation from the judge-advocate who had visited the jail. Marsden took umbrage at the release of prisoners he had sentenced and tendered his resignation. Rather than accept the resignation Macquarie published an order dispensing with his services, conspicuously omitting the customary eulogy. The dismissal drew criticism from Commissioner Bigge.[29]

Given the limited number of *respectable* people, dismissal of magistrates was very difficult, except in very clear circumstances. Governor Brisbane, for example, was able to dismiss five magistrates at Parramatta who had tried to use their office to censure a fellow magistrate, Douglass, who was allied to Brisbane. They then refused to sit on the Parramatta bench with him and were dismissed. Although Brisbane was vindicated, the political cost of the controversy was considerable.[30] Brisbane's experience typified the difficulties involved in holding the magistrates accountable for their conduct and the sort of opposition that could be expected by governors opposed to the interests of the magistracy, as both Governor Macquarie and Governor Bourke could testify. Despite many reports of corruption, illegality, extreme brutality and defiance of the Supreme Court (see below), legislation to indemnify the magistrates rather than dismissing them often proved the more politically attractive option.[31] The magistrates were very powerful men within the colony and the associations of their office muted criticism of them made to England by the governors or through Hall's editorials.[32]

Macquarie had attempted to deal with the problems of limited choice in the magistracy by appointing three outstanding men from the ranks of the emancipists. Initially, Macquarie's emancipist appointments had been a response to the limited number of suitable people on his arrival in 1810. Many of the wealthy Exclusives had been associated with deposing Governor Bligh, hence his selection of an emancipist like Thompson.[33] Other less wealthy free settlers lacked the necessary prestige, as measured by material success. By 1820, the problem of choice had changed. By then, sufficient wealthy free settlers had arrived but they were aligned with the Exclusives and opposed to Macquarie's emancipist policy.[34] He was wary and sought to promote his emancipist policy by rewarding the distinguished service of the emancipist surgeon, Redfern – convicted of involvement in a mutiny at the Nore in 1797. Bigge had told Macquarie at the time that he disapproved of the appointment of emancipists to the magistracy and subsequently detailed his objection in his report.[35] Macquarie told Bigge that to retreat on the appointment of emancipists would be giving too much to the Exclusives. The Colonial Office subsequently told Macquarie to remove Redfern, the sole remaining emancipist magistrate.[36] Redfern's dismissal made it clear that emancipists could not gain access to power through the magistracy, leaving the field clear for the Exclusives. This gave little choice to the governor. Governors Brisbane and Bourke met similar difficulties. Exclusives dominated the magistracy and exercised that power in their own interests, as E.S. Hall, editor of the *Monitor*, editorialised in 1827:

> ...the graziers will, for the above and other reasons too numerous to explain, do their utmost with the government to prevent the distribution of tickets of leave and emancipations to all, but especially deserving convicts. And as government is always influenced by the *magistrates* and civil officers, and as both these classes are graziers to a man, it follows, that nothing but a strong sense of *humanity*, and a patient consideration of those profound principles of political economy which reveal the ultimate expediency of liberal measures, can ever expect to operate on the mind of this government, to pursue towards the convicts the humane treatment of the philanthropic and *people* loving Macquarie . . . the emigrants [i.e. the Exclusives], and even many of the emancipists, are decidedly hostile to the improvement of the convicts, except insofar as coercion and perpetual slavery may tend to reform and humanize them. [Original emphasis][37]

But there was another reason for treading lightly with the gentlemen justices: the government depended on them.

The burden of administering New South Wales and the convict system – apart from a small civil staff attached to the governor – fell entirely on the magistrates. Musters of convicts to keep a check on their movements, recommendations on eligibility for tickets-of-leave, the assignment of convicts by ballot, hearing cases against convicts for breaches of the convict 'code', complaints from convicts and more, all fell to the magistrates. On top of this they administered the matters noted above: police and prisons, master and servant legislation and a number of other local government functions pursuant to local proclamations and legislation; they also conducted the normal magistrates' court functions for cases involving free people. Thus while the governor held the power of appointment and dismissal, his dependence on the magistracy meant that he could not simply refrain from making appointments and that – as the Marsden case had shown – dismissal was an option of last resort. Moreover, the effective operation of the rule of law at local level depended on respect for the magistracy at local level, and hence the governor had to avoid undermining their authority, as his critics, including Bigge and Bent, pointed out.[38]

Despite this dependence, the governor had several techniques at his disposal for the exercise of some control over the magistracy. In the first place, there were Government and General Orders and, after 1823, legislation by which he could direct their actions. Macquarie, for instance, issued orders in relation to convicts' wages, clothing, hours of work,[39] the way in which magistrates were to process tickets-of-leave[40] and the number of lashes which could be given.[41] Magistrates had to list the fines and punishments they imposed and forward them to the government.[42] Legislation in 1832 specified the subject matter of the summary jurisdiction of the justices, where hearings might be held, the number of justices to be present and the types of punishments which could be awarded.[43] It would be naive to think that these laws were followed to the letter, and indeed there is evidence to the contrary in Macquarie's public rebuke to the magistracy that they had failed to follow his ticket-of-leave regultions[44] and from various other sources that justices did not restrict themselves to the number of lashes specified.[45] The vagueness of offences such as 'insubordination' or 'insolence' left plenty of room for interpretation, while multiplying the charges in respect of one set of events allowed limitations on the number of lashes to be evaded.[46] Introducing legislation to define and regulate the summary jurisdiction of magistrates, Governor Bourke laid a list of illegal punishments awarded by the magistrates before the Legislative and Executive Councils.[47] Complaints by the magistrates about the limitations placed on them by this legislation indicate that legislative controls were felt as a constraint, but a series of indemnity acts to protect the magistracy shows that they were by no means a precise control.[48]

There were other means of control. The governors could exercise the prerogative of mercy over sentences and there are several instances of early governors reducing the number of lashes to be inflicted. As the colony grew in area and size of population this became impractical.[49] The prerogative of mercy also extended, as we have seen, to reducing sentences of imprisonment imposed by the magistrates and this was freely used. Restricting the territory over which a justice of the peace might act constituted another means of control for the governor. Following English practice, Macquarie insisted that magistrates be appointed for a specified district and he resisted attempts to create justices who could exercise their jurisdiction anywhere in the colony.[50] He criticised Marsden for sitting outside his jurisdiction and probably saw the potential for more disruption of the Governor's authority if justices who were his political opponents were able to move throughout the colony in their magisterial capacity. This potential was realised in 1834, during Bourke's governorship, when magistrates stacked the Sydney bench to ensure the conviction of one of the governor's allies.[51] The power to confine the geographic jurisdiction of the magistrates had been lost after 1821, when general commissions of the peace created justices for the whole colony.

Numbers of justices provided another point of control, but the need for local administrators limited the extent of this option. During the 1820s and 1830s, difficulties in getting the magistrates to attend to their duties brought calls for more magistrates. This, combined with complaints about the performance of justices who did attend to their duties, led to the creation of the first stipendiary magistrates in 1825.[52] However, stipendiary magistrates (or 'police magistrates' as they were known in the colony), created potential for more control by the central government over the magisterial office. By and large the men appointed were already in receipt of some sort of government remuneration (e.g. officers on half-pay), and supplemented their incomes with the stipend for magisterial duties.[53] Reasons of politics and class had prompted controversy in England over the composition of the magistracy. Stipendiary magistrates had been staunchly resisted in the last half of the eighteenth century in England;[54] the appointment of industrialists to the commission drew criticism in the early nineteenth century.[55]

The rural gentry in England rightfully saw stipendiary magistrates, appointed by central government, as a threat to their authority and a criticism of their performance. Similar sentiments existed in New South Wales. But the illegalities of the honorary magistrates in New South Wales produced cautious acceptance of the experiment with stipendiaries, even from the New South Wales magistracy's fiercest critic, the editor of the *Monitor*:

> ...As to the salary, what is the expense of a salary to any country, in comparison of the inestimable advantages, the indescribable benefits of a pure, discreet, *lawful* administration of the law. The best money that a nation expends, is that which is laid out in the administration of justice. Custom has given rise to many eulogiums on the *unpaid* magistracy of England, but those panegyrics have lately been much called in question, and from the superior tact, discretion, diligence, and steadiness of the

paid part of the English magistracy (the police of London to wit) over the unpaid, we ourselves are more than half converts to the cause of the paid.[56]

Against this, the 1839 Committee on Police and Jails saw the stipendiaries as an interruption of the natural order of things; it saw the removal of stipendiaries as desirable so that gentlemen could school themselves in the art of government against the time when 'the Constitution of this Colony shall have assumed the more congenial form of popular representation'.[57] Friction occurred with the honoraries when police magistrates took the chair at court sittings; and the *Australian* thought that the appointment of stipendiaries demeaned the honoraries.[58]

Increase in control by central government also figured among the criticisms. The appointment of police magistrates constituted an item of government patronage which gave the governor the lever of a salary against the police magistrates; not so, of course, with the honoraries. Some suggested, echoing traditional rhetoric about paid police and magistrates, that the police magistrates were spies for the central government.[59] Certainly they reported to the governor on events in their jurisdiction but the extent to which the government could direct their actions, and the actions of the honoraries, was a matter of some delicacy. Windeyer, who had been both a paid and unpaid magistrate, told the 1839 Committee, in some frustration, that even the idea of a circular letter from the governor to the magistracy about an escaped murderer would be regarded as offensive.[60]

Despite this sort of opposition to police magistrates, there was also opposition on grounds of expense from the governors themselves and from England.[61] But circumstances forced many in the colony and the 1839 Committee to the conclusion that they were a necessary evil:

> ...Your Committee have found, however, that the state and occupations of this community render it impossible in all cases as in the Rural Districts of England, to obtain the services of an unpaid magistracy. There is a marked distinction between a newly formed Society, thinly scattered over a wild and unimproved Country and all necessarily engaged in the active pursuits of life, and the mother country possessing in great numbers men of wealth, and leisure, ready to devote their time and talents to Public objects...where the necessity for an efficient Police is rendered the more necessary from the absence of a resident Gentry.[62]

Ironically the Colonial Office had to remind settlers in New South Wales of their class interests, urging reductions of the numbers of police magistrates, which in that year, 1834, stood at 29 out of 238 magistrates in the colony.

With reference to your observation as to the disinclination of the Inhabitants to give up their time to the discharge of Magisterial Duty, and the necessity which would therefore exist for a future augmentation, if convicts continued to be sent out in large numbers, I think it right to acquaint you that His Majesty's Government will not feel at liberty to sanction the substitution of a stipendiary for an Unpaid Magistracy, excepting under peculiar circumstances, and that therefore Persons of Property, who may be otherwise qualified for the task, must not be encouraged to expect that they can be relieved altogether from a duty, which is required from them as much for their personal interests as for those of the Community at large.[63]

How serious a threat stipendiaries posed to the Exclusives is debatable. First, as the 1839 Committee made clear, they were regarded only as a temporary expedient. Second, one did not lose caste by being appointed a police magistrate: the jobs went to ex-army officers and the sons of the elite.[64] Perhaps this explains the muted criticism; non-gentry appointments would have produced an uproar. Some of the magistrates testified to the 1839 Committee about the similar class interests of the stipendiaries and the honoraries.[65] The contemporary account of free labourer, Alexander Harris, gloomily observes that '...the appointment of paid magistrates was considered some time ago to be an attempt to remedy evils in the administration of the law at the inferior courts,...; but I do not believe that it did any good. The police magistrate gets acquainted with his settler neighbours who are honorary members of the bench; and the same system goes on, only with this difference, that it is at second hand.'[66] Hence, while the appointment of police magistrates offered some potential for a readjustment of power in favour of central government and away from the local elite, it was very little realised in the period under study.

The legal means of ensuring that the power of the justices of the peace were exercised lawfully were more restricted than in England. As detailed in chapter 4, the first and second Charters of Justice did not provide the superior courts with the traditional means of supervising the functions of magistrates, the prerogative writs. The *New South Wales Act* 1823 cured this defect and immediately proved useful to Governor Brisbane, who used the writs to coerce the Sydney bench over the extremely controversial issue of trial by jury.[67] The magistrates had been refusing to convene quarter sessions because of a ruling by the Chief Justice that juries had to be used at these sessions. The Exclusives were opposed to jury trial in the colony and hence the magistrates' refusal to convene quarter sessions. In the event the Supreme Court granted the attorney-general a writ of mandamus compelling them to convene quarter sessions. As a counterpoint, the magistrates complied but issued jury lists omitting the names of emancipists.[68] The technicalities and other limitations of these writs, however, were neatly demonstrated in litigation over the next two years, which unsuccessfully attempted to have the names of emancipists included on the jury lists.[69] The technicalities also left a good deal of room for errors in matters over which magistrates had jurisdiction; the writs are much more limited than appeals which were not provided until 1835.[70]

Despite limited rights of appeal, there were other means of keeping the magistrates within the bounds of law. Civil actions for damages could be brought by aggrieved individuals but not by the central government; thus civil suits did not provide a direct means for the governor to control the magistracy (cf. prerogative writs and criminal prosecutions). The effectiveness of civil suits was limited by indemnity legislation[71] and a deferential attitude on the part of the Supreme Court towards the justices of the peace.[72] Civil remedies were easier to get in cases where the magistrates acted without jurisdiction, but in matters over which the justices had jurisdiction only want of 'probable cause' or *mala fides* would provide a remedy for the litigant.[73]

Apart from the limitations already mentioned, the passive nature of the Supreme Court's power (it had to wait to be moved by a suitor who had standing to sue) constituted a further check on the practical control exercised over the magistrates. And as yet no account has been taken of geographic, economic and political obstacles to the intervention of the court. Even this low level of supervision seemed extreme to the Exclusive spokesman, James Macarthur, who complained to the Molesworth Committee that:

> ...the magistrates for years past have not been supported in the manner which I conceive they ought to be by the Supreme Court of the colony; or at all events there has been an evident disposition to throw difficulties in the way of the magistrates, and to let them be annoyed by legal technicalities, where I conceive the very opposite disposition ought to have existed . . . but I know the magistrates in forming the jury lists were frequently apprehensive of excluding persons who were of objectionable character, lest those parties should commence action in the Supreme Court, and in which case there was scarcely any doubt, from former experience, that the magistrates would have gone to the wall.[74]

Given the illegalities and evasions that the magistrates did practise in New South Wales – as we shall see – the degree of concern about the Supreme Court exhibited by this statement seems at once disingenuous and revealing. Any degree of control by a governor or the Supreme Court excited the indignation of the Exclusivist magistracy; the Supreme Court and the rule of law – 'legal technicalities' – imposed some check on the magistrates' very extensive power but it was far from complete.

From the perspective of a governor's political opponents, the courts provided the most direct and immediate means within the colony of contesting the central authority of the governor. Resort to the Colonial Office, where the Exclusive cause usually gained a favourable hearing, could be kept for desperate causes. Governor Macquarie, and later Chief Justice Forbes, claimed this had been the strategy by which the Exclusives had been able to have every previous governor recalled. For everyday matters, the magistracy provided the Exclusives with an ideal immediate site of opposition. Where this produced conflict with the governor, they too could draw on rule of law ideas to invoke magisterial independence and the traditional associations of their office. If they lost a battle with the governor in the colony, the record of the conflict could then be used against the governor at the Colonial Office.

There are several notable examples of the use of this strategy by the magistrates against each of the anti-Exclusive governors, Bligh, Macquarie, Brisbane, and Bourke. The Parramatta bench established a tradition of using the office to demonstrate political opposition to Macquarie's policies.[75] The bitter opposition of the same bench to the magistrate Henry Douglass, an ally of Governor Brisbane, took the strategy to new and foolish lengths. They accused Douglass of illegalities on the bench which – as an investigation showed – they themselves had practised.[76] Justices of the peace used their office in their campaign against Governor Bourke, which culminated in the stacking of the Sydney bench in *Watt's* case. Bourke subsequently resigned over his colonial treasurer's election as chairman of quarter sessions.[77] These constitute clear examples of the extent to which the office of justice of the peace was politicised. But we have already encountered the case which best demonstrates the Machiavellian intrigues at work in the colony's principal sites of power, the revocation of Hall's assigned convict printer, Peter Tyler. Chapter 4 examined the case at the level of conflict between the governor and the Supreme Court. But this case was a multi-layered affair. The magistrates were deeply involved. The case became a test of strength between the magistrates and the governor on the one side and the Supreme Court, in its attempts to impose the rule of law, on the other.

Both Governor Darling and the magistrates had a fervent dislike of Edward Hall, the radical editor of the *Monitor*. Hall had been a strident critic of Darling. He had also editorialised against the magistrates, accusing them of receiving stolen goods, pocketing thousands of pounds of fines, provoking convicts by sleeping with their wives and then flogging the convict if he complained, refusal to take evidence, torture, harassment under the *Bushrangers Act* and flogging prisoners to obtain confessions.[78] In an attempt to silence his critics in the press, Darling decided to revoke the assignments of Hall's foreman, Peter Tyler, and the *Australian's* court reporter. The latter was arrested while actually at the Supreme Court reporting a case! Hall told Tyler not to comply with the revocation.[79] In the meantime, the Supreme Court decision in *Jane New's* case, referred to in the previous chapter, was handed down. The court held that the governor did not have an unfettered discretion to revoke convict assignments. In apparent deference to the court's ruling, Darling decided not to persist against Tyler. Rather the attack was transferred to the real enemy, Hall. The magistrates decided – and there is a strong suspicion that Darling connived at the plan – to prosecute Hall before the Sydney bench of magistrates for harbouring a runaway convict, namely Tyler, on the basis that his assignment had been revoked![80] Nothing, we can imagine, could have given the gentlemen justices greater pleasure than to strike a blow at their critic, Hall, and simultaneously thumb their noses at the Supreme Court. Hall was convicted and fined before the magistrates. He then took his case to the Supreme Court.

Hall had told Murray, Secretary at the Colonial Office, that the governor's revocation had caused outrage in the whole community because of the governor's 'illegal despotism'.[81] Against the background set by Hall of the illegalities practised by the magistrates and the threat posed to private property by arbitrary revocation of assigned servants, Hall invoked the rule of law against arbitrary power:

> In order, Sir, that you may not think the unbounded authority invested by the late Act of Parliament in General Darling is exercised by His Excellency benignantly in proportion to its extent, and that, *de facto*, the said act 'works well' for His Majesty's very distant and very unprotected Juryless subjects in New South Wales, I beg to lay before you [the facts relating to the revocation of Tyler and the reporter for the *Australian*].[82]

By the time the case got to the Supreme Court, it had assumed the proportions of a constitutional confrontation between the Supreme Court on the one hand and the governor and the magistrates on the other. With Wentworth as his counsel, Hall launched a frontal attack. Wentworth moved the Supreme Court for permission to file a criminal charge against the magistrates for illegally fining Hall. He argued that their refusal to be bound by the ruling in the *Jane New* case amounted to contempt of the Supreme Court.

The three judges of the Supreme Court found that the conviction of Hall was not 'reconcilable to common sense'. '[W]ith much difficulty', the court refused to grant a criminal information against the magistrates in what they called a 'momentous matter'. With similar reluctance and not much conviction, Mr Justice Dowling, a political conservative, went on to find the evidence identifying Governor Darling's Colonial Secretary, McLeay, as the instigator of the prosecution, insufficient. He then delivered a stinging warning to the justices of the peace about contempt of the Supreme Court lest they be tempted to allow themselves 'as magistrates [to] set their opinions against ours, as judges, against the Supreme Court of the Colony. As long as he had the honour to form one of its component members, he would never be treated with contumely. It would be an extraordinary novelty, indeed, if subordinate tribunals were to be allowed to call in question the justice of a Supreme Court.' While pardoning the contempt on this occasion, the court ordered the magistrates to pay court costs.[83] In a later civil action, the Supreme Court awarded Hall damages against the magistrates.[84]

No doubt the reluctance of the Supreme Court to find any involvement of the governor in all of this stemmed from the potential ramifications of a head to head confrontation between the court and the governor. Not to be left out of this politicking, the magistrates used the opportunity to withdraw their services, complaining about their legal liability and the criticism of them by the press, impliedly threatening a boycott of the bench.[85] The incidents demonstrated the considerable political influence of the magistrates. In the first place their access to prosecution process could be used to good effect against their political opponents, or where the governor was the opponent, against his protégés.[86] Second, the affair demonstrated their hostility to, and considerable effective shelter from the supervision of the Supreme Court, even when formally subjected to its jurisdiction. Third, they could use the confusion arising out of attempts to supervise them to strengthen their power. Against Macquarie, they could invoke the rhetoric of independence of the judiciary and the need for the dignity of the magistracy to be upheld.

The same argument about dignity was used against their political opponents, to keep emancipists off the bench. Eventually incidents between Macquarie and the magistrates made up a large part of Bigge's criticisms of Macquarie and contributed significantly to his recall. Similarly the magistrates' position enabled them to resist implementation of policies which they opposed, their opposition to trial by jury being a particular example of this strategy.[87] Ironically, the absence of juries at quarter sessions provided an argument for the Emancipists who contended that many of the abuses committed by the magistrates arose because of the absence of a jury to check their arbitrary decisions.[88] Even in defeat over the *Hall* case, the magistrates had demonstrated their extensive political power and posed a very serious challenge to the authority of the court and the operation of the rule of law in the colony.

The operation of the rule of law at local level forms the other dimension in this analysis. Through the local courts and their control of the police, the magistrates were the main source of legality in the rural areas. But as local landowners and employers of labour, they also posed a threat to the lawful exercise of power. The desire to exercise power on the larger plane deepened this tension. The badge of the magisterial office publicly recognised other achievements, notably material success and respectability. Once gained, however, a seat on the bench endowed the incumbent with lawful authority to make court orders about people's liberty and to prescribe punishments which would be enforced by the state. The exercise of magisterial power served not only to recognise and maintain the authority of the large landowners, but also to enhance their authority at both the central and the local level, not to mention their material interests. At the local level too, the legal system, in this case the magistracy, provided a means of resolving the conundrums of status and power confronted in a new and changing society.

An understandable anxiety about respectability pervades the discourse about free and freed people in the penal colony. Fear of being swamped by an emancipist ascendancy underlay many of the campaigns by the Exclusives until the decision to end transportation in the late 1830s rendered the old rivalry otiose.[89] Surrounded by convicted felons, people like chaplain and magistrate Samuel Marsden – who only had slim claims to high social status in English terms[90] – could tolerate nothing but the clearest demarcation between themselves and the convict/emancipist population. These men's acute concerns about status, enhanced no doubt by the codes of chivalry imported with the military garrisons, led to what seems to modern eyes like extraordinary pettiness. The Emancipists demonstrated similar anxiety, by their efforts to gain public office, the campaign over the right to serve on juries, the furore surrounding their standing to sue and attempts to be accepted in 'society'. Even ownership of landed wealth, the hallmark of civic status in England,[91] could not be relied on, so far as the Exclusives were concerned, in a colony where emancipists were numbered among the largest property owners. Allowing for hyperbole about sod huts, Clark has put it well:

> The foundations of authority in the Old World were absent in rural society in New South Wales. In England, Scotland and Ireland the local Justice of the Peace lived in an imposing mansion; in New South Wales he often lived in a sod hut. In England, Scotland and Ireland the local justice was distinguished by dress, speech and deportment from those to whom he dispensed justice; in New South Wales bush life stripped away most of the differences between man and man.[92]

In the absence of an established class structure, the fund of traditional authority attached to the office of justice of the peace was a valuable prize. The trappings and traditions of the office offered the cloak of respectability to men who could never have satisfied the traditional English criteria. That is not to say, as we shall see, that the local population to whom these office bearers looked for respect could not detect a counterfeit. One convict, no doubt acquainted with the proper conduct of magisterial office, expressed his contempt for the poor fist made of it by an incumbent: 'The Government should not appoint fools to the magistracy'.[93] However, such office bearers could at least command the power of the office and the outward signs of respect and deference which, in the end, however grudgingly given, may well have become mixed up with genuine respect and real authority.[94]

The clearest battles over respectability in the magistracy were waged over Macquarie's emancipist policy, in particular his appointment of emancipists as magistrates.[95] The relevance of this at the local level depended on the argument that the effectiveness of 'the law and its dispensers' depended on the respect they could command from the local population. Bigge attacked Macquarie's emancipist appointments to the magistracy not because of their inefficiency or lack of capacity but because of their former convict status. Describing the emancipist magistrate Simeon Lord, for example, he says:

> In the performance of these duties, he has exhibited a great deal of natural sagacity and shrewdness; but his want of education, and feelings of

self-respect, have, on more than one occasion, exposed the magisterial office to contempt.[96]

Similarly, Bigge comments that since emancipists were excluded from 'society':

> ...how much greater must it [the difficulty] be in raising them to the functions and honours of the magistracy, without diminishing that respect for the law and its dispensers, which it is so important in every country to uphold.[97]

As their name suggested, the Exclusives were concerned to exclude emancipists, in the magistracy as elsewhere, from avenues of attaining status. Disqualifying them from holding office in the magistracy was an important victory. The Exclusives were able to make their personal authority and repectability parasitic on the need for respect for the law and hence the government of the colony. Such arguments about respectability directed upwards by the Exclusives to their English colonial masters struck a responsive chord. Respectability and the dignity of the gentlemen who held the King's Commission for the Peace were part of the English countryside. A few 'trading justices' in England strained the traditional imagery a little; the notion that former convicts in New South Wales could become justices was too much. The Exclusives did not have too much trouble in persuading the British government that emancipists should be excluded from the magistracy. They were not so successful in persuading those 'below' them that they merited respect, as the convict quoted above, and Hall's criticisms illustrate.[98]

Although the magistrates directed their arguments about respectability upwards, the evidence suggests they also appreciated the instability of orders based simply on physical coercion. Ultimately, authority is based on physical coercion but stable orders rely on their legitimacy and resort to force as infrequently as possible: authority may be more or less reliant on physical coercion.[99] Members of the ruling elite in the colony were nervous about the possibility of a convict uprising and, with some reason, about the lack of physical resources at their disposal to combat such an eventuality.[100] The mix of legitimacy and coercion that went into their attempts to establish their authority in the colony – particularly in the rural districts where in 1828 assigned convicts outnumbered free settlers by four to one – has an important bearing on the questions of law and power that we have been pursuing.[101] Respectability has been canvassed above. The physical aspects of subordination at local level also require attention.

From 1788, justices of the peace took summary jurisdiction over breaches of convict discipline and disputes between master and servant. Convict discipline offences like insulting language, refusal to follow orders, unauthorised absence and the vague offence of insubordination could earn the offender brutally severe punishments. In his capacity as a magistrate exercising summary jurisdiction, the first judge-advocate ordered 300 lashes for a convict interfering in a business in which he had no concern, 100 lashes for absence, and Ann Smith to be flogged through the camp for insolence.[102]

The legal basis for these offences is uncertain. They seem to be based on a sort of common law for the penal colony which constructed the offences from a combination of master and servant legislation and the rough and ready justice of the quarter deck to which the justices with military and naval backgrounds were accustomed.[103] The similarity of the convict discipline offences to master and servant legislation produced a creative confusion which led magistrates to overlook legal restraints on their powers over free workers, and to augment their power over the pool of available labour. This 'irresponsible' power over convicts also caused the magistrates to expect the same sort of deference from free labourers.[104] Ironically, it turned out that the jurisdiction they purported to exercise over free workers under English master and servant laws was illegal.[105] This imposed no practical constraint on the magistrates for many years, and was not finally resolved until 1828.

A seat on the local bench gave magistrates the lawful authority to coerce a workforce which they and their class employed. This was indeed a boon, though some limitations applied. A magistrate was forbidden from punishing his own assigned convict workers, but reciprocal arrangements with brother magistrates could obviate any difficulties which might arise. For example, Hall reports a case in which Hannibal Macarthur called in a fellow magistrate to flog Macarthur's convict for lateness caused by a skittish horse.[106] The inclination for one magistrate to give a neighbour a favourable interpretation to a vague charge like insubordination in return for a similar favour on a future occasion would be understandable. The more so when the proceedings took place in private in the magistrate's house, screened from public scrutiny.[107] Exercise of these aspects of the jurisdiction provided not only a means of subordinating the workforce but also the means of cementing the solidarity of the masters and an organisational structure.

Governor Bourke's *Summary Jurisdiction Act* of 1832 attempted to cut back the arbitrariness of the magistrates' power. In the first place it specified the offences over which the magistrates had jurisdiction. The offence of insubordination disappeared, though vague offences such as 'neglect of work', 'abusive language to his or her master or overseer' and 'other disorderly or dishonest conduct' remained.[108] The offences were still vague enough to bear a multitude of interpretations to ensure due deference where masters chose to insist on it. The legislation did however limit the imagination of the magistrates who had been known to have men whipped for not showing proper respect (e.g. not raising one's hat to a magistrate when passing him on the road).[109] This still left plenty of scope. James Wright was a magistrate at Queanbeyan in the late 1830s. He owned 4000 acres at the edge of authorised settlement and grazed his flocks on both sides of the Murrumbidgee, the official frontier. He was master of 40 to 50 assigned convicts at his property, Lanyon, and regularly had convicts before his brother magistrates. Wright was known as a flogging magistrate and should be seen at the extreme end of the spectrum of magistrates in New South Wales. But there are enough stories to make his case instructive. He could rely on his brother magistrates to legitimise his cruelty towards his assigned convicts when he brought them before the court and to collude with him in an endeavour to undo the stipendiary who had attempted to bridle their excesses. This speaks to the breadth of the powers exercised by magistrates in New South Wales, even with the restrictions imposed by Bourke's legislation. The Bench book leaves a grim record:

> Mr. James Wright deposed – I live at Lanyon, the prisoner [John Ward] is employed as a shepherd – On last Tuesday he lost several sheep and has since found all but seven – this is the fourth time this has occurred – he has otherwise behaved well. The prisoner makes no defence.
> Guilty of neglect of duty 75 lashes
> A. J. Faunce.

> James Wright: In the beginning of October the prisoner [Samuel Hayes] was employed thrashing and finding him sitting idle I watched him for 20 minutes, during which he did nothing...On 13 October he was half an hour after the bell had rung for work after dinner. On 27 October I had him work with another man removing a wool shed...I found the two men sitting down smoking their pipes and doing no work. I took out my watch and sat down on a tree to see how long they would remain so...
> 50 lashes.

> James Wright Esq.: I reside at Lanyon, the prisoner [Philip Lee] is under my charge. On the 25th instant he was tried before this Bench and sentenced to punishment. On his return to Lanyon I desired to see his back he refused saying he'd see me dead before he'd show it to me nor

should I get any good of him. He was exceedingly insolent and abusive in his manner and his language...
                              25 lashes for disobedience, and 50 for insolence.[110]

Second, the legislation specified the punishments accompanying these offences. Magistrates did not have the power to impose the death sentence, but their powers over imprisonment, further transportation, the treadmill, floggings, bad reports on ticket-of-leave applications and other punishments had been the subject of tensions between the magistrates and a number of governors. The press, especially the *Monitor*, campaigned vehemently against the magistrates. Hall accused them of a mentality akin to West Indian planters in relation to their bonded workforce and a desire to keep them in perpetual slavery.[111] Macquarie, as discussed, had exercised his prerogative of mercy over prisoners imprisoned at Parramatta, and limited the number of lashes allowed to be ordered by magistrates.[112] The effect of the limitation was at best doubtful, hence the 1832 legislation. Despite the evidence of some sort of dumb insolence from convicts who had endured the lash, it is hard to doubt that the spectacle of the triangle had the desired effect on its audience, if not its victim. Nor was the example used sparingly, as we have seen.[113] Argot like 'Giving a man a red shirt', thirty-second spaces between lashes and the descriptions of blood and flesh thrown around by the lash, convey some of the brutality of floggings. James Wright had doubts about the integrity of the flogger at Queanbeyan, hence his examination of Lee's back. It was a practice not even the police magistrate at Queanbeyan could stomach:

> I have the honour to report for the information of his Excellency the Governor that it has appeared to be a practice with one or more of the assignees in this district to order their assigned servants after they have received corporal punishment, to strip and shew their backs in order that the extent of laceration might be ascertained, and to request that, as such a disgusting practice might tend to insubordination amongst the convict population, His Excellency will be pleased to authorise in all cases a recommendation that the servant be withdrawn.

Governor Gipps would not grant the request in general but did agree to consider individual cases of 'what seems to me a highly disgusting practice'.[114]

Of course the lash was not the only form of punishment open to the magistrates; the treadmill, places of secondary transportation and work on chain gangs added to the array of punishments at their command. The 1832 legislation clarified the legal powers of the magistrates but still left them with a set of awesome sentence options.

As Governor Bourke remarked, the legislation would not have been out of place in a slave code.[115] The legislation also required petty sessions to be held in public at designated places before two or more magistrates.[116] Despite the apparently reasonable nature of these restrictions, Bourke's legislation was trenchantly attacked by the magistracy,[117] and blamed, dubiously, for increases of crime in the colony.[118] Along with trial by jury, the *Summary Jurisdiction Act* turned out to be among the most controversial political issues of Bourke's governorship and formed one of the focal points of the campaign against him. The ferocity of the reaction by the magistrates underlined the importance they attached to their coercive powers and their indignation at attempts to trammel their local autonomy.

Control over the police further enhanced the local power of the magistrates. The importance of the police role warrants separate treatment.[119] Magistrates controlled the local police just as their English counterparts did. Their power to direct and deploy the police – often close to their own properties – provided them with a legal warrant for a small force of private retainers at government expense. Local legislation enhanced this power and provided possibilities for vindictiveness and arbitrary treatment. The most egregious example of the possibilities occurred under *Bushranging Acts* which gave police the power to arrest and detain anyone they suspected of being a convict at large and bring them before a magistrate. The result of such detention was confinement in makeshift lockups on the magistrate's property, long delays and long journeys to verify their status. In this, not only did the rule of law impose virtually no check on arbitrary power, it imposed a substantial burden on freedom of movement; this was justified by contemporaries on the basis that New South Wales was a penal colony. The near-arbitrariness of this system, coupled with the absence of any adequate system of identification, except in Sydney, increased the risks for those moving around the rural areas looking for work.[120] This suited the interests of employers seeking to discipline a mobile workforce, especially at times of labour shortages, and magnified the power of the magistrates.

The magistrates also controlled the prosecution process. Prosecutions, as we have seen, could be used for vindictive purposes. Harris has an example of a prosecution aimed at removing a person from a desirable tract of land.[121] Hall complains of grazier magistrates who had their constables-cum-pound keepers impound the cattle of their enemies. Of course, the magistrates themselves were never prosecuted for allowing their own animals to stray. Retrieving stock from the pound could be a very expensive business.[122] The power of detention and decisions over bail and committal for trial also allowed scope for abuse and de facto punishment of innocent parties. Moreover the discretionary nature of these decisions made it extremely difficult for a would-be plaintiff to prove malice against a magistrate in an action for damages.

Attempts at resistance to this near arbitrary authority can be found. Atkinson has presented evidence of protest at several levels.[123] Frontal attacks on authority were rare although in 1829, for example, there was fear of a convict uprising.[124] Certainly the convicts had numbers on their side but even if the motivation for a general uprising was present, dispersal, lack of organisation and lack of weapons militated against success. The Castle Hill rebellion in 1804 had shown this,[125] as did the abortive rising at Bathurst in 1830.[126] Convicts, however, were prepared to use the courts to call their masters to account and despite the slim prospects of success and risk of reprisals, their actions suggest some point in invoking the rules about their treatment.[127] Sabotage and violence directed at the magistrate or his property were also possible.[128]

People in the country could invoke the rule of law against the magistrates, either by petitioning the governor or by bringing suit in the Supreme Court. Passage of indemnity legislation and cases in the Supreme Court demonstrate that this option had some credibility. However distance, partiality, expense, lack of expertise, reprisals by employers and problems of a convict's credibility in a swearing contest against a magistrate held out low prospects of success for a convict or free labourer aggrieved by the conduct of a justice of the peace.[129] The presence of pro-Emancipist lawyers, such as Wentworth and Wardell, and a vigilant press provided some check on the magistracy in and around Sydney.[130] In the distant areas the introduction of stipendiaries made some difference. Faunce, the police magistrate at Queanbeyan was prepared to write to the governor about James Wright's inspections of the backs of convicts who had been flogged. Perhaps this was a retaliation for the complaints lodged with the governor about Faunce's conduct of his office at Queanbeyan. Gipps sent two other stipendiaries to enquire into the dispute. Alexander Harris makes a reference to this sort of use of the police magistrates – this time to check on the honoraries – in his semi-fictional, *The Emigrant Family*. But Harris says that humane magistrates who would stand up to their peers were exceptional.[131] The unearthing in 1825 of practices existing since the early 1800s – whipping suspects to extract confessions of theft, and then whipping them again to reveal the whereabouts of stolen property – goes some way to support Harris's general assessment, at least up to 1825. Even this abuse came to light through a grand jury rather than the complaint of an aggrieved party. Ironically, it was a grand jury stacked by Exclusives aiming at impeaching one of their opponents, Douglass, who had been appointed to the local bench. As we have seen, the inquiry disclosed that members of the same grand jury had themselves been guilty of the same illegal punishments, and that such practices went back to the colony's earliest days.[132] The extent of such practices became an explicit rationale for the subsequent indemnity legislation.

The ratio between legitimacy and coercion in magisterial authority at the local level in New South Wales is not susceptible of precise measurement. As chapter 6 will show, the convict system offered opportunities for close surveillance despite the vastness of the colony. This left actual or potential insubordinates vulnerable to the array of fearsome punishments at the disposal of the magistrates through the legal system. Figures on the use of flogging, to say nothing of the other forms of punishment, and the bitter complaints from the magistrates about restrictions on their powers, suggest a much higher degree of reliance on coercion than in England at the time, and arguably higher than in the contemporary slave-holding societies. Lack of the respectability normally associated with magisterial office, and a population inured to the rigours of the convict system would indicate a greater resort to coercion than respectability. Yet the use of the courts by free workers and convicts suggests some degree of faith in the normative elements of the system. Criticisms of those magistrates who did not measure up to expectations and praise for upright magistrates from contemporary chroniclers testify to some degree of legitimacy enjoyed by the magistracy. By whatever means, the local power of the magistrates was maintained; they had no serious challengers in the convict period.

The magistracy formed a crucial part of the colonial legal system. Its capture by the Exclusives meant that the shape of state power in the convict period had to be negotiated with them. The office served as a sword and a shield. As a shield, governors could be prevented from prosecuting policies to which the Exclusives were opposed; as a sword the office could be used to injure and harass governors to whom the magistrates were opposed. Other rivals, notably the Emancipists, could be treated similarly. Moreover, the magistracy gave its holders access to the traditional authority of the office and State-sanctioned coercion which was used first to gain and then guarantee the power of the incumbents and the subordination of local populations. The justices stood between the governor and the governed, a position from which they were ideally placed to play a dominant role in colonial politics until the end of convict transportation.

As Maitland said in the passage quoted at the beginning of this chapter, English magistrates were entrusted 'to show what the laws made in Parliament, the liberties asserted in Parliament, really meant to the mass of the people'. But justices of the peace in England and in New South Wales had only an amateur's grasp on the law and, often, strong self-interest in the cases they adjudicated. The office with its traditional associations of status and independence put a great deal of political power in the hands of the Exclusives in New South Wales. It also put the power of the State at local level in their hands, and provided them with instruments of coercion – police, jailers and floggers – to reinforce their power. The rule of law at the local level in New South Wales was an uncertain quantity which could and did spill over into arbitrary power. But it also constrained what might have been. Eventually, the excesses practised by the magistrates up to 1824 were held up to a legal standard. The Supreme Court curbed the magistrates' vendetta against Hall. The complaints of the magistrates in the 1830s reveal the pinch of the legal standard. As the legal system became more sophisticated through legislation, the strength of the Supreme Court and lawyers like Wentworth and Wardell grew. And as the newspapers railed against the illegalities, the magistrates became more bound by the legal system through which they had gained a great deal of their authority.

CHAPTER 6
Policing a Penal Colony

They have an admirable police at Paris, but they pay for it dear enough. I had rather half-a-dozen people's throats should be cut in Ratcliffe Highway every three or four years than be subject to domiciliary visits, spies, and all the rest of Fouché's contrivances.

We have heard much in praise of the admirable effects of the Police in Paris. Certainly the Police of Paris is most dexterously contrived for the purpose of tyranny, but that it is so very efficacious in the prevention of the blackest crimes that deform and afflict human nature we much question.

The Earl of Dudley, 1811[1]

Here we go on in the usual monotony – the same system of Government as when you left us, Douglass at the head in this unfortunate village, keeping up a most detestable system of Police, such as would never be imagined to exist in any English Town – What think you of every stranger coming to the Inns however respectable being questioned as to their name etc. by the Convict Constables of this detestable fellow. He has a Constable in the middle of the Town expressly stationed to report the Ingress and Egress of any, even the Inhabitants of the Neighbourhood – This is placing the Inhabitants in the Situation of Italians in the petty States which are under a foreign Yoke and military government.

Hannibal Macarthur [2]

Standing armies and paid police forces formed part of the demonology in the book of British liberty. The opening quotations exemplify the opposition of the eighteenth-century English gentry to proposals for reform of the administration of criminal law, be they proposals about paid justices of the peace or police. Even in the face of serious threats to order, such as Jacobite revolts, the Wilkite protests, the Gordon Riots and the fears raised by the French Revolution, the gentry refused to countenance such threats to British liberty.[3] They rejected Beccarian principles of certainty of apprehension and punishment in favour of a system of selective terror and mercy administered by the gentry.[4] Paid magistrates and police forces conjured up fears of standing armies which might fall into the hands of central government and a spy system antithetical to fundamental British liberties. Paid police also threatened the control of the gentry over the magistracy and the police; proposals to establish them implicitly criticised the gentry's competence and performance in discharging these tasks.[5]

Hannibal Macarthur expresses precisely these sentiments regarding the constables in Parramatta, constables who were under the control of his foe, Douglass. New South Wales was a closely-watched society; distinguishing the bond from the free and dealing with absconding convicts imposed costs on everyone and was used as a reason to justify intrusive policing practices. This sort of surveillance contrasted sharply with the free society Hannibal Macarthur had known in England. Policing a penal colony presented special problems for British liberty and the traditional means of protecting it, the rule of law.

But there is more than a little irony in Macarthur's complaint. Macarthur was one of the magistrates found guilty of ordering the illegal punishments discussed in the preceding chapter. Consistent with his Exclusivist outlook, Macarthur's concerns lay with the respectable. Members of his class meant to control the means of coercion, not to be controlled by them. That was part of the reason why it was important to control the magistracy: in the traditional English model of policing, justices of the peace appointed, supervised and, if necessary, dismissed the local constables. Unlike contemporary Australian policing which is organised state-wide, the parish constable was the model people worked on in early New South Wales. And like English justices, the New South Wales magistrates jealously guarded their prerogatives over policing.[6]

On the Emancipist side, if 'the laws made in Parliament, the liberties asserted in Parliament' were to mean anything to the 'mass of the people', the power of the police had to be subject to legal control. The English tradition of magisterial autonomy, combined with the sensitivities of the local power struggles, made any sort of control difficult, as we have already seen in the case of the magistrates; the fact that many of the rural magistrates were former military officers and impatient of 'legal technicalities' compounded the difficulties.

At its most basic level, the promise of the rule of law ideology to curb arbitrary power depends on policing. While their power poses a threat to liberty, police also enforce the law, make its orders meaningful and constitute its coercive dimension. The mix between force and law, and who would control that mix, were questions which, like so much else in early New South Wales, were left open. The answers to the questions of policing sprang from English conceptions of governance, but these conceptions had to be adjusted to the peculiarities of the penal colony. The role of police in shaping power in the new colony repeats the themes about law and power which run through this book. The relationship of police to the central authority of the governor (and later the councils), to the magistracy, to the convict and free population, to the Aborigines and to the military, provides a key to general conflicts over the exercise of power in the colony, the establishment of hierarchy and the operation of the rule of law on a day-by-day basis. To understand this, we will need to look at the various structures of policing which emerged in New South Wales.

Governor Phillip appointed Henry Kable a constable of police for Sydney in 1789. Two years later, Henry became the overseer for the Night Watch and went on to serve for seven years as Chief Constable for Sydney. He was dismissed from this position in 1802 for misbehaviour in the execution of his duties. Apparently his trading activities came into conflict with his duties as a constable.[7] The fact that the governor had to rely on convicts as the first police in the colony exemplifies the improvisations necessary in such a peculiar society.

To modern eyes, the measures taken for supervision and control of convicts in the first settlement seem remarkably casual. Phillip's instructions empowered him to create constables but there was no one suitable for the office, other than convicts. Now this already represents a break with tradition, since constables were supposed to be respectable members of the parish, who did duty for a year at a time on an honorary basis. While the tradition had persisted, by the eighteenth century, employment of deputies to do this duty was widespread and the evidence suggests that often the quality of the deputies was poor.[8]

No one seems to have thought about who would act as police in

New South Wales. Phillip did not appoint a Night Watch for some eighteen months after landing, and then he did so only in response to a suggestion from one of the convicts.[9] He divided the settlement into four districts and appointed twelve watchmen, one principal and two subordinates to each district. He appointed convicts 'whose conduct and character had been unexceptionable since their landing'.[10] Working perhaps on the logic of 'set a thief to catch a thief', convicts continued to be appointed to police forces throughout the convict period. So George Barrington, pickpocket to the rich in England, became Chief Constable at Rose Hill weeks after his arrival in 1791.[11]

Perhaps the sparse policing arrangements reflected the traditional assumptions about local constables being appointed from the local respectability, a strange oversight in a place like New South Wales. Perhaps the thinking was predicated on the presence of marines to guard the convicts on the First Fleet. If so, with a fine appreciation of the traditional distinctions between civil and military functions, the marines refused to take on that role. Moreover, they were outraged when Phillip's regulations for the Night Watch purported to regulate them, and the more so when marines were actually challenged by the convict Watch. According to the family history, Henry Kable's first catch was one of the marines. The marines forced Phillip to withdraw the relevant regulation.[12] The principle was established that day-to-day management of convicts and the ordinary tasks of policing were not part of the military regiment's duties. Its functions were to protect the colony from external threat and from general insurrection, along the lines of the English model for the non-involvement of the military in civilian policing. The principle does seem to have been pretty well observed although in the 1830s, for example, Governor Bourke used small detachments of troops to guard iron gangs.[13] Soldiers on leave from their regiment also composed the personnel of the Mounted Police, formed in 1825. Although sworn as constables and directed by Mounted Police regulations to obey magistrates, their status seems to have been ambiguous. The 1839 committee on police reported a less than co-operative attitude by members of the Mounted Police towards the civil magistrates.[14]

Although not called on to deal with external threats, the military did figure in insurrectionary activity on three occasions in the transportation period. Twice they appeared as defenders of the established order: in the Castle Hill rebellion in 1804 and in a revolt by convicts at Bathurst in 1829. And once they took the protagonist's role, in the Rum Rebellion. Their intervention proved decisive on each occasion, demonstrating to all concerned where the ultimate seat of physical power lay. Notably, no civil police appear to have been involved at Castle Hill; during the Rum Rebellion too they seem to have chosen discretion rather than valour. In the Bathurst revolt, a civilian posse and some constables were repulsed, as was a party of Mounted Police; but the convicts capitulated when confronted by the military.[15]

The relationship between the police and the military may be characterised as ambiguous, as indeed it was in England. The military stood as a backstop in times of crisis. But despite their power as the commanders in the colony, the governors could not rely on the support of the military for civil functions and indeed one governor, Bligh, met his downfall at their hands, in the Rum Rebellion. For day-to-day policing of the colony, the military had little or no role for most of the period and, where they did play a role, it was as a reinforcement of the civil power. At least this feature of the British system of liberty persisted in the penal colony.

Governor Phillip's system of police in Sydney, plus the appointment of constables for settlements outside the town, persisted until his successor's arrival in 1796. Hunter reorganised policing and issued police regulations. He divided the town into districts, numbered the houses, and required each district to elect three respectable men as watchmen. Although the English practice of local control over the police would have required the *district* to pay the constables, Hunter offered to meet the expenses from central government funds.[16] Among their other duties, these constables were required to police a system of passports issued by magistrates, as a method of keeping a closer check on the movements of the convicts. Collins, the Judge-Advocate, reported that the police system improved conditions in Sydney.[17] The small size of the colony and its composition necessitated much more central involvement in policing than in England. This established a precedent which would later tell against the local gentry in their contests for power against the central government and shape the pattern of power in the colony.

To round out the description of policing in the early days of the settlement, two further points need to be made. First, the executive functions of justices of the peace were far more significant in this early period than later. Unlike their modern court-bound counterparts, they played an active role in the tasks of policing. The first judge-advocate, David Collins, who was also a justice of the peace by virtue of his position, describes cases where he came upon people committing offences, arrested those concerned, tried them summarily and then sentenced.[18] As late as the 1830s, magistrates were being reminded of their policing duties, though it appears from the need for a reminder that in practice a sharper division was developing between their executive and judicial functions.[19]

Second, it is important to see that besides the official police, overseers of convicts and masters of assigned convicts had a quasi-police role in the sense that they initiated action for offences by convicts. In some cases, employers, such as James Wright at Queanbeyan, had what was referred to as a farm constable for the tasks of policing on his own estate, a role which appeared to involve acting as a sort of go-between with the local constables.[20] The range of offences in New South Wales both against the criminal law and against 'the convict code' – such as insubordination, refusal to work, etc. – broadened the scope for intervention.[21] Additionally, a system of rewards and sentence remissions encouraged private informers – often convicts themselves – to assist in the tasks of surveillance and prosecution. Any calculation of policing in early New South Wales should take account of all these unofficial agents of police, the broadened scope of police action allowed by 'the convict code', and the use of public, exemplary, corporal and capital punishment.[22] It was, as we will see, a very closely policed society, consistent with its status as a penal colony.

Governor Macquarie put the policing of the growing town of Sydney on a more elaborate basis. He established a separate Police Fund in 1810, financed by duties on imports. The Police Fund was placed in the control of a committee comprised of the Lieutenant Governor, the Judge-Advocate, and the new Superintendent of Police and Treasurer of the Fund, D'Arcy Wentworth. Wentworth – who had avoided transportation as a highwayman by voluntarily leaving England – continued the tradition by which the experienced were chosen to perform police work in the colony. He received a salary of 200 pounds as Superintendent and, eventually, 100 pounds per annum as Treasurer.[23] In addition to supervision of police in his capacity as magistrate, he conducted court for summary offences in what became known as the Sydney Police Court.[24] There were some novel aspects to this appointment particularly, again, the payment of Wentworth's salary from central funds in lieu of fees. He effectively became the first stipendiary magistrate in New South Wales; this was another departure from the normal English practice of honorary justices being in charge of the police and sitting in court as part of their honorary functions, although there were two precedents in England, one the Bow Street Magistrates Court and the other the Middlesex justices.[25] This arrangement meant that the important office of Superintendent of Police for Sydney was in the gift of the governor.

Wentworth's appointment continued the system under which, with a couple of departures, the first magistrate for Sydney controlled the constables.[26] The governor retained the power of appointment and dismissal of the chief magistrate and chief constable; he also formulated the police regulations. But appointment and dismissal of the ordinary constables was the prerogative of the magistrates; in Sydney this meant the Superintendent, although Wentworth frequently accepted recommendations from the governor.[27] The magistracy and police of Sydney continued to have a professional cast and the later stipendiary magistrates took on a variety of special tasks on behalf of the governor. For example, Windeyer, stipendiary at Sydney in the 1830s, undertook the inquiry into the conduct of the Queanbeyan bench in 1840, as we have seen, to settle complaints against the local paid magistrate raised by the honorary justices, including James Wright. One of the main complaints was the paid magistrate's supervision of the police, although, looking below the surface, he seems to have been subjected to a vendetta for not submitting to the honoraries. Compared to the situation in Sydney, the relationship between the governor and the rural magistrates in these matters was more distant both geographically and metaphorically, and stayed much closer to English models. The rural justices of the peace exercised a good deal of autonomy in policing, more than was the case at Sydney.

Macquarie repeated the practice of his predecessors in dividing Sydney into five districts (six by 1819) and establishing watch houses in each. By 1819 Wentworth presided over a police establishment for Sydney of 61, comprising an assistant and a clerk, a chief constable, assistant to the chief constable, six district constables and fifty constables.[28] Constables resided in or near their district, at their own expense. Instead of wages they received full rations and a half, plus clothes and rations for their wives and up to two children. Added to the range of duties we associate with contemporary policing, police had a variety of functions relating to the convicts, including apprehending convicts abroad after 9.00 pm. They also performed a range of local government functions: they enforced public hygiene rules, saw that the price of bread set by the bench was observed, monitored the liquor laws, policed the slaughtering regulations and made sure the citizens of Sydney duly observed the sabbath.[29] They were also responsible in general for the tranquillity of their districts and for enforcement of a variety of Government and General Orders. Offenders arrested by the constables would be brought before Wentworth's Police Court the following day. Under the police regulations, Wentworth could order corporal punishment against the convicts; free people could be fined, bound over to keep the peace or committed for trial in the Criminal Court. Wentworth was also in charge of the surveillance of convicts in Sydney and informed Bigge that he knew pretty well where all convicts resided in the town: 'There is scarcely one with whom we are not well acquainted', he told the Commissioner.[30]

Similar arrangements on a smaller scale applied in the towns of Parramatta, Windsor, Liverpool and on the Hawkesbury, where the local magistrates took charge of policing. Quality of personnel was an endemic problem throughout the period. In the case of the rural constabulary especially, Bigge found a want of zeal in the chief constables. He also found that the chief constable at Sydney, Redman, was illiterate, elderly and infirm.[31] Wentworth told the Commissioner that he attempted generally to recruit from emancipists and free persons, for instance, retired soldiers.[32] This was not always possible and persistently led to regretful statements about the necessity to appoint convicts and ticket-of-leave holders,[33] allegations of connivance with malefactors,[34] complaints about the difficulty of getting good personnel[35] and high rates of dismissals and resignations.[36] By 1819 police outside Sydney numbered forty-seven, with eighteen police at Parramatta, sixteen at Windsor and smaller numbers at Liverpool, the districts of Airds, Bringelly and Cooke, and Appin.[37]

The mid-1820s brought significant changes to the policing of New South Wales. The nature and growth of the colony, both in geographic and population terms, imposed strains on the traditional model of constables controlled by magistrates. Commissioner Bigge was critical of the colony's police arrangements on grounds of efficiency and unruly behaviour in the towns.[38] By the mid 1820s, under the impetus of Bigge's recommendations, Governor Brisbane set reforms of the Sydney police in motion. Bigge had recommended appointment of a full-time magistrate of police,[39] payment of salaries rather than rations[40] and commented adversely on police performing non-police functions, such as carrying mail.[41]

In 1825 the Legislative Council considered reports by the magistrates and the new Superintendent of Police, Captain F. N. Rossi, on the state of police and recommended a variety of changes. Significantly the Council, which had a mandate for the whole colony, refrained from making recommendations about the rural police because it felt insufficiently informed. While committee members thought the system may be applicable to Parramatta, they called on the magistrates to furnish information about other districts. The Council's deferral is a measure of the autonomy enjoyed by magistrates over local policing and the fact that the Exclusivist magistracy would not surrender such an important perquisite to an agent of central government so easily. Not only did the Council lack information about local policing arrangements, but it was reluctant to trespass on the magistrates' prerogatives. Rossi, who was appointed as head of police for the whole colony, only became head of the Sydney police.[42] The Council recommended that there be three salaried clerks (that is, not receiving fees), two officers, eight wardsmen, sixteen conductors and forty-eight patrolmen. As well as an increase in numbers, these measures introduced more gradations of rank in the force, recommended that they wear uniforms, carry a staff of office and do exclusive duty as police. Moreover, it recommended the separation of police and jail functions.[43]

The most significant change proved to be the appointment of the full-time Superintendent, Rossi, in 1825. Unlike his predecessors, his was a full-time appointment at a salary of 500 pounds a year. Rossi immediately set about energetically lobbying the colonial government for improvements of the Sydney police. His detailed report in the subsequent year cited the numerous 'robberies and outrages' caused by convicts congregating in Sydney, asserted knowledge among criminals of the insufficiency of the constabulary and stressed the need for strict operation of police and a *Vagrant Act* to combat problems as more convicts became free. With due deference, he praised the zeal and activity of the honorary magistrates but pointed out that they could not be expected to devote their whole time to police work. To cure this he advocated the creation of more police magistrates (also referred to as stipendiary magistrates) and a centrally-organised system of police based in Sydney to combat problems of co-ordination between police in the various districts.[44]

Despite initial reluctance, Governor Darling and the Executive

Council were persuaded by Rossi's case.[45] The installation of an officer with a vested interest in the growth and efficiency of his department made itself felt. Whether the number of 'robberies and outrages' had increased is difficult to know; it might be, as David Philips has suggested for England after the new police, that the rate of crime remained steady and the type prosaic.[46] Fears of a convict insurrection and bushranging were beginning to mount in the colony in the mid-1820s. The Executive Council increased the number and salaries of the Sydney police.

Another of Bigge's ideas – for a Mounted Police patrol – also had an impact on the shape of policing. Once again, this innovation in executive power largely by-passed the honorary magistrates. The idea found form in 1825, in response to attacks by Aborigines and increased threats from bushrangers. The Mounted Police was formed for temporary purposes from the regiments in the colony, despite express reluctance to employ the military for civil purposes.[47] It was very much a makeshift arrangement as the soldiers came from infantry regiments. Horses, which were in short supply in the colony, had to be supplied by settlers. Despite these drawbacks, the Mounted Police proved so effective that they became much sought after by magistrates.[48] Mobility made them particularly successful in pursuit of bushrangers and law breakers in the areas beyond the official settlement. In 1838, for example, it was the Mounted Police, under the leadership of Edward Denny Day, a stipendiary magistrate, who tracked and caught the Myall Creek murderers. The massacre occurred more than a week's travel from the official limits of settlement where there was no magistrate and no local constables. Such was the local sympathy with the killers among the whites, that it is doubtful whether Day's assiduous pursuit of the murderers would have been matched by the honoraries or their constables.[49] But this ledger has to be balanced; the Mounted Police were also extensively used against the Aborigines in the inland prior to the formation of the Border Police in 1839 and, as we will see, they were also guilty of violence towards the Aborigines.[50] The Mounted Police provided a means of dealing with problems which were beyond the capabilities of the rural constables, especially in the remote areas where there were no honorary justices. Indeed, they were so effective that the 1835 Committee on Police called for an increase in numbers.[51] The 1839 Committee reported with satisfaction that the problem of losing experienced troopers when their regiment was transferred out of the colony was to be overcome by making the Mounted Police a permanent force, thus allowing the personnel to remain in the colony.[52]

Their numbers steadily increased towards the end of the 1820s as bushranging became more prevalent. From forty-six men in 1826, the Mounted Police grew to one hundred and four in 1830, and to a maximum of one hundred and forty-four in 1839.[53]

The make-up of the Mounted Police gave rise to the traditional problem of mixing civil and military functions. More than this, while their chain of command led to the centre, their areas of operation overlapped the jurisdiction of the local justices and their constables. To overcome the problem, control of the Mounted Police was divided. The commanding officers of the regiments selected men and officers from among volunteers in their regiments. By the Mounted Police regulations,[54] those selected placed themselves at the disposal of the local magistrates.[55] Despite the fact that Day, a stipendiary magistrate, appears to have exercised effective control of the troopers in pursuit of the Myall Creek murderers, in general it seems that neither officers nor men relished subordination to the civil authority of the magistrates and, for their part, the justices felt unsure of the extent of their authority over the Mounted Police.[56] The officers were sworn as justices of the peace and the non-commissioned officers and men as constables. They nevertheless wore military-style uniform, retained their military pay and status and were stationed in small detachments at various points around the colony. The 1835 Committee recommended that the Mounted Police detachments station themselves closer to the local magistrate or bench of magistrates, but the clash of the different models of policing made the success of this measure unlikely.[57]

The other police force administered by central government, was established in the 1830s. If bushrangers were the catalyst for the formation of the Mounted Police, 'collisions', as contemporaries were pleased to call them, between white squatters and Aborigines led to the formation of the Border Police. As squatters moved further and further inland, violence between them and Aborigines, who were being driven off their traditional land, became more frequent and bitter.

'Collisions' between Aborigines and settlers had occurred since the first settlement.[58] The ambiguous legal status of Aborigines – some hybrid of outlaw, foreign enemy and protected race seemed to be the white attitude – exacerbated the problem. The cases which resolved the ambiguity came nearly 50 years after white settlement.[59] The governors had been instructed to conciliate and protect the

Aborigines, but nevertheless governors from Phillip onward – on the foreign enemy model – were prepared to send troops on reprisal raids against Aborigines. Governor Darling did so, for example, after Aborigines had speared some whites at Bathurst despite the written objections of his Solicitor-General that the action was illegal.[60] Those on the frontier had adopted the practice of shooting Aborigines who represented any sort of threat and others poisoned them. Their attitudes and practices are betrayed by arguments about the Myall Creek defendants, men who had shot some twenty-eight Aborigines – including women and children – in cold blood. Arguments on their behalf claimed they had been singled out for special treatment.[61]

Although the Myall Creek defendants were brought to justice by the Mounted Police, the troopers' record respecting Aborigines was by no means unblemished. Early in the same year, 1838, a party of twenty-three Mounted Police led by a Major James Nunn was sent to 'suppress outrages' by blacks on the Liverpool Plains. These outrages occurred against a background of violence as whites intruded into the lands around Moree. Resistance by the blacks was met by savage reprisals. After initial skirmishes in 1836, one stockman was killed and two others wounded. In response, eighty blacks were shot by a party of Mounted Police. Late in 1837, trouble broke out again, leading to the 'outrages' which precipitated Nunn's expedition: the Aborigines had killed two whites and speared some cattle. Nunn's troopers shot at least twelve Aborigines, probably many more. Their bloodthirstiness provoked official enquiries in Sydney, but dealing with a powerful figure like Major Nunn of the Mounted Police was a far different proposition than dealing with convict and ex-convict stockmen. Governor Gipps pointed out the difficulties of law enforcement '...if offence was given to the Officers or Men of the Mounted Police, who are (as your Lordship knows) all volunteers...'.[62]

To meet the problems of policing on the periphery, Governor Gipps formed the Border Police, a force which would be located in the remote areas. For him it was a means of protecting the Aborigines from white depredations. The squatters favoured the idea too as a method of policing their itinerant workforce in the sparsely populated areas outside the official limits of white settlement. The constables were placed under the command of special justices of the peace, Land Commissioners, who had been established in 1835 to adjudicate land disputes in the squatting districts. Convicts served as constables (many were army deserters from South Africa), and the non-commissioned officers came from the Mounted Police. The

Colonial Office, through James Stephen, approved the plan fatalistically, accepting the inevitability of the extinction of the Aborigines:

> That problem is how to provide for the government of persons hanging on the frontier of a vast pastoral country for which there is no known assignable limit...the Shepherds and Herdsmen of New South Wales must bear a great resemblance to the Nomad Tribes of Russia and Tartary and must I apprehend ultimately become almost as lawless and migratory a Race.[63]

The extension of central authority and the rule of law faced a three-pronged threat at the periphery: from land grabbers relentlessly pushing out from the settled districts with their assigned convicts; agricultural labourers, many of whom were taking the exit option offered at the edge of the frontier; and, on the other side of the frontier, Aborigines resisting the advances into their lands. The attitude of the authorities, however, was mixed.

The central government fiddled with law and order beyond the settled districts throughout the 1830s. Following the recommendation of the 1835 Committee, three visiting magistrates, one each for the north, west and south borders, were established.[64] The appointees were also officers in the Mounted Police.[65] No courts of Petty Sessions sat beyond the boundaries of location until 1847, and there were no resident magistrates to supervise a rural constabulary as was the case in the settled districts.[66]

Land Commissioners had been established in 1835 and were sworn as justices of the peace but they had no constables attached to them. When the Border Police was established in 1839, its constables were placed under the supervision of the Land Commissioners. The quality of personnel and conditions of service in the Border Police managed to be worse than those of any other force in the colony. Convict constables were employed on no pay but full rations, accommodated in whatever huts they could build for themselves, given horses which they did not know how to ride or tend and promised remissions on sentence for good behaviour and return to government service for the whole of their sentence for misconduct.[67] Governor Gipps was unable even to supply cuffs as a distinguishing mark in lieu of a uniform.[68] Never numerous, their numbers ranged from twenty-two in 1839 to a high of eighty-six in 1845, before they were wound up in 1847. In 1846 this represented one constable for every 489 inhabitants (the census did not include Aborigines) spread over a vast area.[69] Even discounting government concerns about expense, the inadequate provision for policing must be taken as an indication that the problems in the distant areas were regarded as a low priority. Despite expressions of concern for Aborigines, the government was not prepared to curb the pastoral expansion.

Gipps had only newly arrived in the colony when news of Nunn's killings reached Sydney. Gipps sympathised with the plight of the Aborigines. But however much he may have wished to see the law of murder applied on the frontier, he was confronted by powerful constraints. First, the law depended on the agencies of enforcement and, on this occasion, they were the law-breakers. On the frontier, the Mounted Police had been the only option. There was little commitment to the Border Police. Second, there was an even more fundamental constraint on Gipps' actions towards the Mounted Police. The logic of colonisation and the white invasion of Aboriginal land required the use of force to quash resistance; the white runholders demanded protection from the government. There could have been more or less force and it could have been more or less indiscriminate. Had the government explicitly condoned white vigilantism, the violence might have been worse. By using the Mounted Police, the State could exert its monopoly over the use of force and still maintain the colour of law on the frontier. But the mix of law and power here was very heavily weighted towards the latter and, in the case of Nunn, it clearly spilled over into lawlessness. The execution of the Myall Creek murderers later that year tipped the balance of law and power back somewhat. Gipps could only have stopped the killing by stopping the invasion. Neither he nor anyone else was prepared to take that course, as Stephen's fatalism showed. The rule of law had only a very tenuous hold at the frontier. The police enforced a very lop-sided version of equality before the law: they punished Aboriginal resistance savagely and only very occasionally intervened on their behalf. The law of murder – in relation to the Aboriginal victims of white settlers – went into virtual suspension as an adjunct to the dispossession of the Aboriginal landowners. As a constraint on arbitrary power, the rule of law at the frontier was an abject failure.

Sydney, on the other hand had become quite a centre for law and order by the 1830s. Such were its pretensions that it even modelled its police arrangements on London. Sydney had three police magistrates by 1834, with the Superintendent of Police increasingly divorced from bench duties and fully occupied with administration of his force.[70] The *Sydney Police Act* of 1833 placed the organisation of police on a legislative basis for the first time in the colony.[71] The Act showed the influence of the London police model[72] but it was supplemented by a host of regulations about public hygiene,[73] town building,[74] licensing carters, porters, etc.[75] and apprehension of convicts at large without a pass.[76] The convict system, together with Acts such as the *Bushranging Act*,[77] the *Vagrancy Act*,[78] and provisions in the *Police Act* to check convicts for passes, meant that the range of duties and extent of surveillance was much greater than for the new London police.

Two police magistrates were appointed to control the Sydney police and they appointed constables who were subject to their orders and to dismissal by them. They also had the responsibility for framing police regulations.[79] From 1825 when there had been 54 police in Sydney, the numbers steadily increased to 103 in 1835 and then, subsequent to the 1835 Committee Report, they jumped to 154.[80] The ratio of police to population in Sydney and the settled districts in 1836 was very high, at one constable to every 133 people; it had been as high as 1:96, in 1828, at the height of fears of a convict insurrection and troubles with bushrangers.[81] By contrast, contemporary police to population ratios in the rural areas of England were 1:1000 and present-day Australian ratios are about 1:500. This high ratio may have been justified by the large number of convicts but, even so, the increase of police did not keep pace with the influx of convicts from England in the early 1830s or the growth of population.[82] The announcement in 1828 that the colony would have to pay for policing out of its own funds – long-delayed and much resented by the upright citizens of Sydney who thought England should pay the price of policing its own transportees – affected thinking about police numbers after that date. If the residents of Sydney were concerned about the rate of crime and controlling the convict population, this is not reflected in proportionate increases of the numbers of police. Indeed the 1839 Committee recommended the reduction of Sydney Police by one-third, transfer of Mounted Police to the distant areas and a slight increase in constables' pay of three shilling and sixpence per day, still less than the four shillings per day which was the going rate for labourers. Constables could earn extra through a half-share of fines.[83]

The 1839 Committee seemed satisfied with police arrangements for Sydney, but not for the colony as a whole. Though not cited as reasons, the end of transportation in 1838, silence about convict insurrection, decline in the number of bushrangers and 'crimes and outrages' in Sydney, the prospect of the colony having to pay for its police (the Committee had suggested a levy on the inhabitants of

Sydney), and perhaps the performance of the Sydney Police, all contributed to the Committee's satisfaction.

Policing of rural areas within the official limits of settlement presented more difficult problems. Rural policing continued, as it had from the foundation of the colony, with local constables under the control of the justices of the peace. The duties of the rural constables derived from their status as common law constables. They were directed in the execution of their common law powers and their duties under legislation by the magistracy. But there was no general police legislation equivalent to the *Sydney Police Act* for the rural police. In addition to the normal police functions in relation to the criminal law, they were also responsible for surveillance of convicts in their areas, for catching runaways, policing the pass system, knowing all the assigned convicts, running convict musters, escorting prisoners to and from petty sessions and to the Supreme Court in Sydney or on circuit (at Goulburn, for example), escorting prisoners to places where more severe corporal punishment could be carried out[84] and a range of miscellaneous duties like process serving and letter carrying.[85]

For this work, the colony relied on 80 rural police in 1820, a number which had increased to 314 by 1840.[86] The magistrates consistently complained about the onerousness of their constables' duties, especially escort duty which was both hazardous from the lack of lockups on the roads (the constables had to handcuff themselves to prisoners before they could sleep at night) and time-consuming. Some of the magistrates estimated the constables' time was almost entirely taken up with escort duty.[87] Many of the punishment options open to magistrates required travel. There were no houses of correction in the interior, the treadmill was located at Sydney and punishments of more than 50 lashes had to be inflicted at a place where there was medical superintendence.[88] One magistrate thought they were getting a poor return on the process. He told the 1839 Committee that the convicts enjoyed the trip to and from the treadmill at Sydney.[89] Be that as it may, the rural magistracy compensated for these shortcomings, as we have seen, by liberal distribution of floggings. Between 1830 and 1837, magistrates ordered 7,103 floggings for a total of 332,810 lashes. In the middle of that period there were 27,340 male convicts in the colony. By comparison, magistrates in England awarded an average of 234 floggings per year over the period 1811–1827.[90] A considerable array of punishment stood behind the magistrates and their sturdy rural constabulary. More than this, there was a layer of informal police below the official constables:

farm constables and supervisers to act as links between the master and the official system, and other convicts who could secure privileges for themselves by informing.

The rule of law did not operate evenly in the settled rural areas. The organisation of rural police in fiefdoms under the local justice of the peace prevented central co-ordination from Sydney. The honorary justices continued to control their constables and central government trod warily around their prerogatives. The problems were increased by the fact that Mounted Police also operated in areas under the jurisdiction of the rural constabulary. Not only did rivalry, lack of co-operation and fisticuffs occur between the different police forces in the colony,[91] but also within the rural police, which was organised on a district-by-district basis. The constables of one district would refuse to assist those of the next.[92] The magistrates communicated, if at all, through the Colonial Secretary's Office, which had a range of other responsibilities. Windeyer, Police Magistrate at Sydney, told the 1839 Committee that had it not been for the sensitivities of the justices of the peace to trespasses on their authority and reflections on their competence, there should have been circular letters sent to all magistrates about crimes committed in one district, descriptions of the offender and details as to possible whereabouts. As it was, he said, an offender who moved from one district to the next was as safe as if he had moved to another country.[93] Be that as it may, as we have seen in the case of the Myall Creek murderers and will see again in the case of escapers in the Queanbeyan district, fugitives were usually caught quickly.

While prepared to concede a reduction in Sydney police, the 1839 Committee called for reforms in the rural police. Part of the problem with the rural police lay in supervision. Witnesses to the 1835 and 1839 Committees testified to the need for stipendiary magistrates both to administer the police and to conduct petty sessions.[94] Calls came from the rural districts for the appointment of stipendiaries. For example, James Wright wrote about his difficulties at Queanbeyan, on the edge of the official limits of settlement. He complained that his free overseer would 'neither do his duty nor quit my service, and he is exerting himself to incite improper conduct amongst my assigned men,...'. Wright described his fruitless series of journeys – totalling 520 miles – in search of a magistrate to take out a summons against the errant overseer.

Wright's letter seeking appointment of a paid magistrate drew a rather frosty response from the Colonial Secretary. Wright was told that a number of appointments had been made and that expense prevented further appointments. The Report of the 1839 Committee conceded the practical difficulties while holding on to the traditional themes about the role of the magistracy. Removal of police magistrates was desirable so that gentlemen could school themselves in the art of government, against the time when 'the Constitution of this Colony shall have assumed the more congenial form of popular representation'. However, the practicalities of the situation could not be ignored:

> Your Committee have found, however, that the state and occupations of this community render it impossible in all cases as in the Rural Districts of England, to obtain the services of an unpaid magistracy. There is a marked distinction between a newly formed Society, thinly scattered over a wide and unimproved country and all necessarily engaged in the active pursuits of life, and the mother-country possessing in great numbers men of wealth, and leisure, ready to devote their time and talents to Public objects...the necessity for an efficient Police is rendered the more necessary from the absence of a resident Gentry.[95]

Successive governors adopted the expedient of employing police magistrates, and from a total of two outside Sydney in 1825, their numbers grew to 29 out of 202 magistrates by 1838.[96] Their control over the costabulary effected an important shift of power away from the honoraries and a reduction in the Exclusives' control over law enforcement in the rural districts.

With few exceptions, the evidence to the 1835 and 1839 Committees came from magistrates, mostly police magistrates. The police magistrates, where available, bore the brunt of police organisation (hence their name) and the running of the magistrates' courts in the rural districts. The availability of a police magistrate relieved the honorary justices of tasks which otherwise would have been theirs to perform. Samuel North, police magistrate at Windsor, gives some idea of the duties of policing a town close to Sydney. He ministered to a population of 6,000 with twenty-one police and three Mounted Police. Two-thirds of his men were free, the remainder held tickets of leave, save the scourger who was a convict. He heard an average of 40 cases per week at court, two-thirds of them involving convicts. Between 1832 and 1835 his police apprehended 230 runaways.[97] In addition, like other magistrates, he wrote monthly reports to the governor on the state of his districts. These were the reports which led to charges that the stipendiaries were spies, a charge which echoes the Earl of Dudley's letter which opened this chapter.[98]

Many of the police magistrates were military officers on half pay, and ex-civil office holders; some were patronage appointments from England.[99] Their pay ranged from to 150 pounds to 300 pounds per annum, but they had to find housing out of their own pockets, not an easy task given the dearth of suitable houses to rent in the rural areas and the expense of building. Alexander Busby complained that the lack of suitable residences caused the police magistrates 'to be thrown on the hospitality of the settlers, the impropriety of which it is unnecessary for me to suggest'.[100] Their applications for increases of pay were rejected by the Committee.[101]

The police magistrates testified that they organised petty sessions. Accounts varied about the difficulty of getting honorary justices to make up the number needed to pass sentences of corporal punishment. Often because of the distances involved, these courts were held at two or three different places in their districts each week. In addition to court duties, of course, the police magistrates had the responsibility for appointing and supervising the constables, a task which, some testified, kept them very fully occupied.[102] Finding suitable men proved more difficult than at Sydney; the pay of two shillings and ninepence per day for rural constables fell short of the four shillings per day paid to labourers; the colony paid their Sydney counterparts three shillings and ninepence.[103] This apparently meagre wage could, however, be supplemented by fair means and foul. Constables were entitled to a share of the fines for some offences and some supplemented their incomes by selling necessities to prisoners in their lockups. Bribes were no doubt another source of income.

The criticisms of the police magistrate at Queanbeyan, A.J. Faunce, reveal some of the difficulties of rural policing. The local honoraries – including the master of Lanyon, James Wright JP – charged that ten prisoners had escaped in a six month period because of the culpable neglect of the constables. The responsibility for these escapes and other irregularities in the policing of the district lay with Faunce. The criticisms look damning until the difficulties he had to overcome are recounted. Most of the escapes occurred on the 64-mile journey to Goulburn, where trials took place. The Inquiry found that there were insufficient constables for this task when the force was at full strength, which was seldom the case because of the lack of suitable people. Nor were there any secure lockups on the journey. The escort party spent the nights on the road in huts belonging to convicts. It was hardly surprising that some escaped. Equally, the constables – led by the police magistrate – recaptured all but one within days of the escape.

Faunce was also accused of hiring Zaccariah Westropp as lockup keeper, a man who was facing charges under the *Hired Servants Act*.[104]

(Ironically, the position had become vacant because the previous incumbent had been convicted of allowing prisoners to escape! One of Westropp's successors held a ticket-of-leave; another was under sentence.) Faunce had known Westropp in the army and thought him a better choice than the other available candidates who were all convicted men. The worthy honoraries also complained that Westropp was not duly sworn and had allowed a prisoner to escape. The Inquiry found that as Westropp had previously assisted the police and that the scourger and the other constables were away on other duties, there was no choice but to appoint the man. Anyway, the prisoner had escaped when Westropp was counting them over to the relieving constable. The Inquiry found that his conduct showed lack of experience rather than lack of care. John O'Connor, on the other hand, was an excellent lockup keeper. His sin involved selling tea, sugar and tobacco to prisoners, 'at prices sufficiently high to merit . . . the character of extortion'. Undoubtedly relieved to have someone who could do the job, Faunce forbade the practice but did not dismiss O'Connor. His colleagues on the Bench took a more rigid view; they dismissed him. The Inquiry supported Faunce.[105]

As noted earlier, Wright's criticisms probably had more to do with Faunce's insufficient deference to the honoraries than it did with his ability as a superintendent of the local constables. Indeed the immediate cause of the Inquiry into Faunce's conduct of the police may have been the Inquiry the previous February into escapes and excessive punishment at James Wright's property. Faunce's evidence was critical of Wright and probably there was a history of conflict between the two over policing issues. Perhaps Wright felt that since he had been instrumental in getting a police magistrate for the area that he ought to be getting better service.[106] Wright was a flogging magistrate and undoubtedly thought that Faunce was too lenient. Faunce criticised Wright's inspections of the flogged backs of his convicts.

Wright and his fellow honorary justices of the peace had probably thought that the advent of a police magistrate would augment their power by putting a paid official at their disposal, while relieving them of some of the more onerous and time-consuming duties. No doubt in some areas this was the pattern. However, the police magistrates could be independent-minded and, as we have seen, they owed their position to Sydney.[107] As far as convicts were concerned, their role offered the possibility of an independent check on the self-interest of their employers. Alexander Harris makes the same point in his story about the young police magistrate who threatened a cruel master with a commission of magistrates unless he gave a full account of his treatment of a dying man.[108] The Queanbeyan Inquiry was such a commission, carried out by two stipendiaries – Charles Windeyer from Sydney and Samuel North. This mechanism tied lines of responsibility both for the magistracy and policing back to Sydney. It was both an extension of the governor's authority and a means of making the promise of the rule of law rather than the rule of men more real in the settled districts by the end of the 1830s. What would Governor Macquarie have given for such a mechanism to deal with his unruly Parramatta magistrates?

Despite Windeyer's frustration at the lack of central control over rural policing, as we have seen there is reason to think he exaggerated the problems. The patchwork of policing meant that the watchful gaze of the State was never far away in the settled districts of New South Wales. Molesworth – half the world away in England – thought the number of police was 'immense'.[109] For all the complaints of the magistrates, the accounts we have from the non-elite suggest rural New South Wales was closely policed. The high ratio of police to population quoted above would tend to confirm the fragmentary accounts left by contemporaries in novel and memoir form. Alexander Harris goes to extraordinary lengths to avoid capture after his escape,[110] and constables are fairly close at hand when a crime has been committed.[111] Accounts of arbitrary abuses of police power are sprinkled through the book.[112] He asserts that masters used the pass system to inhibit movement by free labourers, as well as convict workers.[113] Similarly Ralph Rashleigh seems never to be far from constables and is indeed 'rescued' from a cruel master by a sympathetic constable.[114] Although there were ten escapes from the lockup at Queanbeyan, all but one of the fugitives were captured. Escapers from Wright's farm, which was right on the Murrumbidgee River at the edge of official settlement, were almost always caught. The options for fugitives were limited. They could not live off the bush, the Aborigines were hostile, the Aborigines helped police to track them and strangers moving about in sparsely populated areas stood out.[115]

Other accounts describe the harassment of travellers in rural New South Wales by police and trips of many hundreds of miles to verify their free status. James Demarr, a free person, describes how despite elaborate plans to avoid the police on his journey, he was betrayed to the police and detained for three days before he could satisfy the magistrates as to his identity.[116] The *Bushranging Act* in particular gave an underpaid police force, comprised largely of emancipists and ticket-of-leave men, very wide discretion and left the possibilities for 'paying one's way' wide open. Constables, like convicts, appreciated the opportunity of travel, it seems, from an incident related by J.C. Byrne. Apprehension of the unfortunate traveller afforded the constable an opportunity to visit his sweetheart in Yass.[117] The level of violence used by the police also caused concern. The *Australian* editorialised in 1825, after a man had been shot and killed by police at Parramatta that '...the constables have been too much in the habit of using, in any but a discreet manner, the firearms entrusted to their hands for public safety and personal protection'.[118]

As with English local governance, the presence of relatively autonomous justices of the peace in New South Wales constituted a counter-balance to central authority in general, and to the control of police in this instance. The 1825 *Committee on Police and Gaols* found itself unable to make recommendations about police outside Sydney for want of information, and called on the rural magistrates to make reports. By some mysterious means, Bigge's recommendation for the appointment of a full-time police magistrate was transformed into a post simply for the town of Sydney. Other recommendations for an overall commander of New South Wales police by the 1825 Committee and by subsequent committees in the 1830s met with no success.[119]

One historian has argued that the reason for not adopting the idea of central organisation was expense.[120] Hints in the 1839 Committee Report suggest that the real issue hinged on the now familiar disputes between the gentry and the central government about the control of executive power. In making its recommendation for a general superintendent of police to overcome the problems of organisation, the Committee commented that the cost to 'theoretical' liberty of this suggestion was compensated by practical liberty of security of person and property.[121] This is a familiar argument from eighteenth-century debates about paid police and magistracy. It is the counter argument to the assertion by the honoraries that liberty is best protected by not creating salaried officials and quasi-military forces under the control of central government.[122] The arguments hark back to the canons of English governance discussed in chapter 3, notably, no standing armies, no paid police and decentralised local government via the gentry.

This is obviously the model held by honorary justices in New South Wales and hinted at discreetly in both the 1835 and the 1839 Reports.[123] The evidence of Windeyer about the need to observe proprieties in dealing with the justices of the peace on police arrangements in their districts, cited above, confirms this point.[124] Similarly, the rivalries among the rural police and between the various forces, suggests a desire to retain the power and prerogatives associated with control of police. Alexander Berry JP, for example, ordered his constable to maintain order around his estate and told him who to charge, and who not to charge. Another justice, Murray, had his constable, the flogger and the lockup all located on his property.[125] James Wright and his fellow landowning magistrates at Queanbeyan sought to re-assert their power over local policing when the police magistrate would not fall in with them. The editor of the *Monitor*, Hall, makes the same point when he complains about partiality by the constables in relation to the enforcement of the impoundment laws.[126] The discretion exercised by the magistrates over what would and would not be policed committed great power to their hands in the localities. At the central level too – as Governors Macquarie, Brisbane and Bourke had found on a range of issues – the magistrates of the colony could prove formidable opponents when roused.[127] Attempting to take away their control of police would have provoked violent opposition. There was already suspicion that police magistrates were government spies and, as Lorraine Barlow's current work on the magistracy suggests, animosity about who would take precedence in the rural areas.[128]

But the power of the magistracy was curbed by the creation of police forces outside their control, the Mounted Police and the Border Police. The colonial gentry failed to extend their power to the periphery and their place was taken by forces responsible to central government.[129] Within the settled rural districts, the agricultural commitments of the 'respectable class' meant that they were unable to devote the large amount of time that would have been necessary to sit in court and organise police work. This led to the creation of paid magistrates, whose loyalties were split between the government that paid them and the local influence of the honoraries. Although the magistrates and their constables could act in quite arbitrary ways, their autonomy was whittled back during the 1830s by the use of police magistrates, the passage of Bourke's *Summary Jurisdiction Act*, the publication of Plunkett's manual for justices of the peace and by the exercise of the jurisdiction of the Supreme Court over the magistrates. The rule of law became a more practical constraint on what the justices might do with their constables and made them more accountable to the centre.

From the perspective of those likely to be policed, the long arm of the law reached deep into the settled districts. Legal constraints on police and magistrates improved during the 1830s, but still left a good deal of scope for intervention. New South Wales was a heavily policed society, even if we only look at the official police and disregard overseers, masters, private informants and the military, and allow for geographic dispersion at the periphery. This irked the elite as well as non-elite members of society. Hannibal Macarthur's letter to his brother-in-law in England about the galling character of the Parramatta police, quoted at the beginning of the chapter, expresses the point with feeling. He goes on to hope that 'the respectable and free inhabitants' may be rescued from 'this infamous intrusion of that liberty and freedom of action which is the Birthright of British subjects however distant their fortunes may remove them from the Palladium of British Justice'.[130] The *Bushranging Act* – an Act which, according to Chief Justice Forbes, could only be reconciled with the traditions of English liberty by reference to the fact that New South Wales was a penal colony – continued that 'infamous intrusion' long after Hannibal Macarthur's words had been penned. If the rule of law preserved the balance of power between citizens and the State in England, that balance was struck in a quite different place in the penal colony.

From the outset, central government, consistent with English patterns, had no strong direct control of policing. Control over the execution of the law was mediated through the honorary magistracy and the military, both of which proved to be less than malleable, and the paid police magistrates. Perhaps consensus prevailed between government and elite on this power arrangement. It was familiar enough, being based on the English model. Although stronger central control might have been more consistent with the penal nature of the colony, professional jailers would have been very expensive. Anyway, no sharp divergence on the objectives of policing between government and elite emerged to test the issue of control of police power. The changes in policing that did occur evidenced a government and an elite which felt quite sure of their control and agreed upon objectives. (Or at least their objectives converged: in the case of the Border Police: Governor Gipps wanted to protect the Aborigines and the landowners wanted to control their workforce.)

History from the viewpoint of the ruled presents a picture of control. This evidence is fragmentary and, in some cases, has to be discounted for exaggeration, self-interest and so on; of course, official accounts must also be scrutinised with a similarly critical eye. The use of police in connection with labour and movement is particularly salient, especially for the rural areas. Control of the police by magistrates, who were also employers of rural labour, put the power of the law in the hands of the justices, enhancing their power at both a symbolic and practical level.

At the frontier, control by central government or elites was weak. Nor was there much commitment to the extension of the rule of law at the edge of the frontier. Concern for Aborigines by government did not extend to expenditure for their protection. Nevertheless, as far as whites on the frontier were concerned at least, Harris's account suggests a police presence and quite a long reach in some circumstances.

Such was the confidence of the authorities in Sydney, that they were prepared to countenance reductions during the 1830s in what was admittedly a high police to population ratio. The eighteenth-century approach, as has been argued, relied far more on spectacular capital punishment than certainty of apprehension to deter those who might stray into a life of crime. New South Wales had more of both. The ratios of corporal punishment and surveillance (by police, the military, overseers and informers) were both much higher than for England, consistent with the need to establish a new order in a penal colony. By 1840, policing in New South Wales meant that the rule of law had considerable practical reality both for those who exercised power and those who were subject to it.

A page of the Emancipist petition for trial by jury of 1819 ('To HRH the Prince Regent in Council, The Humble Petition of the gentlemen, clergy, settlers, Merchants, Landholders and other free Inhabitants of His Majesty's Territory of New South Wales...'). From the *Forbes Papers*, Mitchell Library, State Library of New South Wales.

CHAPTER 7

The Campaign for Trial by Jury

The trial by jury, or the country, per patriam, is also that trial by the peers of every Englishman, which, as the grand bulwark of his liberties, is secured to him by the great charter, 'nullus liber homo capiatur, vel imprisonetur, aut exulet, aut aliquo alio modo destruatur, nisi per legale judicium parium suorum, vel per legem terrae.'

. . ., so long as this palladium remains sacred and inviolate, not only from all open attacks, (which none will be so hardy as to make) but also from all secret machinations, which may sap and undermine it, by introducing new and arbitrary methods of trial, by justices of the peace, commissioners of the revenue, and courts of conscience.

Blackstone[1]

. . .THAT the Criminal Court appears to your Petitioners to be rather a Court Martial than a Court of Law. . .this Court is not at all calculated to administer and distribute impartial Justice to the numerous free and respectable Population of the Colony: that it cannot command that veneration, awe and respect, which ever ought to attend upon a Court of Justice, a Court in its formation and proceedings contrary to all our habits, feelings and opinions as Englishmen,. . .we do not consider our lives and our liberties can be so well secured, as those of British subjects should be, nor can the laws of our Country be administered with sufficient purity and impartiality . . . THAT your Petitioners most humbly beg leave to approach Your Royal Highness, and ardently and most humbly pray, That Your Royal Highness of your grace and clemency may be pleased to extend to us, His Majesty's Subjects in this Territory, that great and valued inheritance of our Ancestors, Trial by Jury, . . .

The Emancipist Petition of 1819[2]

By 1819 the practical wisdom of the ancient constitution in providing for trial by jury had been amply demonstrated in New South Wales, at least to the Emancipists. Their petition recites their cultural affinities but it also lists the defects of the colonial court system and rehearses complaints going back to the early days of the colony by Governors Hunter, Bligh and Macquarie, and Judge-Advocate Ellis Bent.[3] They could have added Governor King to their list.[4] Hunter, King and Bligh, and those settlers who petitioned Bligh for trial by jury in 1808, were reacting against manipulation of the Criminal Court by 'the Faction', namely John Macarthur and the officers of the Rum Corps. These early lessons about law and the legal system confirmed the age-old wisdom about trial by jury, expressed pungently by Blackstone and fresh in the mind of any politically aware English person in the late eighteenth century, through the trials of John Wilkes and his followers. Wilkes himself had his predecessors in the seventeenth century, people like the Leveller, John Lilburne, who appealed over the heads of the government and its judges to the jury as the source of English justice.[5]

As we have already seen, the rule of law configures political power in a particular way: it imposes an obligation on government to justify its actions to independent courts according to the 'artificial reason and judgement of the law.' It impedes arbitrary exercises of power and thus safeguards individual liberty.[6] The independence of courts is a critical part of this equation. And the English variant of the rule of law did not settle for just any sort of court. As Blackstone makes clear in the quotation – and the great constitutional cases of the seventeenth and eighteenth centuries had driven home the point – judges unchecked by juries also constituted a threat to English liberty. Judicial independence might have been guaranteed by the *Act of Settlement* in 1701, but eighteenth-century English people remembered the seventeenth and viewed judicial independence with a suitably critical eye. The jury checked the possibility that courts might be supine in the face of power; this was, as Brewer puts it, 'a constitutional cliché in the eighteenth century'.[7] The colonists of New South Wales had more reason to be concerned. Not only were the colonial judges dismissible by the British government, but the 'new and arbitrary methods of trial' in the colony – the panel of military officers and the assessors in the Civil Court – had demonstrated obvious partiality in cases involving the military.

But important as juries may have been in guaranteeing the independence of the courts, trial by jury took on an additional dimension in New South Wales. By 1819, wealthy emancipists controlled the commerce of the colony and they wanted the political power to go with it. The right to serve on juries symbolised citizenship and for the Emancipists that was the crucial issue. It explains why trial by jury stood at the head of the Emancipists' first-ever petition to the king, why they sent an agent to London to represent them on the question and why it continued to be a burning political issue for them over the next two decades.

The Exclusives, on the other hand, regarded themselves as the only class fit to exercise political power in the colony; the idea that emancipists might sit in judgment over those who had come free, much less that they might vote and stand for office, appalled them. Both factions in the colony recognised the political significance of the jury issue, even though their arguments were framed in terms of a debate over its judicial significance and practicality. The clearest proof of this may be found in James Macarthur's 1836 manifesto on behalf of the Exclusives. Abandoning the earlier opposition to jury trial, he argued that those with a convict record were unfit to take a place on such an important institution as the jury. In support of the argument, Macarthur quotes the following passage from de Tocqueville's, *Democracy in America:*

> ...political laws owe their chief support to the enforcement of the penal laws; if this support be wanting, the law sooner or later loses its force. He who is invested with decision of political matters, is in truth the master of society. But the institution of the jury places the people, or at least a Class of the people, in the judgment seat. This institution in fact, therefore, places the direction of society in the hands of the people, or of the class from which the juries are taken.[8]

Allowing for some hyperbole, Macarthur and de Tocqueville were right to identify the political significance of trial by jury. The undemocratic state of New South Wales, together with the vexed question of the emancipists' civic status, heightened the political significance of the jury issue in the penal colony. Property qualifications – applicable to both jury service and the right to vote – could be relied on as a measure of civic virtue in England. That was not true in New South Wales – at least according to the Exclusives – because many emancipists easily satisfied the property qualification. The Exclusives would have to rely on the convict taint as a mark of disqualification. The jury issue became a crucial test of status, especially as the prospect of a colonial legislature came closer. The Emancipist leader, William Wentworth, did not need de Tocqueville to tell him this. His book, published in 1819, identified the issue for New

South Wales: competence to serve on juries meant competence to vote for and to be a member of the representative political institutions which would eventually be granted to the colony.[9]

Significantly, Macarthur's selections omit any reference to de Tocqueville's points about jury service as a form of political education. De Tocqueville thought that jury service had morally uplifting and educative effects on those who participate in civil cases and that 'the jury is both the most effective way of establishing the people's rule and the most efficient way of teaching them how to rule'.[10] Of course, Macarthur did not want to suggest that emancipists could be educated to power. The Exclusives were no democrats and sought to protect their influence and political authority in the colony from the onset of popular institutions. They correctly saw the jury issue as the harbinger of liberal, egalitarian views which would undermine their eighteenth-century aristocratic pretensions and the privileges they enjoyed in the colony. The fear of an 'Emancipist ascendancy' fuelled their opposition, as James Macarthur later admitted.[11] For a long time they were able to persuade an uninterested English administration, whose own experience convinced it of the nuisance value of juries, to withhold jury trial from the 'turbulent' penal colony.[12] This enabled the Exclusives to continue to dominate colonial policy through their contacts in England and their monopoly on the nominated Legislative Councils introduced in the colony in the 1820s.

But the growth of liberal, egalitarian ideas – most clearly evidenced by the French and American revolutions, the abolition of slavery and also by the introduction of de Tocqueville's ideas about American democracy – also had implications for the Emancipist side of politics. Once the convict barrier to enfranchisement had been overturned, the logic sustaining the property qualification became the next target. After the abolition of transportation, wealth became the new line of political cleavage in the colony, a line which would split the old, wealthy, Emancipist leadership – especially Wentworth – off from its erstwhile constituency. Trial by jury was granted to New South Wales in the middle and late 1830s, followed closely by representative institutions in 1842. While the Exclusives won the contest over the magistracy, their loss of the jury issue symbolised the failure of their grand plan to constitute themselves as a ruling oligarchy in New South Wales.[13]

Historians of early New South Wales have failed to see the significance of the jury issue.[14] They have either overlooked it altogether, or portrayed it in terms of its utility as a process of obtaining proper verdicts, or treated it as a relatively minor matter of civil liberties. The campaign for trial by jury was not primarily about the practicality, efficiency or fairness of the jury as a judicial institution, despite substance in the claims of partiality in some cases and the far-reaching implications of some of those cases. It was about political power. The campaign for trial by jury shows again how the complex of ideas and institutions associated with the rule of law enabled the Emancipists to draw on a rich heritage: the Magna Carta, the jury as the 'bulwark of British liberty', their rights as true-born Britons, and the celebrated cases in the seventeenth and eighteenth centuries in which juries had stood firm against oppression. The rule of law heritage allowed the political argument to proceed subliminally in legal form. This was a particularly useful strategy for the Emancipists. For former convicts to have made explicit political claims in a penal colony would have seemed very odd indeed.

The campaign for trial by jury falls into a number of phases. The manipulation of the legal system by Macarthur and his officer colleagues in the period up to the Rum Rebellion in 1808 confirmed those opposed to the rum monopolists in their English prejudices against the involvement of the military in civil affairs. It also demonstrated the political importance of control of the courts in the exercise of power in the colony. Governor Macquarie's arrival in 1808 marked a new phase. His emancipist policy – the full reinstatement to society of the growing and increasingly wealthy group of emancipated convicts – encouraged especially the more economically successful to aspire to political power.

We have already seen how the courts became a de facto parliament for the early conflicts between the governor and the rum monopolists and the subject of complaint from smallholders and others who found themselves opposed to the military entourage. The court's lack of expertise, as well as its military paraphernalia, struck the early inhabitants of the colony, experienced as they were in these matters, as odd mutations of the system they knew at first-hand. But apart from these concerns, English notions of the rule of law were sorely tried by the absence of trial by jury. It was not only that the colony's courts clashed with the jury tradition, but also that the independence of those courts – a key part of the guarantee offered by the jury system – was so obviously in question in the early colony.[15]

Some of the important departures from the traditional English model of separation of the courts and the executive have been detailed in chapter 4. But, over and above those oddities, the replacement of juries – the instrument which placed a body of citizens between the state and the accused – by the panel of officers, offended doubly. Not only were there no juries but their replacement was supplied by the military!

The military panels differed from juries in fundamental ways. Trial by jury – to be put on one's country – involved trial before twelve residents of the county in which the crime occurred. Although the laws and the assize judge who tried cases came from central government, the verdicts came from local people who were not in the employ of that central government. Juries were selected from the names of those in the county who satisfied the property qualification, a qualification which was usually less stringent than the qualification for the vote. The roll of those eligible to serve on juries was maintained by the sheriff of the county, but the selection of a jury took place in open court before the trial. Sheriffs who stacked the jury list could be challenged and the parties had the opportunity to remove jurors who might be partial. The jury's role was to determine the facts of the case, to apply the law explained by the judge to those facts, and come to a unanimous verdict.[16]

The selection of the military panels which sat with the Criminal Court in New South Wales knew no such niceties. Military officers rather than local residents tried the cases. Formally, the governor held the legal power to nominate the six officers to sit on the Criminal Court with the judge-advocate. In practice, when the governor convened the court, the commanding officer of the garrison supplied the names of the next six of his officers from a rotating duty roster which he drew up. The list was supplemented by naval officers if a ship was in port.[17] Unlike the traditional jury selection procedure in open court, this process took place away from public scrutiny. Aside from the limited pool of officers to choose from, the system was open to abuse whenever a case touched on the interests of the military. The process did not even have the appearance of fairness in such cases. The absence of any right to challenge either the basis on which the roster was drawn up or the particular officers who were to serve compounded the injustice of the arrangement.

The practical problems of this process became clear almost immediately. It seems that the marines shared civilian distaste for military involvement in civil affairs. Service on the Criminal Court became the subject of conflict between Governor Phillip and the officers who found the duty distasteful and demeaning. Phillip suggested that the name of the officer who did not want to serve be passed over on the roster – a solution which showed the flexibility of the roster system – but was informed that all the officers had the same objection. Phillip resolved the problem by drawing the officers' attention to the terms of the statute.[18]

There were other examples of the problems caused by the composition of the Criminal Court, especially if a member of the military was the defendant or one of their opponents was in the dock.[19] The court's legitimacy in local eyes had already been diminished by the manoeuvrers of the Rum Corps before Bligh's arrival in 1806. Indeed the first calls for trial by jury had come in Governor Hunter's time. Hunter saw the wisdom of providing the colony with the Criminal Court, as did his successor, King. King put the point with delicacy: '...it certainly will be more satisfactory to the inhabitants of the colony at large to see every advance toward the complete trial by jury'.[20] King's advice was echoed in addresses of welcome from the 'settlers' to his successor, Bligh. Nettled by John Macarthur's presumption in speaking for the whole colony in welcoming the new viceroy, they disowned Macarthur, coupling their economic grievances against the rum monopolists with earnest entreaties about the due administration of the law. Although the composition of the Criminal Court was not explicitly mentioned, three out of their seven requests to Bligh called for justice according to the established law. A year later, Bligh wrote that the 'superior people' wanted the military out of the courts which they regarded as partial. Bligh thought there were enough free people to serve on juries and thus to resolve the problem of partiality.[21]

The conflict over the military influence over the colony's courts became most acute in the period leading up to the Rum Rebellion. Understandably, Bligh's conflict with the Rum Corps led him to distrust a selection procedure which put their commanding officer, Johnston, in charge of selecting the officers who would determine criminal cases which were central to that conflict. Late in 1807, one of Bligh's allies, Gore, faced charges before the Criminal Court. Bligh correctly saw Gore as the subject of a vendetta by Johnston and believed that the Court would be stacked. To forestall this, Bligh exercised the power formally conferred on him by statute to select the panel to hear the case. Johnston protested to Bligh about the departure from the established practice and the usurpation of the prerogatives of the commanding officer. Bligh remained unmoved. Undoubtedly, Bligh had the statutory power to do what he had done, as had his predecessors and successors. But he was the only one to have done so. Having lost the skirmish in the colony, Johnston tried to turn the issue to advantage by complaining to his superiors in England about the governor stacking the panel.[22]

In some ways, Bligh's assertion of his power to select the members of the panel was quixotic since – except when naval officers were available – his choice was still limited to officers of the Rum Corps. Despite the governor's considerable formal and actual power over the courts, the contest for the power locked in the legal system was by no means uneven.

Bligh's forced departure after the Rum Rebellion provoked renewed calls for trial by jury to offset the influence of the military. Not surprisingly, one of these calls came from Bligh himself, but he also carried a petition back to England, signed by 833 free settlers, including the judge-advocate and several justices of the peace. The requests went to the heart of their complaints against the monopolists. They wanted freer trade and trial by jury.[23] Their assessment of the courts' partiality gave added point to the claims for trial by jury.[24] For his own part, Bligh thought the 'Benches of Magistrates and Courts of Justice are mockeries of what they represent. . . .'.[25]

The petition fell on deaf ears, as would the other criticisms, for many years to come. But critics of the military panel system did not confine themselves to the method of selection. The fact that there was no challenge to a member of the panel, that they were judges of both the facts and the law – even when the judge-advocate had legal training – that they were the military subordinates of the governor, and that their verdict need not be unanimous, all represented substantial departures from English jury practice. These departures provoked criticism, both before and after Bligh's time.[26] But the experience of the manipulation of the Criminal Court in the period leading up to the Rum Rebellion confirmed the importance of trial by jury in the minds of many of the colonists.

The English government, convinced about the need for a legally qualified judge-advocate, sent Ellis Bent to fill the post and required him to report on the desirability of introducing trial by jury. By that stage political lessons about the significance of the legal system in the colony had been well learned. In the absence of any other political forum, the autocratic power of the governor might be contested and party interest furthered by astute manipulation of the courts. Only when this strategy was on the brink of failure and Macarthur likely to be convicted, did Macarthur and his colleagues resort to force and depose Bligh. But the Rum Rebels appreciated the tenuousness of their position and returned to the courts so that Macarthur could be tried and acquitted. It was a rather hollow attempt to use the court forum to denigrate Bligh, justify their own position and cloak their rebellion with whatever legitimacy the legal system could lend to it. However, one of the important legitimating features of British justice – the jury – was absent in New South Wales. And Macarthur and his colleagues had sullied its replacement.

Judge-Advocate Bent's report on the state of the colony's legal system in 1810 recommended the introduction of trial by jury and that free settlers and emancipists of some years' standing be allowed to serve on them.[27] A Select Committee of the House of Commons reported to the same effect in 1812, after hearing evidence in favour of trial by jury from several prominent colonists, as well as from Hunter and Bligh.[28] Governor Macquarie, consistent with his pro-emancipist policy, strongly supported the requests. However, Earl Bathurst, His Majesty's Secretary of State for the colonies viewed trial by jury as unsuitable for convicts. And, since he thought that jury trial could not be extended to the free settlers without extending it to the convicts as well, he decided not to allow it at all. The Emancipists were to receive this response repeatedly in the ensuing years. The other stock response adverted to a lack of sufficient people competent to serve on juries, a claim denied as early as 1808 by Bligh and again in 1810, 1812 and 1821. This of course begged the question as to the measure of competency. Nevertheless, the new Charter of Justice issued in 1814 did not include provision for trial by jury,[29] and the English government told the colonists that the state of the colony was such that the display of military uniforms on the bench of the Criminal Court was still a necessary precaution.[30] There would be no juries for the Supreme (civil) Court either; the new judge, Jeffery Bent, would continue the procedure of sitting with assessors rather than a jury.

Until 1814, the opposition to trial by jury had come mainly from the English government. Factionalism in the colony and the memory of the Rum Rebellion worried Bathurst, the Colonial Secretary, hence his opinion about the need for a show of military force on the colony's Criminal Court. But, Macquarie's pro-emancipist policy was provoking opposition and that opposition began to find voice in the courts. As we have seen, the new judge of the Supreme Court, Jeffery Bent, was aligned with the Exclusives and one of his first official acts was to deny emancipist lawyers admission to practise. Macquarie's pro-emancipist policy may not have given the growing and increasingly wealthy body of former convicts much cause for concern about their legal status. Emancipists had brought legal actions, appeared as counsel before the courts, and even been appointed to the magistracy.[31] Bent's ruling signalled a strong challenge to the policy.

Worse was to come. In 1820, hard on the heels of the Emancipist petition for trial by jury, Jeffery Bent's successor on the Supreme Court, also on the Exclusive side, augmented the theme by denying emancipist lawyer, Edward Eagar, standing to sue. The threat posed to emancipists by this ruling cut the ground from under Emancipist calls for trial by jury, and radically questioned their status. It also threatened their dominance of the colony's commerce: how would they enforce their contracts and recover their debts if they could be denied access to the courts? The advent of professional judges had struck severe blows to the Emancipist cause. And all this at a time when Commissioner Bigge's presence in the colony presaged significant change. The Emancipists needed an issue and an advocate to retrieve their position.

In 1819 William Charles Wentworth was reading for the Bar in London.[32] Then 27, Wentworth had been born in the colony and identified as an Australian. His mother was a convict and his father, D'Arcy, 'volunteered' for transportation during his second trial for highway robbery. He was in fact acquitted but perhaps his aristocratic family connections, who had secured him a post on the second fleet to Botany Bay, suggested that he really should go. D'Arcy succeeded handsomely in the colony, was favoured by Governor Macquarie and, as we have seen, became the Superintendent of Police for Sydney. Young William, 'the Native Son', had already staked his claims for leadership before leaving for England. He had demonstrated his bushmanship as a member of the first party of Europeans to cross the Blue Mountains and tried his skills with his wits and his pen in skirmishes with the Exclusives during Macquarie's battles over emancipist magistrates and lawyers.

The Bar was a great school for the inheritors of the seventeenth-century Whig constitution. It educated Wentworth in the 'artificial reason and judgment of the law', it taught him the glories of struggles between judges and kings, it married the rule of law tradition to Wentworth's obvious potential for political leadership in the colony. The Magna Carta, Coke, Hale, the Glorious Revolution, the independence of the judiciary, Blackstone and great struggles to protect that 'palladium of British liberty' – trial by jury – formed the basic currency of the apprentice barrister's professional culture. Even during his stay in England, Wentworth remained in contact with

Emancipist politics. He was in England when Edward Eagar and the emancipist doctor (and disappointed magisterial candidate), William Redfern, arrived with the Emancipist petition concerning the legal status of emancipists. Wentworth assisted them in lobbying for the Emancipist cause. Together with his barrister friend, Robert Wardell, he returned to New South Wales in 1824. If Henry and Susannah Kable's law suit marked the first crucial moment in shaping the exercise of power in New South Wales along legal lines, William Wentworth's return to the colony as a barrister and founder of the *Australian* newspaper marked the second. He was a culture bearer for rule of law ideas. His ability to cast political issues into a legal mould so that he and Wardell could use the courts as a forum – and a sympathetic forum at that, with another rule of law adherent in Chief Justice Forbes presiding – repeatedly left political opponents, like Governor Darling, spluttering with frustration.[33] The campaign for trial by jury was the clearest demonstration of this strategy and Wentworth made it the *cause célèbre* in the Emancipist platform.

Wentworth published his book on New South Wales in 1819. The book not only became a standard reference on New South Wales in England but also a political manifesto for the Emancipist cause. It called for trial by jury and, more radically, for representative institutions. The conjunction of these issues was no accident. Eligibility for jury service carried a property qualification and was a mark of respectability in England and had been bracketed with the claim for representative institutions by the American revolutionaries. According to his biographer, Wentworth had an additional motive for linking the two, since the popularity of the jury issue among the emancipists was sure to establish Wentworth as their leader for the time when representative institutions were granted to the colony. Although his fellow Emancipists were prepared to confine themselves to the jury issue for the time being, Wentworth's concern with representative institutions reveals the larger political purposes behind the campaign for trial by jury.[34]

The year 1819 marked the beginning of a concerted campaign for civil and political rights for emancipists centred on the jury issue. Early in 1819 Macquarie granted permission for a public meeting of 'landholders, merchants and other respectable members of the community'.[35] They proposed to discuss a number of resolutions relating to trade and agriculture. Buried among issues like the distillation of spirits and the duties on oils, skins, wool and timber, in resolution four, was a call for trial by jury. The meeting resolved to draft a petition. In the drafted document trial by jury took pride of place at the head of the petition, accompanied by supporting argument. In the course of a month the petition gathered 1,260 signatures including, according to Macquarie, 'All the Men of Wealth, Rank or Intelligence throughout the Colony'.[36] Emancipists figured prominently on the list, including the lawyers Edward Eagar, a prime mover on the jury issue,[37] and George Crossley. Macquarie endorsed all the claims of the petition and took the opportunity to reiterate the recommendations he had made on trial by jury in 1811. The petitioners also took the opportunity of drawing his Royal Highness' attention to the fact that, 'Hindoo in India, the Hottentot in Africa and the Negro Slave in the West Indies' enjoyed the privilege of trial by jury whereas they, who were Englishmen, were suffered to remain as the sole exception.[38] They went on to make a series of criticisms about the Criminal Court: the occurrence of cases in which the judge was personally interested; the fact that the judge-advocate was prosecutor, committing magistrate, grand jury, judge and petit juror; the absence of a right to challenge the members of the court, or to appeal; and the military character of the court. They complained – as the quotation opening this chapter records – that a court composed in this way could not administer the laws impartially nor command the respect of the population.

But the claims to status in the petition were dealt a severe blow in 1820 when Eagar became involved in a contretemps with Mr Justice Field in the Supreme Court. His suits were refused on the basis of a plea of convict attaint in two cases; in one of these cases Mr Justice Field was the defendant. His Honour was pleased, no doubt, to cite the authority of an English case, *Bullock v Dodds*: that in England pardons were not effective until issued under the Great Seal. Due to an oversight in England, governor's pardons issued in New South Wales purporting to restore the recipient to the full rights of a British subject, had not conformed to the correct procedure. Commissioner Bigge, himself a former Chief Justice in the West Indies and no supporter of the Emancipists, considered Field's decision to be contrary to the intention of the Act specifically empowering the governor to grant pardons, and unjustifiable in the state of the colony.[39] Certainly the custom in the colony had always been to accord emancipists the right to sue. Instructions to the governors to grant them property in fee and the provisions in the Act empowering the governor to grant pardons, effective while the person remained in the colony, exhibited an intent to restore the civil capacities of emancipists.[40] Moreover, their economic and numerical dominance in the colony constituted good grounds to distinguish the English case. Mr Justice Field was disposed to decide otherwise.

Macquarie's policy had induced a degree of complacency amongst the Emancipists. Despite setbacks like Bent's refusal to admit the emancipist lawyers, many of them had become quite wealthy by 1819 and had considerable business interests and property. Some had risen to positions of status such as the magistracy. Field's decision struck at them all. It meant that their rights to hold property, make and enforce contracts and to give evidence in court could be nullified. Their status and positions in the colony were set at naught. The jury issue, which the petitioners saw as the next advance in formally acknowledging their position in the colony, was pushed into the background by the radical challenge to their legal status.

The Emancipists convened another public meeting to send a new petition to England reciting the devastating effects of the rulings, praying for confirmation of their legal status, and indirectly querying the impartiality of the courts:

> ...your Petitioners, retrospectively and prospectively, are to be considered as Convicts attaint, without personal liberty, without property, without Character or Credit, without any one Right or Priviledge belonging to free Subjects; And are now, after thirty Years of good Conduct and Industry, whereby they have attained to Wealth, Character and Rank in Society, to be thrown back at once and for ever to that state of degradation from which they have by worthy Conduct, they hope, not undeservedly arisen.[41]

The petition bore the signatures of 1,367 Emancipists and was carried to England, with Governor Macquarie's endorsement by two of their number, Eagar and Redfern.[42]

The issue of the legal status of emancipists was quickly resolved but it once again underlined the importance of the courts and the legal system in the politics of the colony. And there was another setback in the wind. Even as the ship carrying Eagar and Redfern set sail, Macquarie received a rebuke from England for his appointment of Redfern to the magistracy.[43] Events like these heightened the need to confirm the full civil and political competence of emancipists and the jury issue was the vehicle for that confirmation.

Bigge devoted the second volume of his report to the state of the legal system in the colony, finding against the Emancipists on the jury question.[44] While going to some lengths to avoid being linked in the colony with the Exclusives, he found association with the Emancipists distasteful.[45] Bigge did recommend removal of the legal disabilities under which emancipists suffered, although he thought they constituted a useful control on the 'contentious and litigious spirit' in the Emancipists.[46] But the colony was not yet sufficiently mature for trial by jury, according to the Commissioner. In this he found a supporter in John Macarthur who thought trial by jury would 'seal the destruction of every respectable person' in the colony.[47]

Bigge's reasons for advising against trial by jury were essentially the same as those relied on in 1812 by the Secretary of State, Bathurst: insufficient numbers of competent jurymen, factionalism in the colony and the unfairness of extending the privilege to one section of the community and not the other. Conceding the general support in the colony for trial by jury, Bigge attacked the 1819 petition claiming several of the signatories had not meant to endorse the immediate introduction of trial by jury, or did not understand it to mean that emancipists would serve on juries.[48] It is difficult to believe that anyone familiar with the politics of the colony who had read the petition before signing it could possibly have made such mitakes. Trial by jury figures at the head of the petition, an emancipist was secretary to the committee which drew it up, and it referred to requests going back to 1800 for trial by jury. The reference to these few dissenters seems a quibble, given Bigge's avowal of the general support for the measure.

Bigge then turned to the insufficient numbers of competent jurymen. He commissioned the magistrates to survey their districts to see how many people met the freehold property qualification and, in the case of emancipists, the magistrates' estimate of their character. (This repeated work done by the magistrates for the 1819 petition.) He found 329 settlers or free-born people and 587 emancipists with freeholds, a total of 916. Bigge, however, was only prepared to allow that 100 of the emancipists would be acceptable as jurors, making a total of 409.[49] He makes no reference to remarks on the character of these people, which he had solicited from the magistrates, preferring to rely on other sources as well as his own observations. Eagar claims that many of the magistrates had signed the 1819 petition and promoted the objects of the meeting.[50] Bigge's reluctance to mention their responses on this important point is odd and his own figure ungenerous.[51] The conclusion, even on his figures, that this was an insufficient number is not supported by figures on how many juries or jurors would be required. He regarded the proposition as self-evident. Nor was he prepared to canvass possible compromises such as offering litigants an option of trial by jury, a mixture of officers and civilians, different property qualification or six man juries. The suggestion that the jury question be postponed until factionalism in the colony had died down was hardly meritorious when this constituted one of the principal causes of the factionalism. In any case it ignores the general support from all areas of the colony, with a few significant exceptions in the Exclusive ranks, evidenced by the 1819 petition and the Commissioner's own observations.

The explanation for the Commissioner's recommendation on the jury question lies in his opposition to emancipists occupying positions of prestige and influence in the legal system, such as the magistracy, and hence, in the political life of the colony. Due to their numerical majority, emancipists would have played a dominant role on juries. The Commissioner, while prepared to grant them access to the courts as litigants, certainly did not countenance conferring the politically more significant power of the jury on emancipists. The result favoured the *status quo* in which Exclusive interests predominated. This precluded any awkward precedents as to the civic competence of emancipists.

Despite Eagar's best efforts in London, the new legislation of 1823 for the colony of New South Wales did not allow trial by jury.[52] The problem of the governor's lack of legislative capacity was cured by the provision of a nominated Legislative Council of seven, the first departure from the autocratic authority of the governors. Aside from this, the Act concentrated almost exclusively on the legal system in the colony. As outlined in chapter 4, it abolished the old courts and replaced them with a single Supreme Court and a Chief Justice. The Chief Justice presided in both the civil and criminal jurisdictions, but the system of military officers sitting with the judge in criminal cases persisted. In civil cases, if both parties agreed, a jury could be empanelled.[53]

But the real spark for the jury issue came from the provision for courts of quarter sessions, courts of intermediate jurisdiction between the magistrates courts and the Supreme Court. Unlike the sections in the Act relating to the Supreme Court, there were no provisions about the mode of trial in quarter sessions.[54] It did specify that convicts under sentence should be tried summarily for non-capital offences, leaving it open to inference that trials for those who were not prisoners should be conducted with juries, as they were in England. Acting on his attorney-general's advice, the new governor issued a proclamation convening quarter sessions once a month in Sydney. The magistrates delayed, apparently concerned about the wisdom of the attorney-general's opinion and the legality of jury trial. The *Australian* was unkind enough to suggest they were dragging their feet:

> We are happy to find that Mr. Campbell [a magistrate] is friendly to juries; but he must pardon us for persisting in our belief that the majority of his order are not, or at least were not, a month since, of his way of thinking.[55]

The attorney-general sought an order in the Supreme Court compelling the magistrates to convene the quarter sessions and the new Chief Justice, Francis Forbes – relying on perfectly sound principles of statutory interpretation – granted the order. The *Australian* hailed the decision, which coincided with its first edition, as a triumph for the Emancipists over the wishes of the Exclusives and their 'tool', Commissioner Bigge. It denounced attempts to preserve class distinction in the colony through the ruse of insufficient jurymen.[56] The triumph was dampened by the resourceful magistrates who, now accepting the attorney-general's advice on the ineligibility of emancipists for jury service, published a list of jurors excluding all emancipists.

Wentworth and Wardell – using their newspaper the *Australian* to amplify their courtroom exploits – attacked the partiality of the magistrates.[57] Campbell, one of the magistrates who had supported trial by jury, denied the charges but, as we have noticed, the *Australian* would not exonerate the majority of his brother magistrates from bias.[58] Given the dominance of Exclusives in the magistracy, there can be little doubt that they were continuing the traditions of 'Botany Bay jurisprudence'.[59]

No doubt the advent of Wentworth and Wardell to argue the cause of the Emancipists both in court and in the press influenced the development of the issue. Hostile reactions appeared in the press, both editorially and in letters to the editor. The *Sydney Gazette* seized on the wording of the Governor's pardon which purported to restore the recipient to 'all the rights of a free subject',[60] and declared those opposed to emancipists serving on juries to be 'enemies to public liberty and British freedom..., enfranchising a quarter of the population and degrading the remaining three quarters'.[61] One letter labelled opposition to the Emancipists as 'illaudible in all its bearings, clogged with manifest partiality and unfairness, and injurious to the common interests of every branch of the community', while another suggested that the Emancipists might respond by boycotting free settlers and foreclosing on the mortgages they held.[62]

Repeated attempts to litigate the issue in 1825 and 1826 failed and, as the 1827 date for the expiry of the *New South Wales Act* approached, a legislative strategy became more important. The Emancipists had been buoyed by the fact that the limited experiment with trial by jury had been so successful; even magistrates who had opposed it wrote to the newspapers announcing their satisfaction with the operation of trial by jury.[63] Governor Brisbane[64] and Chief Justice Forbes agreed with their assessment. In justification of his interpretation of section 19 of the *New South Wales Act* 1823, Forbes assayed some legal positivism:

> . . .I had always been of the opinion that the clause admitted of an experiment upon the trial by jury – and I remember the effect of this clause being the subject of a conversation between Mr. James Stephen and myself at Downing Street. . .In giving effect to the new act, the constitution and power of the Court of Sessions [staffed by a bench of magistrates], became a point of great importance – feeling that I might be called upon to give a judicial opinion upon the act, I retired altogether from the question and left it with the Attorney-General, under whom it had originated. . . .I was fully aware that the only substantial difficulty in the way, was the prejudice of a few leading persons of the free population – As to the want of members, or the apprehension of an undue bias, I soon found they were chimeras, which would vanish before the light of a Court of Justice...My judgment satisfied all the parties. The Sheriff's dissenting opinion goes to the policy not the law – but as my province was limited to the law, and entirely liberated from any consideration of policy, I do not feel that even his opinion is at variance with mine. . . .the experiment of juries has entirely succeeded.[65]

Unfortunately for the Emancipists, the Colonial Office took a dim view of the jury trial experiment and considered it contrary to the intent of the 1823 Act.[66] They had decided in the forthcoming legislation to put an end to the experiment.[67] Meanwhile, John Macarthur junior had been cultivating the acquaintance of the Under-Secretary at the Colonial Office, Robert Wilmot-Horton, dining with him and supplying him with information about New South Wales. He wrote to his mother, '...as we are in high favour here, I doubt not that we shall obtain whatever we shall ask for'.[68]

When the draft of the *New South Wales Bill* arrived in the colony, the Emancipists realised that they had once again been outmanoeuvred on the jury question. The Colonial Office was proposing that the issue be determined in the colony by the governor and Council. Because of Exclusive dominance of the nominated Council, that meant further delay on the jury question. The delay would give the Exclusives time to consolidate their position in the colony and deflect the Emancipists from campaigning on the issue of representative institutions.

Eagar in London had realised in 1826 that trial by jury was by no means a foregone conclusion. Although the Emancipists proposed both trial by jury and elective institutions, the fear of losing the jury issue and the unlikelihood of securing representative institutions forced them to concentrate on trial by jury. Eagar produced a pamphlet attacking the 1827 Bill and in 1828 presented another petition from a public meeting in the colony calling for trial by jury. Despite this petition, and the evidence of all those who had gone before, the Colonial Office announced that on balance the local authorities favoured the existing system. Accepting the Exclusives' arguments, factionalism was given as the reason for continuing to withhold trial by jury; every case would be an opportunity for revenge. Presenting the Bill to Parliament, Huskisson dismissed attempts to introduce an amendment to allow trial by jury. Despite the evidence, he said that the experiment in quarter sessions had proved unsuitable.[69] Only unsuitable to some – the Emancipists had been outmanoeuvred.

Three changes to the system of trial by jury did eventuate in the 1828 legislation.[70] First, the Act abolished jury trial in quarter sessions until it was established in the Supreme Court. Second, a Supreme Court judge could in his discretion grant trial by jury in *civil* cases on the application of either party. And most importantly, third, the legislation allowed the King in Council (i.e. the King plus ministers) to grant the governor and his Council the power to introduce trial by jury. In civil cases where juries were summoned, the magistrates again took a narrow construction of a local ordinance which allowed those attainted of felony to serve on juries only if they had received a pardon. In 1829 the magistrates refused to include emancipists on jury lists. This was cured by legislative amendment.[71]

Governor Bourke arrived in the colony in December 1831 with instructions to expedite the extension of trial by jury. The Order of the King in Council – allowing the Legislative Council in New South Wales to extend trial by jury – had been issued. But Bourke found his Council opposed to any further extension of the jury system and decided to proceed circumspectly. He first proposed to extend trial by jury to any case in which an officer of government or a military officer was involved. This removed the possibility of blatant bias where the governor might select the panel in a case where he had a personal stake in the outcome[72]

In the following year, 1833, using his casting vote to secure passage of the Bill, Bourke put through the Act which finally extended jury trial to all criminal cases (although the defendant could request military panels), against the wishes of those who wanted 'to keep the Emancipists in a state of disfranchisement'. The Act was to last for two years. At last the battle had been won; at least temporarily.[73] The expectation of major legislation in the colony kept the issue alive. The leading proponent of the Exclusives' case, John Macarthur's son, James, published a book stating his views.[74] He attacked trial by jury and listed a number of cases of alleged abuse,[75] relying heavily on the evidence of Mr Justice Burton, one of the three judges of the Supreme Court:

> That portion of the emancipated convicts, who have become possessed of wealth by dishonest means, comprising the great majority of the persons belonging to that class who sit upon juries and now lay claim to political power, are strongly actuated by the desire to degrade others to the same level which they themselves have fallen; – a feeling men are but too prone to indulge under such circumstances.
>
> ...it has been seen that the convicts 'consider the colony theirs by right, and the free settlers as interlopers on the soil:' . . . If the emigration of industrious and respectable families of the labouring and middle classes is to be encouraged, . . . it surely becomes the bounden duty of government, and of the legislature, to pause and weigh well what would be the probable operation, as regards these emigrants, of such a feeling on the part of the emancipated convicts, armed with political privileges. On the other hand, it may be safely asserted, that no mischievous effects would be likely to arise to the emancipated convicts, by their exclusion generally from the judgment seat and from political power.[76]

Significantly he did not cite the opinions of the other judge or those of the Attorney-General or the Solicitor-General, all of whom favoured jury trial. The opinion of the old enemy of the Exclusives, Chief Justice Forbes, in favour of trial by jury, drew a scathing attack. Even the Exclusives now advocated trial by jury, save they would have excluded emancipists, or as many emancipists as possible. Under strong questioning on successive occasions from the Molesworth Committee, James Macarthur modified his view from excluding emancipists as a class – other than those few who held the king's pardon – from jury service, to allowing those who could demonstrate rehabilitation to serve, to excluding those who could be shown to be of bad character.[77] The issue had, however, been lost.

Macarthur's linkage of the jury and political power in the passage quoted gives the clue to the significance of the jury issue. Interestingly, when jury trial was optional, defendants continued to choose the military panel in 38 per cent of cases before the Supreme Court and in 68 per cent of quarter sessions cases.[78] The day-to-day operation of juries, politically important though it was in some cases, was not as important as the mark of political status conferred by enrolment on the jury lists. Macarthur quotes these figures to undermine the Emancipist case, but his own arguments show that the practical operation of juries, was not the real issue. Bourke's legislation was confirmed in 1839 when the option of the military panel was abolished. But the more fundamental issue had been lost.[79] By 1839 the decision to end transportation had been taken and the representative institutions were a short couple of years away. Electors qualified for those institutions by satisfying the property qualification. The convict taint would not operate to disqualify emancipists from the political franchise.[80]

In the early colony, the legal system's significance as the only check on the authority of the autocratic governors made the courts a crucial political forum. Seizure of that forum, particularly the Criminal Court, by the New South Wales Corps showed the potential of the courts for opposing the governor's authority and for safeguarding the interests of those who controlled them. Out of this situation the first calls for trial by jury were raised.

As Exclusive and Emancipist factions emerged, variations were played on the original theme. The Exclusives looked beyond the colonial courts to London, to secure their interests. However, through the magistracy especially, they could exercise the authority conferred on them by the State in the day-to-day life of the colony. It was a situation they sought to preserve, for example, by excluding the emancipists appointed by Macquarie from the magistracy. A lessening of the courts' intrusiveness and a sympathetic governor in Macquarie lessened Emancipist emphasis on trial by jury for the decade from 1810.

From 1819, however, the campaign for trial by jury assumed major significance. By that time a significant and growing number of wealthy emancipists perceived New South Wales as a free settlement rather than a penal colony and moreover, one that belonged to them by dint of their labour and enterprise. Their legal and political status had seemed fairly assured but was rocked by the court decisions against Eagar. Trial by jury became a proving ground of that status. As the 1820s progressed and political power was devolved, the dominance of Exclusives on the nominated Councils granted by the 1823 Act meant that it became even more important for the Emancipists to settle the question of their status to serve on juries. From that basis they could push claims for representative institutions and their share of political authority in the colony. In addition to de Tocqueville's propositions about the direct political power exercised by juries in day-to-day deliberations,[81] in New South Wales the jury issue provided the arena of conflict for rival theories of citizenship. The jury issue, with its powerful rhetoric about the Magna Carta and the rights of British subjects, translated from an issue of direct power via the jury box into a symbolic one which did serve to qualify the Emancipists for their share of political authority in the colony.

William Charles Wentworth. From a portrait by James Anderson, 1872. Mitchell Library, State Library of New South Wales.

CHAPTER 8

Conclusion

In 1840, Henry Kable was still alive aged 77; he died in 1846. Susannah had died in 1825. Young Henry was in his mid-50s. Susannah and Henry had 11 children. Some of them had married and had children of their own. Those of Henry and Susannah's progeny who owned a house worth more than 200 pounds and were male, were eligible to sit on juries and vote for the first representative assemblies.[1] New South Wales had changed dramatically since their parents had waded ashore 52 years earlier. But the fact that their parents had come to New South Wales as convicts would not bar them from participating fully in the newly-granted, free institutions of the colony. Henry himself could have served as a juror, voted or even stood for the new Legislative Council. They all probably felt some of the social stigma of their convict origins. But their whole story could have stopped at the end of a rope in Norwich Castle Jail, or at the side of the hulk, when the baby was turned back, or at Lord Sydney's door – if some of their cleanskin fellow citizens looked down their noses occasionally, the Kables could afford to look back with satisfaction at the great changes they had seen.

The Kables had played their part in those changes. Henry and Susannah's children, and their children, added to the number of free-born people in the colony. Henry's shipping partnership with fellow-convicts Lord and Underwood made an important contribution to the growth of the colony's economy. But Henry and Susannah's greatest impact on the colony flowed from their suit against Captain

Sinclair. Because from that moment on, the day-to-day structure of power between convict and ship's captain, convict and convict, convict and master, convict and Exclusive, convict and governor had new possibilities.

The rule of law tradition gained a foothold with the Kables' case. But it was just that . . . a foothold. The case meant that exercise of power in the penal colony would be open to scrutiny against a legal standard, not the standards of prison discipline or martial law, or the arbitrary standard of the governor. This did not mean that power would always be exercised lawfully; power was used brutally and illegally by convicts against one another, by settlers against Aborigines, by police against Aborigines, by masters against assigned convicts, by magistrates against suspects and so on. The point is that the rule of law offered a check against 'power's all-intrusive claims'.[2] While the foothold was small, the guarantees against abuse were also small. But people in the colony soon saw the possibilities for exercising and augmenting their power over one another in a legitimate way: through the courts.

The courts became a sort of broking house of power in New South Wales. As one of the core elements of the rule of law complex, courts had an established place in English political ordering. But their place, like so much else in topsy-turvy New South Wales, was not so clearly established. Some were surprised that courts were provided at all for a penal colony. The right of convicts to resort to them was by no means clear. By serendipity or a judgement about the necessities of the settlement, Henry and Susannah were allowed to bring their suit. Their case established a precedent which opened the doors of the superior courts to convicts and emancipists. But the precedent would have come to little if the courts – strangely constituted as they were – had played the dutiful role expected of them by the early governors. Not only were the courts prepared to rule against powerful individuals in the colony – like the captain of Henry and Susannah's ship – but they were also prepared to rule against the most powerful individual in the colony, the governor. The courts provided the forum in which the rule of law model could be elaborated.

None of this was foreordained. This book has not been a story about the inevitable triumph of British institutions. Henry and Susannah's case shows – as do so many of the other incidents described here – how easily things could have turned out differently. Chance combinations of circumstances, the peculiarities of cases, the predilections of this judge, that governor, some British politician and so on, meant that the outcomes were always in doubt. This has been a story about how people in the colony were able to use their political and legal traditions and the legal mechanisms open to them in a penal colony to shape and reshape the power structures of the new society. It has not been a story about the virtues or appropriateness of those institutions. It has been a story of how the inhabitants of New South Wales – and especially the three major parties to the politics of the colony, the governor, the Emancipists and the Exclusives – were able to shape their arguments and turn the rule of law ideology to their advantage in their struggles to establish the terms upon which power in the colony would be exercised and by whom.

For the governor, the legitimacy of his administration depended the lawfulness of his commands and the lawfulness of their execution. He could have secured the compliance of the convicts by arbitrary physical force. But regimes of this sort tend to be inefficient and short-lived. More importantly, to do so would have conflicted with the English political culture which, as Blackstone said, even recognised the rights of convicts.[3] The governor was vulnerable to charges of illegal force both in the colonial courts and in London. Despite frustrations over the legal technicalities experienced by military men like Macquarie and Darling, and despite some slips from grace, they conformed to the legal constraints on their power.

There were good reasons for them to do so from their own point of view as colonial governors. They governed by laws addressed to the population at large. They depended on their functionaries – the police and the magistrates – to make the rule of law meaningful in the localities. They also depended on the law as a method of supervising these functionaries. Hence Governor Macquarie's orders to the magistrates concerning tickets of leave and Governor Bourke's *Summary Punishments* legislation. Hence Governor Gipps' enquiry into Major Nunn's Mounted Police killing of Aborigines. The rule of law is a two-edged sword: the governors could not hold their subordinates to the legal standard unless they observed the legal standard in their own conduct of office.

For the Exclusives, the first lessons about the use of the courts came during the period leading up to the Rum Rebellion. John Macarthur knew about the defect in the governor's legislative power. He and his fellow officers – both as litigants and members of the panel of officers who sat with the judge – used the courts to defy attempts by the governors to interfere with their interests and to harass their opponents. They also saw the advantages of the magistrate's court. They colonised the magistracy and bitterly opposed attempts by Macquarie to appoint emancipist magistrates. The office of justice of the peace was a rich prize in the struggle for power and authority. Not only did it carry with it the traditional, English gentry associations, it also gave control of the police into their hands and put them in the judgment seat. From here they could assert the independence of the bench against governors who were unsympathetic to their concerns or who tried to interfere with their discipline of the convict workforce. They could also establish their authority over the local population.

For the Emancipists, the courts and the rhetoric of the rule of law offered their best chance to share in power. The governors came equipped with a seemingly autocratic authority and the trappings of office. The Exclusives had wealth, patronage links in England and they were cleanskins. Surely they were the natural aristocracy. The Emancipists had to find a strategy which could overcome the advantages of their opponents and the taint of their own convictism.

Wealth helped. By 1819, many emancipists owned enough property to satisfy the traditional qualification for the franchise. And they looked to a future in which they would take their share of political power. Macquarie's policies had encouraged them to consider themselves restored to all the rights of free-born Britons. There had been some setbacks, for example, when Bent refused to admit the emancipist attorneys to practise and in the controversy over the emancipist magistrates. But success with the jury petition would resolve their status and confirm their entitlement to their English rights and liberties. Representative institutions would follow.

The Emancipists' expectations turned out to be premature but the rule of law strategy gave them a powerful weapon to wield both in the colony and in England. Wentworth could don Wilkes' cap of British liberty in the press and in the courts over so many issues: jury trial, illegal punishments inflicted by Governor Darling, torture by the magistrates, Darling's attempt to censor the press, the magistrates' prosecution of Hall. Governor Darling could become the symbol of oppression in a classic rule of law text.

Blackstone had promised that British settlers took the laws of England with them when they planted new colonies; but he said nothing about the rule of law in a penal colony, nothing about how English laws would apply to people who were civilly dead, transported in place of death. This book has taken up that story. It is about the transportation of those rule of law ideas to Botany Bay.

The rule of law theme has generated a great deal of debate in recent years following Edward Thompson's now famous post-script to

Whigs and Hunters and Douglas Hay's essay, 'Property, Authority and the Criminal Law'.[4] The burden of their argument is that the rule of law maintained and enhanced the authority of the eighteenth-century English ruling class, while at the same time imposing checks on the arbitrary use of that power. The extension of that political culture to the Antipodes allows us to pursue those arguments in a radically different context.

The rule of law is a political concept. It refers to a set of ideas about the configuration of political power in which rules, legal reasoning and courts mediate, constrain and legitimate political power. But whereas Thompson and Hay describe rulers using and being bound by the rule of law in a society with a highly developed authority structure, in New South Wales we see parties using rule of law ideology as the medium in struggles over political power in a new and very unusual society.

The penal and military nature of the settlement at Botany Bay suggested that the rule of men – in particular, the governor – would prevail. But was the distinction between law and arbitrary power – the rule of law and the rule of men – so sharp in New South Wales? Is the distinction so sharp in general? This has been a controversial point among those who write about the rule of law. For example, Thompson's critics have claimed that he draws too sharp a line between law and arbitrary power. Cromwell's admonition to Sir Mathew Hale, that 'if they would not let him rule by red gowns, he was resolved to govern by red coats',[5] shows a much closer connection between the rule of law and arbitrary power than the opposition of these concepts suggests. The English Civil War stood as the threat behind Cromwell's warning. And yet Cromwell himself saw the distinction. He puts the options quite boldly: either the rule of law or the force of arms. The executioners of Charles I had confronted a similar choice. Their solicitude for legal form in executing their monarch sprang from a fear of renewed armed strife.[6] And similarly, the bloodless revolution of 1688 chose the rule of law as its insurance against a slide back into the violence of the Civil War and its aftermath. Similarly, the eighteenth century's respect for the rule of law depended on the memory of the seventeenth-century alternative.

Similarly too, the Rum Rebels in New South Wales chose to use armed force against Bligh but then attempted to enlist the forms and rituals of the rule of law to legitimate their actions. As we have seen in both the treatment of the Aborigines and in the illegal punishments handed out by magistrates, arbitrary force was used in the penal colony. So it is true to say both that the colony was no stranger to the rule of law and to arbitrary power. That the choice between law and the use of arbitrary force has been quite stark. But for the most part in New South Wales the choice of armed rebellion – even for the Emancipists who stood to gain most from it – was not considered. They chose constitutional paths.

But the relationship between the rule of law and power is more complex than this; not all force is arbitrary. The claim to monopoly on the use of physical coercion lies behind political authority.[7] Political legitimacy is the way polities mostly avoid resorting to openly coercive strategies.[8] The relationship between power and authority is variable;[9] they are closely related but at some times resort to coercion will be closer than at others. In seventeenth-century England physical coercion was close to the surface; in the eighteenth it was much less so. The enormous amounts of capital and corporal punishments inflicted in New South Wales meant that the mix between force and consent was weighted much more heavily towards force than was the case in England. In Bathurst's refusal to accept Judge-Advocate Bent's entreaty to dispense with the military trappings of the Criminal Court, the Colonial Secretary says quite explicitly that the government wanted to keep the idea of coercion before the public eye and to use the colonial court for that purpose.[10]

This last example brings out some of the connections between power, authority and the rule of law. Power is the ability to exert one's will over others, for example, by the use or threat of physical force, or by economic dominance. Authority, on the other hand, is the ability to get people to obey because they believe in the rightness of the command or the ruler's entitlement to issue orders. Authority is power that has become legitimate.[11] To speak of legitimate authority is a tautology; by definition, authority can only be legitimate. The rule of law is a way, and a very powerful one, both to legitimate power and to exercise it. This is in addition to being an important way of constraining rulers, the point Thompson stressed in the now famous passages in *Whigs and Hunters*.[12]

The rule of law was an unusually strong legitimating force in eighteenth-century English politics. Majesty, justice and mercy produced the consent necessary for the maintenance of authority.[13] But how convincing would all this be in a penal colony, one composed of those who had been at the butt of eighteenth-century British society and whose intimate experience of the criminal justice system had more to do with the stench of the jails and hulks than it did with ermine robes and assize balls?

As far as I can tell, it seemed still to be convincing and important. The convicts – and later the Emancipists – did not reject the rule of law ideology. They did satirise it in their songs and mimicry but there is little evidence of outright rejection. They did criticise its operatives – especially in the magistracy and the police forces – but not the idea of the rule of law itself. John Grant, Alexander Harris, Edward Smith Hall, Edward Eagar and William Wentworth all made a sharp distinction between the office and its incumbents. They used the rule of law to contest the power of their opponents, to assert their own status and to hold those in authority – courts, magistrates, police and Governors – to a legal standard in the exercise of that authority.

But although the establishment of courts and legal rules and legal argumentation – the core elements of the rule of law notion, described in chapter 2 – profoundly shaped the exercise of power in New South Wales and meant that the exercise of power was susceptible to the challenge of legality, it is important to see that this did not guarantee particular outcomes. Legal reasoning does not produce 'right answers' in the way that arithmetic does. But it is not arbitrary either. For most cases the conclusions flow neatly from their legal premises; but the difficult cases, such as the controversial and unusual cases which brought Chief Justice Forbes and Governor Darling into conflict, call for displays of art, the 'artificial reason and judgment' which Coke emphasised. The rightness of these decisions formally depends on the system's decision making rules and informally on the assessment of other practitioners of the legal aesthetic.

Early New South Wales shows one more thing about the rule of law: that its use as an instrument of power is not confined to rulers. Susannah and Henry Kable demonstrated that. This is not just the point that the rule of law acts as a constraint on the power of rulers, that it is a shield against oppression. In early New South Wales, rule of law ideas served as a sword, not just a shield, for a variety of people battling over the partition of power in a relatively open setting. Susannah and Henry Kable used it at first against Captain Sinclair; Henry and his partners also used it later to ruin other ships' captains and commercial rivals as well. John Macarthur used it as part of his strategy to 'ruin' governors who opposed his plans. The Exclusives used it through the plottings of the brothers Bent, through the magistracy and the police. They employed it to push the Emancipists into a subordinate role both economically and politically. The Emancipists used it – most strikingly on the jury issue, but also through court room strategies and rule of law rhetoric in the newspapers – to fight against the Exclusive plan to impose an hereditary disability on them. And both Emancipists and Exclusives used it against governors whose policies ran counter to their interests.

Both sides – but more especially the Emancipists – conscripted the rule of law to transform New South Wales from a penal colony to a free society. Little by little, over the fifty-year period, they were able to set up the conditions which effected that redefinition. The Kables' court case was an important first step. The appointment of the first qualified judges and the arrival of more qualified lawyers, allowed rule of law ideas to grow. The confrontations between Macquarie and the Bents forced the metropolitan power to re-assess its policy towards its penal colony, and to make the major changes contained in the 1823 legislation: the Legislative Council and the reformed court system.

These changes – especially in the courts – strengthened the conditions for the exercise of the rule of law. They were promptly put to use in the Emancipist cause to contest the power of Governor Darling and the Exclusivist magistracy, and to push the claims of the Emancipists on the jury question. The advent of a free press at this time enabled the Wilkite tactic – hitching press and the rule of law ideology in tandem – to be employed to great effect.

The 1830s completed the transition from penal colony to free society. The provision of the criminal jury trial option in 1833, which also allowed emancipists to sit on juries, broke through one of the last major barriers. Even then, however, contingency was a major factor. In the 1830s England transported more convicts to Australia than it had sent in the whole of the period up to 1830. What could have been more plausible than the old policy: continued postponement of free institutions because of the nature of the colony and its population? But events had moved on in England. By the 1830s the ascendancy of the Whigs, the Benthamite radicals and the prominence of the anti-slavery campaign meant that transportation to New South Wales had to confront fundamental shifts in English politics. Although the evidence to the Molesworth Committee overwhelmingly favoured continued transportation, the Report recommended its cessation. It was not so much that the Report did not fit the evidence, but that the evidence did not fit the political climate.

Once the decision to end transportation had been taken, punishment ceased to be a major part of the rationale for New South Wales. The political alignments changed from bond versus free to the traditional criterion of English politics, landed wealth. This was no democracy. The Emancipists' campaign had defeated the threat to exclude them on account of the convict taint and forced England to reassess its view of New South Wales as a penal colony. From this point new contests about authority would begin in different institutions and mediums. But that is another story.[14] Representative institutions were granted in 1842 and responsible government a decade later. New South Wales had become a free society.

APPENDIX 1
Historical Boundaries of Australia, 1788–Present

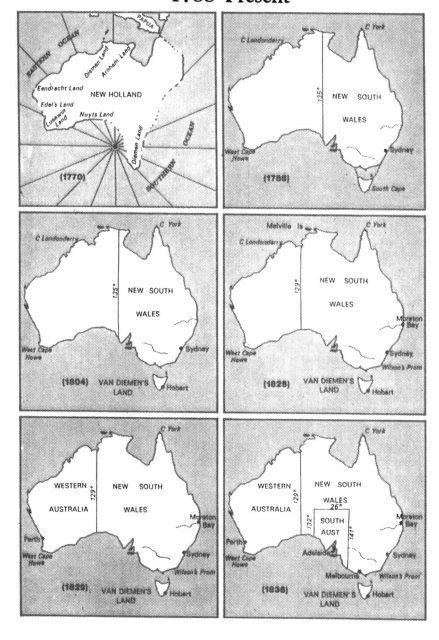

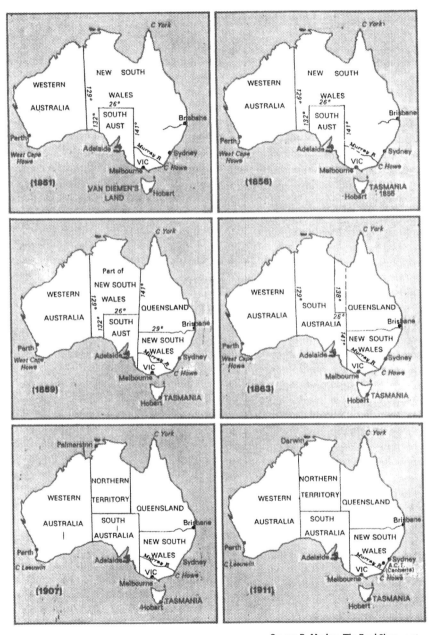

Source: R. Hughes, *The Fatal Shore*, xxvi

APPENDIX 2
Population of New South Wales

	Total	No. of Convicts	Pop. %
1788	1,024	717	74.2
1800	4,958	1,558	31.6
1810	10,452	–	–
1820	23,939	10,873	45.4
1830	46,276	18,571	40.1
1840	129,463	38,305	29.6

Source: C.M.H. Clark, *Select Documents in Australian History*, 405–6

APPENDIX 3
Convicts Transported to New South Wales

1787–89	1,010
1790–99	6,079
1800–09	4,030
1810–19	13,584
1820–29	21,956
1830–39	31,661
1840–41	1,684
	80,004

Source: L. Robson, *The Convict Settlers of Australia*, 170.

APPENDIX 4
Composition of New South Wales Population

	Convicts	Emancipists	Free Born	Free Immigrants
1828	15,668(43%)	7,530(20%)	8,727(24%)	4,673 (13%)
1841	26,453(23%)	18,257(16%)	28,657(24%)	43,621(37%)
1851	2,693(1.5%)	26,629(14%)	81,391(43%)	76,530(41%)

	Convict/Eman./Free Born	Free Immigrants
1828	31,915(87%)	4,673(13%)
1841	73,367(63%)	43,621(37%)
1851	110,713(59%)	76,530(41%)

Source: R. Ward, *The Australian Legend*, 37–8. See ch.1, n.35, for some qualification of these figures.

APPENDIX 5
Governors of New South Wales 1788–1851

A. Phillip	26.01.1788	–	10.12.1792
(F. Grose)	11.12.1792	–	12.12.1794
(W. Paterson)	12.12.1794	–	11.09.1795
J. Hunter	11.09.1795	–	27.09.1800
P. King	28.09.1800	–	12.08.1806
W. Bligh	13.08.1806	–	26.01.1808
(G. Johnston)	26.01.1808	–	28.07.1808
(Joseph Foveaux)	29.07.1808	–	08.01.1809
(W. Paterson)	09.01.1809	–	31.12.1809
L. Macquarie	01.01.1810	–	01.12.1821
T. Brisbane	01.12.1821	–	01.12.1825
(W. Stewart)	01.12.1825	–	18.12.1825
R. Darling	19.12.1825	–	21.10.1831
(P. Lindsay)	22.10.1831	–	02.12.1831
R. Bourke	03.12.1831	–	05.12.1837
(K. Snodgrass)	06.12.1837	–	23.01.1838
G. Gipps	24.02.1838	–	11.07.1846
(M. O'Connel)	12.07.1846	–	02.08.1846
C. Fitzroy	03.08.1846	–	01.01.1851

(Names of acting governors in brackets)

Notes

Preface

1. See R. White, *Inventing Australia* (Allen and Unwin, Sydney, 1981), ch.1.
2. In the American setting, see S. Diamond, 'From Organization to Society: Virginia in the Seventeenth Century' (1958) *American Journal of Sociology*, 457 and D. Rutman, 'The Virginia Company and Its Military Regime' in D. Rutman (ed.), *The Old Dominion* (University of Press of Virginia, Charlottesville, 1964).
3. This fiction is laid bare by H. Reynolds, *The Law of the Land* (Penguin, Melbourne, 1987b).
4. Quoted in Stanley Katz' introduction to Blackstone's *Commentaries* I, 16.
5. Blackstone's *Commentaries* I, 104–5.
6. D. Hay, 'Property, Authority and the Criminal Law' in D. Hay *et al.*, *Albion's Fatal Tree* (Pantheon, New York, 1975) and E.P. Thompson, *Whigs and Hunters* (Pantheon, New York, 1975).
7. C. Currey, *Sir Francis Forbes: The First Chief Justice of the Supreme Court of New South Wales* (Angus and Robertson, Sydney, 1968a).

Chapter 1

1. Regarding Susannah, see Mr Justice G. Nares to the King, 13/5/1783, HO 47/3; and Lord Sydney to the Justices of Assize for Norfolk, 19/5/1784, HO 13/2 f.84. For Thomas Dunn, see Mr Justice J. Eyre to the Secretary of State, 24/4/1784, HO 47/1. On the pardon system generally, see P. King, 'Decision Makers and Decision Making in the English Criminal Law, 1750–1800' (1984) *Historical Journal* 27, 27; the

seminal article by D. Hay, 'Property, Authority and the Criminal Law' in D. Hay et.al., *Albion's Fatal Tree* (Pantheon, New York, 1975); cf. J. Langbein, 'Albion's Fatal Flaws' (1983) 98 *Past and Present* 96.

2   Notice of the hanging appeared in the *Norfolk Chronicle* 8/4/1783. The reprieve for Henry junior is in Lord North to Sir James Eyre, 1/12/1783, HO 13/1, f.300. No correspondence about the grandfather or the other man, Carman, could be found.

3   HO 42/8–9, ff.331–2. On Norwich Castle see B. Green, *Norwich Castle: A Fortress for Nine Centuries* (Jarrold, Norwich, 1970). On eighteenth-century jails see J. Innes, 'The King's Bench Prison in the Later Eighteenth Century' in J. Brewer and J. Styles (eds.) *An Ungovernable People* (Rutgers University Press, New Jersey, 1980).

4   Lord Sydney to the Sheriff of Norfolk, 21/10/1786; Lord Sydney to Henry Bradley (Captain of the hulk *Dunkirk*), 21/10/1786, HO 13/4, ff.273–4.

5   Lord Sydney's order to receive Henry and the baby was given on 7/11/1786, two days after Susannah had been delivered to the hulk, HO 13/4, f.280. The letter from the Captain is Bradley to Under-Secretary Nepean, 16/11/1786, HO 42/10 f.235. A month later he reported that he had received two other female convicts with babies. Quotation from the *Norfolk Chronicle*, 11/11/1786. The London *English Chronicle* carried the story on 2/12/1786 and a letter about the subscription the following Thursday. Correspondence about the case went on through December. One correspondent to the *Universal Daily Register*, 21/12/1786, thought the whole affair had been blown out of proportion. Simpson received gifts of 10 pounds from Lord Chedworth and 6 guineas from Lady Cadogan.

6   Cited in R. Hughes, *The Fatal Shore* (Knopf, New York, 1986), 143.

7   D. Hainsworth, *The Sydney Traders* (Melbourne University Press, Melbourne), 123 and App.E.

8   I am indebted to the article by Sir Victor Windeyer, 'A Birthright and an Inheritance' (1962) *University of Tasmanian L.R.*, 635, for these points.

9   Blackstone, *Commentaries* IV, 373–82.

10 *Field v Eagar, Eagar v de Mestre*. See ch.6.

11 The Kables' story is pieced together from a range of sources in addition to those specifically noted. I thank the descendants of the Kables, Mrs Z. Campbell, Mr and Mrs A.E. Dawson and Commander P. Kable for access to material in their possession. See too the seminal article by Sir Victor Windeyer, *op. cit.*, n.8. See too, J. Cobley, *Crimes of the First Fleet Convicts* (Angus and Robertson, Sydney),46 and 135. On legal standing, see ch.6.

12 For the Norwich petition see HO 42/8–9, ff.331–2. Often the Under-Secretary had to disappoint the petitioners: Lord Sydney to the Magistrates at York, 23/10/1786, HO 13/4, f.274. See generally J. Howard, *The State of the Prisons in England and Wales* (Patterson

Smith, 1973). The debate among historians about the reasons for choosing New South Wales has been lengthy. See, for example, D. Mackay, *A Place of Exile: The European Settlement of New South Wales* (Oxford University Press, Melbourne, 1985). For an English criminal justice historian's point of view, see J.M. Beattie, *Crime and the Courts in England 1660-1800* (Oxford University Press, Oxford, 1986). The main proponent of the contrary view is Alan Frost, *Convicts and Empire: A Naval Question* (Oxford University Press, Melbourne, 1980). The debate is summarised in R. Hughes, *op.cit.*, ch.2. On transportation to America see A.E. Smith, 'Transportation of Convicts to the American Colonies in the Seventeenth Century' (1934) *American Historical Review*, 9, 232; and A. Ekirch, *Bound For America: The Transportation of British Convicts to the Colonies, 1718-1775*, (Clarendon, Oxford, 1987).

13 A. McMartin, *Public Servants and Patronage* (Sydney University Press, Sydney), 8-11.
14 See J.M. Beattie, *op.cit.*, n.12, ch.9.
15 The petition is dated 7/8/1786, PRO HO 42/9 f331. Hughes, *op.cit*, n.6, 56-67.
16 A. McMartin, *op.cit.*, n.13, 14-17. Transportation to America is discussed in K. Morgan, 'The Organisation of the Convict Trade to Maryland: Stevenson Randolph and Cheston, 1768-1775' (1985) *William and Mary Quarterly*, 42,201. See too A. Smith, *op. cit.*, n.12; and A. Ekirch, *op. cit.*, n.12.
17 A. McMartin, *op. cit.*, n.13, 18.
18 See ch.6.
19 D. Hainsworth, *op.cit.*, n.7, 13-16 and passim.
20 H. Merivale, *Colonisation and the Colonies* (Longman, London, 1861), 103-7.
21 J. Murrin, 'The Great Inversion, Or Court Versus Country: A Comparison of the Revolution Settlements in England (1688-1721) and America (1776-1816)' in J.G.A. Pocock, *Three British Revolutions* (Princeton University Press, New Jersey, 1975), 370; and D.Lovejoy, 'Two American Revolutions 1689 and 1786' in *ibid.*, 258.
22 Bentham wrote incessantly to important figures in criticism of New South Wales. See for example Romilly to Bentham, 28/8/1802, Bentham to Dumont 20/8/1802, Bentham to Abbott 2/9/1802, Bentham Papers, BL, Add. MSS.33543, ff. 601-3, and to Fox, *ibid.*, Add. MSS. 47569 f.129.
23 Darling to Hay, 6/2/1827, PRO, CO, 323/149, f.167.
24 See J. Pocock, *The Machiavellian Moment* (Princeton University Press, New Jersey, 1975), esp. part 2.
25 See T. Parsons, 'Was John Boston's Pig a Political Martyr?' (1985) *JRAHS*, 71, 163.
26 M. Craton, J. Walvin and D. Wright, *Slavery, Abolition and Emancipation* (Longman, New York, 1976), 231 ff.

27 On anti-slavery opinion in England, see Craton *et al.*, *ibid.*; S. Drescher, 'Public Opinion and the Destruction of British Colonial Slavery' in J. Walvin, *Slavery and British Society 1776–1846* (Macmillan, London, 1982), 22; and J. Walvin, 'The Propaganda of Anti-Slavery' in *ibid.* 49.
28 See Drescher, *ibid.*; Walvin, *ibid.*; and Craton, *ibid.*, n.26, 279.
29 D. Hay, *op.cit.*, n.1.
30 J. Langbein, 'Shaping the Eighteenth-Century Criminal Trial: A View from the Ryder Sources: (1983) *University of Chicago L.R.*, 50, 1.
31 See the seminal article on this by Hay, *op. cit.*, n.1. See too the replies by Langbein and King, cited in n.1, and J. Beattie, *op. cit.*, n.14.
32 E. O'Brien, *The Foundation of Australia* (Sheed and Ward, London, 1939). Part 1 has an excellent treatment of these ideas.
33 See D. Philips, "A New Engine of Power and Authority': The Institutionalization of Law Enforcement in England 1780–1830' in Gatrell *et al.*, *Crime and the Law* (Europa, London, 1980), 155; and D.Neal, 'The Role of the Justices of the Peace in Relation to Popular Protest in Eighteenth Century England', 1979, Unpublished manuscript.
34 See Hay *et al.*, *op.cit.*, n.1.
35 See Appendices 2–4, pp.200–1. I am indebted to an anonymous reviewer for pointing out two matters in relation to these statistics. In the early 1800s the proportion of the population which was convict dropped to a low of 36 per cent, and possibly lower. However, due to the very low rate of free settlement during this period, the great majority of the remaining population were emancipists. Appendix 4 assumes that all children born in the colony had convict parents. While the great majority of them had, in the relevant period (i.e. up to 1840), the assumption has to be qualified. W. Vamplew, *Australians: Historical Statistics* (Fairfax, Syme, Weldon, Sydney, 1987), 104 has a table which breaks down the population components for the whole period; there are some minor variations from the figures shown in the appendices but they do not affect the points made above.
36 On mercantile expansion, especially among the emancipists, see Hainsworth, *op.cit.*, n.7. See too Hirst, *Convict Society and Its Enemies* (Allen and Unwin, Sydney, 1987).
37 Quoted in M.H. Ellis, *John Macarthur* (Angus and Robertson, Sydney, 1973), 270. See too G. L. Haskins, *Law and Authority in Early Massachusetts* who makes the same point about distance and autonomy.
38 Quoted by Hughes, *op.cit.*, n.6, 324.
39 Saxe-Bannister to Darling, 9/9/1826, PRO CO 323/146, f.208. See too ch.6.
40 The case was *R. v Jack Congo Murrell* (1836) 1 Legge 72. The case is discussed by A. Castles, *An Australian Legal History* (Law Book Co., Sydney, 1982), 526–9.
41 See H. Reynolds, *The Law of the Land* (Penguin, Melbourne, 1987b), chs.1–3; and *Frontier* (Allen and Unwin, Sydney, 1987a), esp. part 2;

and Castles, *op.cit.*, n.40, , chs. 1, 2 and 18. On the failure of the police to make the rule of law meaningful at the periphery, see ch. 6.

42 Some of the Exclusives suggested, for example, that the children of convicts ought not sit on juries. This proposal of an hereditary disability provoked sharp responses from the Emancipists. See ch.7.

43 Some of the contemporary commentators on the strong factionalism in the colony were: P. Cunningham, *Two Years in New South Wales II*, 139–43; Darling to Hay 10/12/1825, PRO, CO 323/146, f.128 ff; Eagar responded to Commissioner Bigge's use of factionalism to deny trial by jury by saying that the factionalism was itself caused by such measures, as well as by Judge Field's conduct (see ch.6), HRA IV, I, 454. Sturma quotes James Macarthur's 1849 admission that the Exclusive cause had been fanned by fears of an Emancipist ascendancy, *Vice in a Vicious Society* (University of Queensland Press, St Lucia, 1983b), 30.

44 John Macarthur told Governor Darling on first meeting that he had succeeded in disposing of any who were obnoxious to him. Darling observed that he did not except governors from the statement. Darling to Hay, *ibid.*

45. *Bigge Report* I, 89. See too T.G. Parsons, 'The Commercialisation of Honor: Early Australian Capitalism 1788–1809' in G. Aplin, *Sydney Before Macquarie* (University of New South Wales Press, Sydney, 1988), 104–7, 111.

46 *A Statistical, Historical and Political Description of the Colony of New South Wales* (Doubleday, Sydney, 1978), 364 ff.

47 V. Windeyer, *op.cit.*, n.8, 645.

48 See chs. 4 and 6.

49 H.V. Evatt, *Rum Rebellion* (Angus and Robertson, Sydney, 1938); Hainsworth, *op.cit.*, n.7; and J. Ritchie, *Lachlan Macquarie* (Melbourne University Press, Melbourne, 1986), 100–104, who cites the impartial assessment of the botanist, George Caley. The debate over the Rum Rebellion has revived recently: see A. Atkinson, 'Jeremy Bentham and the Rum Rebellion', JRAHS (1978) 64, 1; T.G. Parsons, *op.cit.*, n.45; R. Fitzgerald and M. Hearn, *Bligh, Macarthur and the Rum Rebellion* (Kangaroo Press, Sydney, 1988).

50 H.V. Evatt, *ibid.*, 78–9.

51 E. P. Thompson, *Whigs and Hunters* (Pantheon, New York, 1975), 263.

52 See chs. 5 and 7.

53 For example, Ellis, *Lachlan Macquarie* (Angus and Robertson, Sydney, 1969), chs. 20–21, sees only venality, ulterior motives and self-promotion in the opposition of the colony's judges, the Bents, to Governor Macquarie. Similarly, Shaw dismisses Chief Justice Forbes' opposition to Governor Darling as legal pedantry, an irritant to a governor who had to be concerned with administration, not law, see *Heroes and Villains in History* (Sydney University Press, Sydney, 1966), 21. Hirst accuses the Bents and a successor, Wylde, of acting to preserve their own and the law's independence, not for the general good, and lacking

an appreciation of the special needs of authority in a penal colony, *op.cit.*, n.36, 116. See chapter 2. Hughes, *op.cit.*, n.6, does not cite the legal and constitutional histories in his bibliography. The local legal system only intrudes at the margins of his account.
54 See especially the Emancipist rhetoric in the campaign for trial by jury, ch.7.
55 *Mostyn v. Fabrigas* (1774) 1 Cowp. 161; see too *Campbell v. Hall* (1774) 1 Cowp. 204.
56 For example, Bligh complains about Henry Kable and his emancipist partners Lord and Underwood suing ship's masters and ruining them, HRA 1, VI, 148–9. Atkinson documents the preparedness of convicts to take their masters to court, 'Four Patterns of Convict Protest' (1979) *Labour History* 37, 29. Paula Byrne shows extensive use of the courts by women, 'Women and the Criminal Law: Sydney 1810–1821' (1985) 2*Push From the Bush* 21, 2.

Chapter 2

1 J.Locke, *Second Treatise of Government* (Bobbs-Merrill, New York, 1952), 32–3. Blackstone echoes these sentiments, *Commentaries*, I, 121–2.
2 Darling to Hay, 9/2/1827, Private Correspondence, PRO CO 323/149.
3 Hughes' book, *The Fatal Shore* (Knopf, New York), was published in 1986. There have been two major recent revisionist histories of New South Wales in the last few years. John Hirst's, *Convict Society and Its Enemies* (Allen and Unwin, Sydney, 1983), and a collection of essays edited by Steven Nicholas, *Convict Workers* (Cambridge University Press, Cambridge, 1988). Both the revisionist accounts play down the extent to which punishment set the tone in New South Wales. Hughes incorporates a good deal of Hirst's thesis without coming to grips with the tensions this sets up in his own more bloody account. While the revisionists provide a valuable corrective to a simplistic rendering based on brute force, they over-correct by draining almost all the blood from the story. The penal purposes of the colony cannot be pushed to the margins and the important differences between free workers, slaves, immigrants and convicts should not be elided. I have outlined my objections to John Hirst's book more fully in 'Free Society, Penal Colony, Slave Society, Prison?' (1987) *Hist. Studs.* 22, 497. His reply follows my article. Hirst complains that he has been misread and that New South Wales was not a free society at the outset. But he seeks to avoid the consequences of that concession by setting up an artificial divide between a society's political and legal institutions on the one hand and the conditions of everyday life on the other. Although Hirst accepts that New South Wales was not a free society, he still insists that it was a 'unique society', not a penal

colony. He does not respond to my argument about what constitutes a penal colony except to say, 'point to a penal colony elsewhere in which half the convicts were employed by ex-convicts and it was regarded as bad form to call convicts by that name'. New South Wales was not Devil's Island and not everyone there was a convict. But, as I argue in the text, New South Wales turned on a penal base and that point is in danger of being forgotten in the revisions. Some commentators, taking Hirst's views to an extreme, now seem to regard New South Wales as some sort of triumph for British civilisation; see, for example, J. Carroll, 'Original Sin or Paradise Regained?' (1987) *Quadrant* May, 10. The book by Nicholas and his colleagues takes a quite different line from Hirst and seeks to assimilate New South Wales to other immigrant experiences. While there is much to admire in both books, to understate the penal dimension of life in New South Wales is a fundamental misunderstanding.

4   Blackstone wrote that even convicts had rights under law and could not be transported without legal authorisation,. *op.cit.*, n.1, 130.

5   J. Hirst, 81, 107; R. Hughes, *op.cit.*, n.3, 586–7. On legal rights of slaves, see n.19.

6   Bentham to Dumont, 20/8/1802, BL Add. MS, 33543, ff.603; Sir John Romilly is quoted in Fletcher, *Landed Enterprise and Penal Society* (Sydney University Press, Sydney, 1976), 1. Earl Bathurst to Bigge, *Bigge Report*, III, Appendix; John Grant, BL Peel Papers, Add. MS 40, 357 ff. 37–45 (John Grant); G. Loveless, *The Victims of Whiggery* (Cox, Kay, Hobart, 1946), 26–7; Chief Justice Francis Forbes, Catton Papers DCL, WH 2790, 6/2/1825; Peter Cunningham, *Two Years in New South Wales* (Libraries Board of S.A., Adelaide, 1966), II, 20.

7   Geoffrey Blainey, *A Land Half Won* (Macmillan, Melbourne, 1980), 34ff. and 49; L. Robson, *The Convict Settlers of Australia* (Melbourne University Press, Melbourne, 1965), 162; C.M.H. Clark 'The Origins of the Convicts Transported to Eastern Australia, 1787–1852' (1956) *Hist. Studs.* Pt. I, 7, 121, 122–3; Brian Fletcher, *op.cit.* n.6, 1–2; W.K. Hancock, *Australia* (Jacaranda Press, Sydney) 1; R. Ward, *The Australian Legend* (Oxford University Press, Melbourne, 1978), 36 and *Finding Australia* (Heinemann, Melbourne, 1987), ch.VI; J Ritchie, *Lachlan Macquarie* (Melbourne University Press, Melbourne, 1986), 200–2; and M. Sturma, *Vice in a Vicious Society* (University of Queensland Press, St Lucia, 1983b), 8; D. Hainsworth, *Sydney Traders*, 220–1; R Hughes, *op.cit.*, n.3, 168.

8   *R v Jack Congo Murrell* (1836) 1 Legge 72. The relevant law is discussed in A. Castles, *An Australian Legal History* (Law Book Co., Sydney, 1982), ch.2. On settled colonies V. Windeyer, 'A Birthright and Inheritance: The Establishment of the Rule of Law in Australia' (1962) *University of Tasmania L.R.*, 635; E. Campbell, 'Prerogative Rule in New South Wales, 1788–1823' (1965) *JRAHS* 50 (3), 161. S. Woinarski thought that the settlement was strictly military and penal

and that this vested despotic power in the governor's hands, 'The History of Legal Institutions in Victoria' (unpublished Ll.D. thesis, University of Melbourne, 1842), 14–16; H. Reynolds, *The Law of the Land* (Penguin, Melbourne, 1987). On the Bushranging Act, see for example, Governor Bourke's evidence to the Molesworth Committee (*Molesworth Report*), 238.

9 Merivale's comment is in *Colonisation and the Colonies* (Longman, London, 1861) 107. For some of the English views, see R. White, *Inventing Australia* (Allen and Unwin, Sydney, 1981), ch.1.

10 A. Ekirch, *Bound for America: The Transportation of British Convicts to the Colonies 1715–1775* (Clarendon, Oxford, 1987); A.E. Smith, 'Transportation of Convicts to the American Colonies in the Seventeenth Century' (1934) 39 *American Historical Review* 39, 232; and Mackay, *A Place of Exile: The European Settlement of New South Wales* (Oxford University Press, Melbourne, 1985).

11 See Hirst, *op.cit.*, n.3; and Nicholas, *op.cit.*, n.3.

12 E.S. Morgan, *American Slavery, American Freedom* (Norton, New York, 1975), 60–1.

13 The population statistics are derived from L. Robson, *The Convict Settlers of Australia* (Melbourne University Press, Melbourne, 1965), 170; C.M.H. Clark, *Select Documents in Australian History* (Angus and Robertson, Sydney, 1962), 406; and R. Ward, *The Australian Legend* (Oxford University Press, Melbourne, 1978), 37–8. See Appendices 2, 3 and 4. See too ch.1, n.35 for a note on the figures..

14 For a survey see O. Patterson, *Slavery and Social Death: A Comparative Study* (Harvard University Press, Cambridge, Mass., 1982).

15 See especially M. Tushnet, *The American Law of Slavery 1810–1860: Considerations of Humanity and Interest* (Princeton University Press, New Jersey, 1981); and E. Genovese, *Roll, Jordan Roll: The World the Slaves Made* (Pantheon, New York, 1972).

16 For example, Genovese, *ibid.*; M. Hindus, *Prison and Plantation: Crime, Justice and Authority in Massachusetts and South Carolina 1767–1878*; E. Morgan, *op.cit.*, n.12; K. Stampp, *The Peculiar Institution* (Knopf, New York, 1956); and Tushnet, *ibid.*

17 See n.15.

18 Both Hirst, 207 and Hughes, *op.cit.*, n.3, 586–7, for example, discount the rights of American slaves.

19 On legal rights, see Genovese, *op.cit.*, n.15, 37–43; Hindus, *op.cit.*, n.16, 130ff., 158, 253; and Tushnet, *op.cit.*, n.15, 20–9. On customary rights, see Genovese, *ibid.*, 585–660; Stampp, *op.cit.*, n.16, 54–85 and ch.3; P. Morgan, 'Work and Culture: The Task System and the Work of Low Country Blacks, 1700–1880' (1982) *William and Mary Quarterly* 39, 563; and E. Morgan, *op.cit.*, n.12, 317–20. For the legal position of slaves in the British West Indies, see *Great Britain, Report of the Select Committee on Slavery*. In particular see the evidence of the solicitor, Andrew Dignum, who served as parish-appointed Defender

of Slaves in Jamaica from 1818–1831. He testified that each parish in Jamaica appointed a Defender of Slaves and that he represented slaves charged with serious offences which were tried before judge and jury (cf. New South Wales where jury trial was not available either to convict or free until the mid-1830s). On the legal rights of Roman slaves, see W. Buckland, *The Roman Law of Slavery* (Cambridge University Press, Cambridge, 1908).

20   Genovese, *ibid.*, 535–40; Hindus, *ibid.*, n.16, 142. For Genovese's critics, see the special issue of (1976) *Radical History Review* 3. See esp. E. Perkins, 'Roll, Jordan, Roll: A Marx for the Master Class' *ibid.*, 41. See too C.L.R. James, 'The Slaves' in L. Comitas and D. Lowenthal, *Slaves, Free Men and Citizens: West Indian Perspectives* (Doubleday Anchor, New York, 1973), 4.

21   Genovese, *ibid.*, 38–41, 178–9.

22   *Op.cit.*, n.3, 103–4.

23   Great Britain, *Report of the Commissioner of Inquiry in the State of the Colony of New South Wales (Bigge Report)* I, 119.

24   Patterson, *op.cit.*, n.14, 101. Roman slaves were indistinguishable from other citizens. Proposals to identify them in some way were rejected by the Senate because it might have given them a dangerous sense of their numerical strength. Slaves were estimated to be about twenty-five per cent of the population, R. Barrow, *Slavery in the Roman Empire* (Barnes and Noble, New York, 1968), 20–1.

25   See the *Transportation Act*, 24 Geo. II, Sess 2, c.56, as amended by S.8, 5 Geo. IV c.84 and the discussion in C. Currey, *Sir Francis Forbes: The First Chief Justice of the Supreme Court of New South Wales* (Angus and Robertson, Sydney, 1968a), 244–5, 341–8. See too W. Nicol, 'Ideology and the Convict System in New South Wales' (1986) 22 *Historical Studies* 1–7. See too ch.4.

26   See the discussion of flogging below. On convict resistance see Atkinson, 'Four Patterns of Convict Protest' (1979) *Labour History (Australia)* 37, 28; and see Hirst, discussion of plantation labour, *op.cit.*, n.3, pp.64– 5. On slave resistance in the West Indies see *Great Britain Select Committee on Slavery*, *op.cit.*, n.19. For American examples, see Genovese, *op.cit.*, n.15, 585–660; E. Morgan, *op.cit.*, n.12, 155; Stampp, *op. cit.*, n.16, 86–140; and G.M. Frederickson and C. Lasch, 'Resistance to Slavery' (1967) *Civil War History* 13, 315.

27   On killing slaves, Genovese, *ibid.*, 37; Hindus, *op.cit.*, n.16, 136; and Tushnet, *op.cit.*, n.15, 72–5. On legal and peer restrictions on cruelty, Genovese, *ibid.*, 41–3; Hindus, *ibid.*; and Stampp, *op.cit.*, n.16, 175, 177–91. For the West Indies, see *Great Britain, Select Committee on Slavery*, *op.cit.*, n.19, 557, 561 and *passim*.

28   Thirty-three lashes was the average for court ordered flogging in the American South during the 1830s, Hindus, *ibid.*, 145–6. Stampp quotes a planter as saying 15–20 lashes as generally sufficient, *ibid*, 175. On New South Wales see Hirst, 181 and the discussion of

flogging below. On the West Indies, see B. Higman, *Slave Population and Economy in Jamaica 1807–34* (Cambridge University Press, Cambridge, 1976), 181 and *Great Britain, Select Committee on Slavery*, ibid.
29 Genovese, op.cit., n.15, 416; and Stampp, op.cit., n.16, 201, 414–7.
30 Genovese, op.cit., n.15, 119–20, 142, 146; and, Stampp, 162–3, 228. *Great Britain, Select Committee on Slavery*, ibid. On naval floggings and the physical effects of the cat, see J. Neale, *The Cutlass and the Lash* (Pluto Press, London, 1985). On flogging of other forms of indentured and free labourers, see S. Nicholas, op.cit., n.3, ch.12.
31 See Hirst, n.3, 76
32 On convict food and Bigge's reaction, see Hirst, op.cit., n.3, 46–51; Nicholas, op.cit., n.3, 183–7. Some disputed that the convicts had better food, see Governor Bourke's comment in N. Townsend, 'Document: Bourke's Comments on the Molesworth Committee', (1982) *Push from the Bush* 12, 67. On the comparison between slave and European diets in the nineteenth century, see Genovese, op.cit., n.15, 57–70; and on slave food generally, Stampp, op.cit., n.16, 282–9; R. Sutch, 'The Care and Feeding of Slaves' in P. David et al., *Reckoning With Slavery* (Oxford University Press, Oxford, 1976), 231. The arguments made by the West Indian planter Rose Price are cited in M. Craton, J. Walvin, D. Wright, *Slavery, Abolition and Emancipation* (Longman, New York, 1976), 320–1.
33 Hirst, 28.
34 Dr Morgan Price, *Molesworth Report* Evidence, 268. The convict quotations are from Hughes, op.cit., n.3, 129–32.
35 G. Loveless, *Victims of Whiggery* (Cox, Kay, Hobart, 1946), 26–7.
36 B. Bettelheim, *The Informed Heart* (Paladin, London, 1970), 68
37 K. Marx and F. Engels, *The Communist Manifesto* (Pelican, Harmondsworth, 1967), 93–4; K. Marx, *Gründrisse* (Vintage, New York, 1973), 604–8; *Capital* (Foreign Languages Publishing House, Moscow, 1957), I, ch.24, esp. 790–3; M. Weber, *The Protestant Ethic and the Spirit of Capitalism* (Scribners, New York, 1958),21–4; *Economy and Society* (University of California Press, Berkeley, 1978), II, 698–9. For analyses of the effects of ideology on day-to-day life under slavery see Tushnet, op.cit., n.15, 31–2, and for contemporary England, S. Hall et al., *Policing the Crisis: Mugging, the State and Law and Order* (Macmillan, London, 1978), 139–77.
38 See the comments of a colonial commentator on the store of mental images involved in transportation compared with imprisonment, quoted by Hirst, 108.
39 See below, for a discussion of the relative success of these ideologies and the consequences of that success.
40 Catton Papers DCL , WH 2790, 6/2/1825. Editor of the colonial newspaper, E.S. Hall, made a similar observation about the planter mentality, see *The Monitor* 15/12/1826.

41 Ibid. The Quaker missionary, Backhouse, made the same comment in relation to convicts in Tasmania, A *Narrative of a Visit to the Australian Colonies* (London, 1843), 156.

42 E. Goffman, *Asylums* (Anchor, New York, 1962); G.M. Sykes, *The Society of Captives* (Princeton University Press, New Jersey, 1968); M. Ignatieff, *A Just Measure of Pain: The Penitentiary in the Industrial Revolution 1750–1850* (Macmillan, London, 1978); M. Foucault, *Discipline and Punish* (Vintage, New York, 1979).

43 Riots arising from the conditions in prisons, arguably endemic to their very structure as institutions, dotted the 1970s. Prison guards either do 'deals' with inmates who maintain order, or engage in particularly brutal reigns of terror such as 'the reception biff' (beating a prisoner on arrival with clubs), random beatings in cells, requiring prisoners to look down when speaking to a guard, etc. For the example of New South Wales in the 1970s, see D. Brown and G. Zdenkowski, *The Prison Struggle* (Penguin, Melbourne, 1982), esp. section 3.

44 Hindus, *op.cit.*, n.16, 5–6. De Beaumont and De Tocqueville report maxima of 39, 20 and 13 for prisoners in New York, Connecticut and Maryland respectively in their early nineteenth study of prisons in the United States, *On the Penitentiary System in the United States and its Application in France* (S. Illinois University Press, 1964), 204.

45 On flogging in New South Wales, see A.G.L. Shaw, *Convicts and the Colonies: A Study of Penal Transportation From Great Britain and Ireland to Australia and Other Parts of the British Empire* (Melbourne University Press, Melbourne, 1977), 200–3.

46 Brown and Zdenkowski, *op.cit.*, n.43.

47 On 'overstint' see, Hindus, *op.cit.*, n.16,; R. Petchesky, 'At Hard Labor: Penal Confinement and Production in Nineteenth-Century America' in David F. Greenberg, *Crime and Capitalism: Readings in Marxist Criminology* (Mayfield, Palo Alto, 1981), 341; R. Sheldon, 'Convict Leasing: An Application of the Rusche-Kirchheimer Thesis to Penal Changes in Tennessee, 1830–1915' in D.F. Greenberg, *ibid.*, 358. Both K. Preyer, 'Penal Measures in the American Colonies: an Overview' (1983), 326, and D.F. Greenberg, 'Crime, Law Enforcement and Social Control in Colonial America' (1982) *American Journal of Legal History* 26, 293, present overviews of penal practices in the American colonies.

48 The book is by Hindus, *op.cit.*, n.16. Genovese's review is, 'Slavery in the Legal History of the South and of the Nation' (1981) *Texas L.R.* 59, 969.

49 G. Blainey, *The Tyranny of Distance* (Sun Books, Melbourne, 1980), x.

50 G.L. Haskins, *Law and Authority in Early Massachusetts* (Archon, New York, 1968), argues that the entrepreneurs of the Massachusetts Company, drawing on the experience of the meddlesome interference suffered by Virginian colonists from the London Company office in London, planned to transfer their corporation across the Atlantic.

This would also make it more difficult to revoke the corporate charter, 11–12. A similar point is made by S. Diamond, *The Creation of Society in the New World* (Rand McNally, New York, 1963). See too ch.1.
51 Quoted by Hirst, 208–9.
52 See n.13.
53 See Nicholas, *op.cit.*, n.3; and Hirst, 169–88.
54 The contribution of convict labour to the establishment of New South Wales is particularly well documented in Nicholas, *op.cit.*, n.3. The percentage of slaves in state populations in the first half of the nineteenth century ranged from 57% in South Carolina to 1.3% in Delaware. A rough average is 32%, Stampp, *op.cit.*, n.15, 32.
55 *Op.cit.* n.37.
56 H.L.A. Hart, *Punishment and Responsibility* 4–5. In a widely regarded article Herbert Morris points out the profoundly different consequeces of incarcerating people for punishment rather than for rehabilitation. The comparison between the prison and the asylum is apt here. To treat criminals rather than to punish them, he argues, denies their humanity. 'Persons and Punishment' (1968) *The Monist* 54, 475. Similarly, sentencing structures based on retributivism have been determinate. By contrast rehabilitation has led to indeterminate sentences based on the time taken to be 'cured' rather than a fixed measure based on just desert. Ideas like these also affected day to day conditions in New South Wales through policies recommended, for example, in the Bigge Reports. Loveless, *op.cit.* n.6, 40, noticed the effect of policy shifts in Tasmania: 'I can assure my Lord Stanley, who boasted a few years since that he would make transportation worse than death, that his cruel and diabolical purpose is more than accomplished; for it would be doing such unfortunate men a kindness – a favour; it would be granting them an unspeakable privilege to hang them in England, and so prevent their exposure to the cruelties, miseries, and wretchedness connected with the present system of transportation to the Australian colonies.' See too Shaw, *op.cit.* n.45, esp. ch.9, 'Increasing Severity'.
57 Holmes, *The Common Law* (Macmillan, New York, 1968), 7.
58 New South Wales, *Report of the Committee on Police and Goals, 1839*, Evidence, 93 and 95. Of course many of the concerns of this committee, and another on the same subject in 1835 and the controversies over who should pay for the police in the 1840s turned on the very fact that New South Wales was used by England as a place to send convicts. See ch.6.
59 See Hirst, *op.cit.*, n.3, 95, 107, 138.
60 E. Durkheim, *On the Division of Labour in Society* (Free Press, New York, 1933), 70–85; R. Barthes, *Mythologies* (Cape, London, 1972), 43; S. Hall et al., *op.cit.*, n.37, 18–28; M. Sturma, *op.cit.*, n.7, chs.. 2, 3; and D. Philips, *Crime and Authority in Victorian England* (Croom Helm, London, 1977), chs. 1, 2. See too E.P. Thompson's reference to the

analytically disabling tendency of the crime label, in *Whigs and Hunters* (Pantheon, New York, 1975), 193–4.

61 John Hirst, for example, makes repeated references to the convicts as 'professional thieves' and 'professional criminals', *op.cit.*, n.3, 32–3, 73, 83, 143.

62 L. Robson, *op.cit.*, n.7; A.G.L. Shaw, *op.cit.*, n.45. The long debate over the nature of convicts sent to Australia is generally based on the following works: G.A. Wood, 'Convicts' (1922) *JRAHS* 7, 177; E. O'Brien, *The Foundation of Australia* (Sheed and Ward, London, 1937); C.M.H. Clark, *op.cit.* n.7, 121–35, 314–27; M.B. and C.B. Schedvin, 'The Nomad Tribes of Urban Britain: A Prelude to Botany Bay' (1978) *Hist. Studs.* 18, 254; the two works by Shaw and Robson, and most recently, Hughes, *op.cit.*, n.3, 155. It certainly fails to evince the sensitivity to crime and the criminal process shown by Philips, *op.cit.*, n.60, for example. The work of a team of historians at the University of New South Wales on the socio-economic backgrounds of convicts transported to Australia also suggests that the professional criminal tag is inappropriate, see Nicholas, *op.cit.*, n.3.

63 Robson, *ibid.*, 18.

64 Robson, *ibid.*, 178. Cf. Shaw's study of the total transported convict population which shows 25 per cent of the convicts transported from England came from London. Over one-third of the English convicts came from the urban areas of London and Lancashire. These were disproportionately *first* offenders, 151–2.

65 Robson, 91.

66 Robson, 209. In both groups the information was not recorded in over half the cases.

67 Robson, 89–91.

68 Robson, 190

69 Robson, 182.

70 Nicholas,*op.cit.*, n.3, esp chs. 5 and 6.

71 Robson, 210. The next largest category is animal theft, 14 per cent. Shaw's data shows 90 per cent of the English convicts committed some form of theft, 153–4.

72 Shaw, *op.cit.*, n.45, 164. He has a better opinion of the Irish convicts, 166 ff.

73 On bias in crime reporting, Philips, *op.cit.*, n.60, ch.1, esp. 17–21. See too Sturma, *op.cit.*, n.6.

74 Philips, *ibid.*; Nicholas, *op.cit.*, n.3, 74, summarises some of the English work. In addition, Jennifer Davis, Peter Linebaugh and Raphael Samuel all have work in progress on crime, culture and work in late eighteenth/early nineteenth-century London.

75 'Of course, many of the juveniles were professionals.' Shaw, *op.cit.*, n.45, 161. See too Robson, 18.

76 Shaw, *op.cit.*, n.45, 160.

77 See for example, W. Ullathorne, *The Horrors of Transportation Briefly Unfolded* (Dublin, 1938), 20; F. Crowley, 'Working Class Conditions in

NOTES TO PAGES 49-52 215

Australia 1788–1851' (unpublished PhD thesis, University of Melbourne, 1949), 38.
78 Hirst, 57–69; Nicholas, *op.cit.*, n.3, 180–3.
79 A.H. King, 'Police Organization and Administration in the Middle District of New South Wales 1825–1851' (MA thesis, University of Sydney, 1956a), 271–2. Shaw, *op.cit.*, n.45, 202. N. Townsend cites the following average number of lashes: 1831 = 58, 1834 = 38, 1837 = 45, and the ratio of one convict in every five flogged, in 'A "Mere Lottery": The Convict System in New South Wales Through the Eyes of the Molesworth Committee' (1985) *Push From the Bush* 21, 66. Cf. Nicholas, *op.cit.*, n.3, 180–3.
80 Bourke tendered a list of illegal punishments in support of his legislation, A.H. King, *Richard Bourke* (Oxford University Press, Melbourne, 1971), 162. Only eight years previously an enquiry had found that illegal floggings ordered by magistrates had been widespread in the colony since the early days, Great Britain, *Papers Relating to the Conduct of Magistrates in New South Wales, in Directing the Infliction of Punishments Upon Prisoners in that Colony*, House of Commons 1826. The extent of the practice was thought serious enough to warrant indemnity legislation retrospective to 1788! See 6 Geo. IV No. 18 (1825).
81 On the use of the courts by convicts, see A. Atkinson, 'Four Patterns of Convict Protest' (1979) *Labour History* 37, 28, and N. Townsend, *op.cit.*, n.79, 66. On court protection of slaves see n.19 above and the sources cited.
82 King, *op.cit.*, n.79, 272. Fletcher's deposition is in New South Wales, *Inquiry into the Queanbeyan Bench, 1840*, Appendix.
83 As Catholic chaplain, Ullathorne was in a good position to observe his charges at close quarters: *op.cit.*, n.77, 20–7. I am indebted to Ullathorne's biographer, Paul Collins, for this point. Harris, *Settlers and Convicts* (Melbourne University Press, Melbourne, 1953), 12; T. Crofton Croker, *Memoirs of Joseph Holt: General of the Irish Rebels, 1798* (Henry Colburn, London, 1838), vol 2, 118–23; Backhouse, *op.cit.*, n.41, 438., 443, 447, 455, App. O. On James Wright, see New South Wales, *Inquiry into the Queanbeyan Bench, 1840*, ff.17–9.
84 Genovese, *op.cit.*, n.15, 65.
85 *Op. cit.*, n.77, 20–7.
86 Crowley, *op.cit.*, n.77, 38.
87 Harris, *op.cit.*, n.83, 13.
88 Backhouse, *op. cit.*, n.41, 455.
89 *Op.cit.*, n.3, 69.
90 Crowley, *op.cit.*, n.77, 48–9.
91 Shaw, *op.cit.*, n.45, 205–11; Loveless, *op.cit.*, n.35, 36; Hirst, 77; see the evidence of Chief Justice Forbes to the Molesworth Committee, *Molesworth Report*, 86–7. The Catholic chaplain, Ullathorne, gave the same evidence, *Molesworth Report*, 27. Hughes gives a brilliant account of Norfolk Island and of Maconochie's battles, *op.cit.*, n.3, ch.13.

92 M. Clarke, *His Natural Life*, ch.15; P. Grabosky, *Sydney in Ferment: Crime, Dissent and Official Reaction 1788–1973* (Australian National University Press, Canberra, 1977), 66. The execution rates are calculated on population figures of 50,000 in New South Wales and 12,000,000 for England in the 1830s. There were some 26,000 male convicts in New South Wales at this time.

93 See D. Hay, 'Property, Authority and the Criminal Law' in D. Hay et al., *Albion's Fatal Tree* (Pantheon, New York, 1975), 17; and J. Walter, 'Grain Riots and Popular Attitudes to the Law' in J. Brewer and J. Styles, *An Ungovernable People: The English and Their Law in the Seventeenth and Eighteenth Centuries* (Rutgers University Press, New Jersey, 1980), 47.

94 See chap 4.

95 On standing to sue see ch.7. On the social distinctions see Hughes, *op.cit.*, n.3, 341–2.

96 A.H. King, *op.cit.*, n.79, 76–9, and App.L. Policing is discussed in detail in ch.6.

97 D'Arcy Wentworth to Commissioner Bigge, in J. Ritchie, *The Evidence to the Bigge Reports* (Heinemann, Melbourne, 1971), I, 48.

98 Harris, *op.cit.*, n.83, 75–84, 142ff.; 165ff.; J. Tucker, *The Adventures of Ralph Rashleigh* (Currey O'Neil, Melbourne, 1981), 163; J. Demarr, *Adventures in Australia Fifty Years Ago* extracted in R. Ward and J. Robertson, *Such was Life: Selected Documents in Australian Social History, 1788–1850* (Ure Smith, Sydney, 1969), 248–52; and J.C. Byrne, 'Twelve Years Wanderings in the British Colonies 1835–1847' in Ward and Robertson, *ibid.*, 244–8.

99 Hannibal Macarthur to P. King, *King Papers* I, f.259, ML. See ch.5.

100 See ch.5.

101 A. Castles, *An Australian Legal History* (Law Book Co., Sydney, 1982), 47–50; and J. Bennett, 'The Status and Authority of the Deputy Judge Advocates in New South Wales' (1958) *Sydney L.R.* 2, 502. See also ch.7.

102 Bent to Liverpool, 19/10/1811, *HRA* IV, I, 59.

103 A. Castles, 'The Judiciary and Political Questions' (1975) *Adelaide L. R.* 5, 294; J. Bennett, 'The Establishment of Jury Trial in New South Wales', (1961) *Sydney University L. R.*, 3, 483. See also ch.7.

104 *HRA* IV, I, 171.

105 See ch.7.

106 Eagar to Commissioner Bigge, in J. Ritchie, *op.cit.*, n.97, II, 10–11.

107 Sturma, *op.cit.*, n.7, 30.

108 E.P. Thompson, *The Making of the English Working Class* (Pelican, Harmondsworth, 1968), 9–11.

109 For comments from the free and the freed, respectively, see the quotation from Governor Darling and Edward Eagar, above, and the quotation from Hannibal Macarthur at the head of ch.6. For the colonial masters, see the instructions from Bathurst to Bigge, also quoted

above, and at the Colonial Office, James Stephen's comments about reconciling the demands of a colony with those of a gaol, quoted in King, *Richard Bourke, op.cit.*, n.80, 139–40. Numerous witnesses to the Molesworth Committee refer to New South Wales as a penal colony: see e.g. *Molesworth Report*, Mitchell, 79; Lang, 264–5; Bourke, 232; Burton, 78; Breton, 136; James Macarthur, 9–13; cf. Parry 70–2.
110   See ch.3.
111   Many of these will be choices of degree and will depend on the relative opportunities open to other members of the society. As Philip Pettit puts it: 'the choices should be sufficiently rich by local standards for him to count as a full member of the community.' See, 'The Freedom of the City' in A. Hamlin and P. Pettit (eds.), *The Good Polity* (Blackwell, Oxford, 1989).

Chapter 3

1   From the preface to M. Hale, *The History of the Pleas of the Crown* (Professional Books, London, 1971). I am indebted to my colleague Michael Bersten for drawing this to my attention.
2   John Grant was a gentleman, transported to New South Wales. He wrote this ode as he was being re-transported to Norfolk Island, for writing a seditious letter to Governor King, *Peel Papers*, Add MSS 40357, ff 37–45, BL.
3   See Evatt's view, quoted in ch.1, pp.21–2. C.M.H. Clark, *A History of Australia* (Melbourne University Press, Melbourne), II, 38, for example, has this view of Chief Justice Francis Forbes. See ch.4, on the courts, for my argument that Ellis and Shaw have misunderstood the conflict between Governors Macquarie and Darling, respectively, and their judges. The leading constitutional histories are A.C.V. Melbourne, *Early Constitutional Development in Australia* (University of Queensland Press, St Lucia, 1963) and W. G. McMinn, *A Constitutional History of Australia* (Oxford University Press, Melbourne, 1979). John Hirst, *Convict Society and Its Enemies* (Allen and Unwin, Sydney, 1983) is an honourable exception to this parallelism.
4   Hughes' reference to Forbes' conflict with Governor Darling has the judge adopting the position that convicts had no rights, *The Fatal Shore* (Knopf, New York, 1986), 304. Nothing could be further from the truth, as Currey's biography, *Sir Francis Forbes* (Angus and Robertson, Sydney, 1968a), 341–8, would have revealed to him. On rights see Hughes, *ibid.* 19. His extensive bibliography does not refer to this book, Currey's other judicial biography, *The Brothers Bent* (Sydney University Press, Sydney, 1968b), nor to Castles, *An Australian Legal History* (Law Book Co., Sydney, 1982), nor to Melbourne or McMinn, *op.cit.*, n.3.
5   See ch.4.
6   A. Goodhart has classical references to the idea of the rule of law, not

of men. 'The Rule of Law and Absolute Sovereignty' (1958) *University of Pennsylvania L. R.* 106, 943, at 944. See too F. Hayek, *The Constitution of Liberty* (University of Chicago Press, Chicago, 1960), 164. But the phrase 'the rule of law' does not seem to have had the currency in the seventeenth and eighteenth century that it has, probably under Dicey's influence, in the twentieth: see A. Dicey, *Introduction to the Study of the Law of the Constitution* (Macmillan, London, 1939). Contemporaries tended to refer to the same ideas as British birthrights, the ancient constitution, Magna Carta, Habeas Corpus, legality, etc. I have not found the phrase used in Blackstone, for example, nor in the writings of the colonists in New South Wales, though the concepts are very strong in both.

7 D. Hay, 'Property, Authority and the Criminal Law' in D. Hay *et al.*, *Albion's Fatal Tree* (Pantheon, New York, 1975), 17; E. P. Thompson, *Whigs and Hunters* (Pantheon, New York, 1975).

8 See nn. 10 and 11, below.

9 F. Hayek, *The Road to Serfdom* (University of Chicago Press, Chicago, 1944), and *op.cit.*, n.6.

10 J.G.A. Pocock, *The Ancient Constitution and the Feudal Law: A Study of English Historical Thought in the Seventeenth Century* (Cambridge University Press, Cambridge, 1957). The collection of essays edited by Pocock, *Three British Revolutions: 1641, 1688, 1776* (Princeton University Press, New Jersey, 1980), shows the influence of his thesis. See too H. Nenner, *By Colour of Law: Legal Culture and Constitutional Politics in England 1660–1689* (University of Chicago Press, Chicago, 1977); A. Mockler, *Lions Under the Throne* (F. Muller, London, 1983); M. Landon, *The Triumph of the Lawyers: Their Role in English Politics 1678–89* (University of Alabama Press, 1970); C. Hill, *The Intellectual Origins of the English Revolution* (Oxford University Press, Oxford, 1980); Hayek, *op.cit.*, n.6.

11 The debate was started by E.P. Thompson, *op.cit.*, n.7 and Douglas Hay, *op.cit.*, n.7. Extrapolations and criticisms from Marxists and non-Marxists have been numerous. Among them see: J. Brewer and J. Styles, *An Ungovernable People: The English and Their Law in the Seventeenth and Eighteenth Centuries* (Rutgers University Press, New Jersey, 1980); S. Redhead, 'Marxist Theory, The Rule of Law and Socialism' in P. Beirne and R. Quinney, *Marxism and Law* (Wiley, New York, 1982), 328; S. Picciotto, 'The Theory of the State, Class Struggle and the Rule of Law' in *ibid.*, 169; N. Poulantzas, 'Law' in *ibid.*, 76; A. Hunt, 'Dichotomy and Contradiction in the Sociology of Law' in *ibid.*, 74; D. Brown and G. Zdenkowski, *Prison Struggle* (Penguin, Melbourne, 1982); A. Merritt, 'The Nature and Function of Law: A Criticism of E.P. Thompson's *Whigs and Hunters*' (1980) *British Journal of Law and Society*, 7, 194; M. Horwitz, 'The Rule of Law: An Unqualified Human Good?' (1977 *Yale L.J.* 86, 561; P. Anderson

Arguments Within English Marxism (New Left Books, London, 1980); B. Fine, *Democracy and the Rule of Law* (Pluto Press, London, 1984).
12 H. Nenner, *op.cit.*, n.10; D. Hay, *op.cit.*, n.7.
13 Lawrence Stone argues that the consequence of judicial independence was to free the judges to develop the country ideology of individual liberty in the eighteenth century, clearly exemplified in the General Warrants Case. See his, 'The Results of the English Revolutions of the Seventeenth Century' in J.G.A. Pocock, *op.cit.*, n.10, 23.
14 Hay, *op.cit.*, n.7.
15 J.G.A. Pocock, *The Machiavellian Moment: Florentine Political Thought and the Atlantic Republican Tradition* (Princeton University Press, New Jersey, 1975).
16 Thompson's critics have attacked him for over-stating the dichotomy between law and power. I will discuss this aspect of the debate in ch.8.
17 E. Coke, 'Prohibitions del Roy' I 77 E.R. 1343. See Pocock, *op.cit.*, n.15, for the provenance of the phrase. Blackstone also uses it, and refers to judges as living *oracles* of the law, *Commentaries* I, 77. Many volumes have been written on legal reasoning. See, e.g., J. Stone, *Legal Systems and Lawyers Reasonings* (Maitland, Sydney, 1964). See too M. Krygier, 'Law as Tradition' (1986) *Law and Philosophy* 5, 237 for his discussion of legal styles of argument.
18 For example, Hay stresses equality before the law of all social classes, at both ends of the social scale. He goes on to notice, however, that this only operated where the laws were applicable, thus masking the class nature of eighteenth-century legislation, *op.cit.*, n.7, 33. Jennings makes a similar point in his rebuttal of Dicey: see his *The Law and the Constitution* (University of London Press, London, 1933); and see H. Jones, 'The Rule of Law and the Welfare State' (1958) *Columbia L.R.* 58, 143. Hayek, *op.cit.*, n.6, 154 says classification is permissible so long as those inside and outside the designated category agree to it.
19 For Blackstone, the term separation of powers meant the division of government between King, Lords and Commons, *Commentaries* I, 52ff. He did, however, attach great importance to the independence of the judges and the courts in applying the settled law, *ibid.* I, 136–8, 257–71. I am indebted to David Lieberman for his assistance with Blackstone. Other eighteenth-century writers, D. Hume, *Essays: Moral, Political and Literary* (Oxford University Press, Oxford, 1963), 39; and W. Paley, *The Principles of Moral and Political Philosophy* (London, 1814), lay a similar stress on the separation of powers.
20 L.L. Fuller, *The Morality of Law* (Yale University Press, New York, 1964), 159–62; *contra* A. Goodhart, *op.cit.*, n.6; W. Friedmann, *The Planned State and the Rule of Law* (Melbourne University Press, Melbourne, 1948).
21 E.P. Thompson, cf. Redhead and Anderson, *op.cit.*, n.11.
22 The primary disputants here are L. Fuller, *op.cit.*, n.20, and H.L.A.

Hart, 'Positivism and the Separation of Law and Morals' (1958) *Harvard L.R.* 71, 593 and *The Concept of Law* (Oxford University Press, Oxford, 1961).

23 Those adopting this approach in the context of the rule of law include Goodhart *op.cit.*, n.6, and Friedmann, *op.cit.*, n.20; J. Raz, *The Authority of Law* (Clarendon Press, Oxford, 1979), 210–14, 219–29; and Wade in his introduction to A. Dicey, *op.cit.*, n.6, xciii.

24 Poulantzas has correctly attacked the notion that Stalin's terror can stand as an example of socialist legality, *op.cit.*, n.11, 190. Goodhart makes a similar point in relation to Hitler, *op.cit.*, n.6, 947–50. See too Jones, *op.cit.*, n.18, 149.

25 Fuller's eight canons of legality are set out in *op.cit.*, n.20, 33–41.

26 *Ibid.*, 159–62.

27 See J. Stone, *op.cit.*, n.17, and R. Dworkin, *Taking Rights Seriously* (Harvard University Press, Cambridge, 1987), for extended recent analyses of judicial reasoning, a major pre-occupation of jurisprudence. Picciotto points out the inherent tension between general rules laid down in advance and the requirement of certainty, *op.cit.*, n.11, 177; cf. Hayek, *The Constitution of Liberty*, *op.cit.*, n.6, 206.

28 See T. Kuhn, *The Structure of Scientific Revolutions* (University of Chicago Press, Chicago, 1962).

29 See the discussion of this issue in ch.4, text accompanying notes 107–112.

30 Goodhart, *op.cit.*, n.6, and Raz, *op.cit.*, n.23.

31 Anderson, *op.cit.*, n.11, 197; Hunt, *op.cit.*, n.11, 92.

32 R.W. Connell and T. Irving, *Class Structure in Australian History* (Longman Cheshire, Melbourne, 1980).

33 M. Landon, *op.cit.*, n.10 at 9, and the works cited at n.10.

34 Mockler, *op.cit.*, n.10, 27–33, and see Coke, *op.cit.*, n.17.

35 The first edition of Montesquieu, *The Spirit of the Laws* was not published until 1748. Pocock argues that the idea of separation of powers was the consequence of attempts to specify more closely the functions of the legislature, executive and judiciary. Note that while Blackstone stressed the importance of independent courts, the closest he comes to the idea of separation of powers is the mixed constitution of King, Lords and Commons which, for him, combined the features of monarchy, aristocracy and democracy, *op.cit.*, n.19, 52ff.

36 *Act of Settlement*, 1701, 13 Wm. III c.2..

37 Nenner, *op.cit.*, n.10, xiv, 3, 79, 110; R. Bendix, *Kings or People* (University of California Press, 1978) ch.9; Pocock, *op.cit.*, n.15, 19, traces the origins of the legal profession's claim to monopoly over the 'artificial reason' of the law to Fortescue. Blackstone tells how the king no longer exercises judicial power, *Commentaries* I, 77, 257–8.

38 L. Stone, *op.cit.*, n.13, 96; H. Dickinson, *Liberty and Property: Political Ideology in Eighteenth Century Britain* (Methuen, London, 1977), 63–4, 89, 162; J. Locke, *The Second Treatise on Government* (Bobbs Merrill,

New York, 1952); Blackstone, *Commentaries*, I, 121–4; D. Hume, *op.cit.*, n.19, 39, 95, 118, 125; A. Smith, *Lectures on Jurisprudence* (Oxford University Press, Oxford, 1978), 271–2; and Bentham, *Bentham Papers* BL, Add. MSS 33543, f603.

39 Maynard is quoted in Nenner, *op.cit.*, n.10, 8. Blackstone, *Commentaries*, I, 277–8. Various devices to avoid the jury were complained about by Blackstone, *ibid*. See too E.P. Thompson, *op.cit.*, n.7, 151–5, for a description of attempts to get around juries, and Brewer, 'The Wilkites and the Law' in Brewer and Styles, *op.cit.*, n.11, 128. In the American case, the grievance was that the *Sugar Act* provided for trial by an Admiralty judge alone and was assessed by the colonists as depriving them of the right to jury trial as guaranteed by the Magna Carta. See the essays by D. Lovejoy and J. Murrin in J.G.A. Pocock, *Three British Revolutions*, *op.cit.*, n.10, 258 and 380, respectively.

40 Of course, 'no taxation without representation' was a rallying cry of the American Revolution (e.g. Murrin, *ibid.*), but it was also a complaint of the 'middling sort' in England who were subject to heavy excise tax. J. Brewer, 'English Radicalism in the Age of George III' in Pocock, *op.cit.*, n.10, 323, 339ff; and Dickinson, *op.cit.*, n.38.

41 See ch.6. References to the debates and a discussion of the issues in relation to paid police forces may be found in D. Philips, "'A New Engine of Power and Authority': The Institutionalization of Law Enforcement in England 1780–1830" in Gatrell, Lenman and Parker, *Crime and the Law: The Social History of Crime in Western Europe Since 1500* (Europa, London, 1980); and D. Neal, 'The Role of Justices of the Peace in Relation to Popular Protest in Eighteenth Century England' (Unpublished MS., 1979). See too Pocock, *op.cit.*, n.15, 410–427, and L. Stone, *op.cit.*, n.13, 57–8.

42 C. Hill, *op.cit.*, n.10, 256; and G. Aylmer, *The Struggle for the Constitution* (Blandford, London, 1963), 35–6.

43 H. Nenner, *op.cit.*, n.10, ix.

44 D. Hay and E. P. Thompson, *op.cit.*, n.7; L. Stone *op.cit.*, n.10, 94; Brewer, *op.cit.*, n.40, 348. The idea emerges from the contemporary writers. See works cited in n.10.

45 Thompson, *op.cit.*, n.7, 263.

46 Blackstone, *Commentaries*, I, 52ff. See too L. Stone, *op.cit.*, n.13, 90. Blackstone's revolution blunting ideas were rejected by the American colonists, Stone, *ibid.*, 99.

47 D. Hay, *op.cit.*, n.7, 56; N. Poulantzas, *op.cit.*, n.11, 1983; P. Anderson, *op.cit.*, n.11, 197.

48 See n.46.

49 Hay, *op.cit.*, n.7.

50 See n.19.

51 J. Brewer, 'The Wilkites and the Law', *op.cit.*, n.7, and J. Brewer, *op.cit.*, n.40, 348; and Dickinson, *op.cit.*, n.38, esp. 89.

52 J. Langbein, 'Albion's Fatal Flaws' (1983) *Past and Present* 98, 1.

53 J. Brewer and J. Styles, *op.cit.*, n.11, 20.
54 On John Grant, see M. Hazzard, *Punishment Short of Death* (Hyland House, Melbourne, 1984), ch.10; on shipboard convict plays, see P. Cunningham, *Two Years in New South Wales* (Libraries Board of S.A., Adelaide, 1966), II, 237; on 'sea lawyers' see Hughes, *op.cit.*, n.4, 154.
55 On litigiousness, see Governor Bligh's criticism of Kable, Bligh to Windham, 31/10/1807, HRNSW VI, 148–9; see too Governor Darling to Hay, 6/2/1827, PRO, CO 323/146 and 323/149; and Commissioner Bigge on the question of whether the expedient adopted by one of the colony's judges, the non-suiting of emancipists whom he considered to be too litigious, could be supported, *Bigge Report* I, 136ff. On complaint to and about magistrates, see A. Atkinson, 'Four Patterns of Convict Protest' (1979) *Labour History* 37, 28. See too M. Sturma, *Vice in a Vicious Society: Crime and Convicts in Mid-Nineteenth Century New South Wales* (University of Queensland Press, St Lucia, 1983b). Paula Byrne has work in progress on the use of the courts by women, part of which is published in, 'Women and the Criminal Law: Sydney 1810–1821' (1985) *Push From the Bush* 21, 2.
56 See the articles by D.S. Lovejoy and J. Murrin in J.G.A. Pocock, *Three British Revolutions*, *op.cit.*, n.10;
57 As a measure of the mistrust of the radicals in the colony among the military, see T. G. Parsons, 'Was John Boston's Pig a Political Martyr?' (1985) *JRAHS* 71, 163.
58 The Governor of Minorca had to pay substantial damages in a suit for wrongful imprisonment brought on his return to England. The case occurred only shortly before the settlement of New South Wales and was well-known in colonial circles. See *Mostyn v Fabrigas* (1773) Cowp. 161.
59 Cited in V. Windeyer, 'A Birthright and Inheritance' (1962) *University of Tasmania L.R.* 1, 635.
60 *Ibid.*, 643–4.
61 See ch.4.
62 Forbes to Under-Secretary Horton, 20/9/1827, HRA IV, I, 735–6. See too M. Roe, 'Colonial Society in Embryo' (1956) *Hist. Studs*, 7, 153; and M. Sturma, *op.cit.*, n.55, 184.
63 What pleases the Governor has the force of law. Quoted in Currey, *The Brothers Bent*, *op.cit.*, n.4, 115.
64 Forbes to Wilmot-Horton, 14/8/1824 *Catton Papers* DCL ABC WH 2753–55.
65 H.V. Evatt, *op.cit.*, n.3, ch.36; and A. Atkinson, 'The British Whigs and the Rum Rebellion' (1980) *JRAHS* 73, 84–6; R. Fitzgerald and M. Hearn, *Bligh, Macarthur and the Rum Rebellion* (Kangaroo Press, Sydney, 1969).
66 See Ellis, *Lachlan Macquarie* (Angus and Robertson, Sydney, 1969), 339.
67 Darling to Hay, 6/2/1827, PRO CO 323/149 f190.

68 *Molesworth Report*, 221–2.
69 Reproduced in James Macarthur's book, *New South Wales: Its Present State and Future Prospects* (London, 1837).
70 J. Mudie, *The Felonry of New South Wales* (Whaley, London, 1837).
71 Saxe-Bannister to Darling, 9/9/1826, PRO CO 323/146 f208.
72 Darling to Hay, 11/9/1826, PRO CO 323/146 f202.
73 See ch.6
74 *R. v. Jack Congo Murrell* (1836). See Castles, *op.cit.*, n.4.
75 See Castles, *ibid.*, 76
76 See ch.6.
77 See chs.4 and 5.
78 See ch.7.
79 See ch.4.

Chapter 4

1 A. Smith, *Lectures on Jurisprudence* (Oxford University Press, Oxford, 1978), 271.
2 Forbes to Horton, 20/9/1827, HRA, IV, I, 735–6.
3 It had been argued that England did have a fundamental law in such documents as the Magna Carta, but no one in the seventeenth century was prepared to push this to its logical conclusion, H. Nenner, *By Colour of Law* (University of Chicago Press, Chicago, 1977), 17. The supremacy of Parliament allows it in theory to overrule Magna Carta and the Bill of Rights by legislation. English courts could only declare legislation procedurally defective. They could not declare legislation unconstitutional in the way that written constitutions allow the US Supreme Court or the Australian High Court to overrule their respective legislatures. Lawrence Stone comments that courts such as these would have delighted Coke. See 'The Results of the English Revolutions of the Seventeenth Century' in J.G.A. Pocock, *Three British Revolutions 1642, 1688 and 1776* (Princeton University Press, New Jersey, 1980), 99.
4 For example, W. Tench said that had it not been for the clause, they would not have known how to run the courts, cited in V. Windeyer, '"A Birthright and Inheritance": The Establishment of the Rule of Law in Australia' (1962) *University of Tasmania L.R.* 1, 652. Governor King justified his exercise of legislative power and overruling of the court on the nature of the colony, see M. Roe, 'Colonial Society in Embryo' (1956) *Hist. Studs.* 7, 199.
5 Section 24, 4 Geo. IV. C.96 (1823). Section 29 of the Act required the Chief Justice to certify that colonial legislation was 'not repugnant to the law of England, but is consistent with those laws, so far as the circumstances of the said Colony will admit'.
6 See the discussion of the 'artificial reason of the law', ch.3.
7 E. Nepean to Lord Sydney, 9/11/1786, ML, MS An 5311.

8   27 Geo. III, c. 2 (1787).
9   *Ibid.*
10   See e.g. Governor Phillip's Second Commission, HRA I, I, 2.
11   4 Geo. IV, c.96, s.4.
12   A warrant containing a charter is part of the machinery of executive government. Usually it has to be based on legislation but in the case of the Civil Court in New South Wales there was no such legislation. Windeyer argues that the Crown could establish courts in Crown colonies without legislative authorisation, *op.cit.*, n.4, 638, 649. He also argues that New South Wales, although established by statute, was in fact a crown colony and that this is recognized both in the language of the statute (i.e. 27 Geo. III, c. 2) and the other documentation, such as the Charter of Justice, *ibid.* 649. This is important on the issue of the legal validity of the governor's orders in the colony.
13   The First Charter of Justice, HRA IV, I, 6.
14   *Ibid.*
15   How long the practice of allowing convicts under sentence to sue persisted after the Kables' case is unclear. In the early 1800s, the convict lawyer George Crossley pleaded his conviction to avoid being sued. Governor King responded by granting him a full pardon. Woinarski comments that the colonists' belief about this was wrong and that felons could *be* sued, but not sue in English law, 'The History of Legal Institutions in Victoria' (Unpublished Ll.D. thesis, University of Melbourne, 1942), 187. The Select Committee on Transportation 1812, heard evidence that convicts under sentence could not sue or be sued (*Great Britain, Report of the Select Committee on Transportation,* 1812), 6–7. Emancipists, ticket-of-leave holders, and holders of conditional pardons, who technically were still under attaint, but did use the courts, *Bigge Report* I, 131 and II, 7. Convicts under sentence certainly used the magistrates' courts. They may also have used the Civil Court more than this evidence suggests. The issue of emancipist legal status came up sharply in the early 1820s, see below.
16   HRA IV, I, 6, at 10. Blackstone confirms that British settlers take with them such of the law of England as is applicable to the circumstances of the colony. *Commentaries* I, 104, a legal nostrum the colonists were more than ready to quote. This applied to the convicts too, hence the provision of the Criminal Court for trial of new crimes committed in the colony. Blackstone makes the point that even convicts retain rights such that they can only be transported pursuant to their own consent or by legislative authorisation, *ibid.*, 133. The other methods of colonisation (conquest, cession, charter) had different legal consequences, notably with respect to recognition of the rights and legal systems of indigenous people. See Windeyer, *op.cit.*, n.4; 649 and A. Castles, *An Australian Legal History* (Law Book Co., Sydney, 1982), chs.1 and 18. These doctrines are tellingly analysed by H. Reynolds, *The Law of the Land* (Penguin, Melbourne, 1987b).
17   *Mostyn v. Fabrigas* (1774) Cowp. 161

18 See C. Currey, *The Brothers Bent* (Sydney University Press, Sydney, 1968b), 157.
19 Bentham, *A Plea for a Constitution* (London, 1803); James Stephen's opinion can be found in HRA IV, I, 412. The point is discussed by Windeyer, *op.cit.*, n.4, 649; Castles, *op.cit.*, n.16, 35–8; E. Campbell, 'Prerogative Rule in New South Wales 1788–1823' (1964) *JRAHS* 50, 161; and S. Woinarski, *op.cit.*, n.15, 100–2. It may be that on a necessity argument, pre-1823 the governors had a limited legislative power.
20 Judges in England held office during good behaviour while those in the colony held during royal pleasure. The commissions for judges of the Supreme Court made this explicit. See e.g. Jeffery Bent's commission, HRA IV, I, 94. In the case of judge-advocates it seems to have been implied.
21 Judge Advocate Ellis Bent and his brother Jeffery were recalled. See below. Ellis Bent had called for removal by the King only, C. Currey, *op.cit.*, n.18, 60. Governor Darling tried unsuccessfully to get Chief Justice Forbes 'retired' and suggested his health as a pretext. Castles, *op.cit.*, n.16, suggests that the colony was too small and faction-ridden to grant judges life tenure. The Exclusives complained that the judges were too vulnerable to dismissal at the behest of the governor, M. Roe, *The Quest for Authority in Eastern Australia 1835–1851* (Melbourne University Press, Melbourne, 1965), 43.
22 Hunter to Portland, 21/9/1799, HRNSW III, 547.
23 King to Hobart, 7/8/1803, HRNSW V, 187.
24 Bligh to Castlereagh, 28/10/1808, HRNSW VI, 787.
25 The petition is dated 1/1/1808, HRNSW VI, 411. Bligh's letter is to Windham, 31/10/1807, HRNSW VI, 355.
26 Great Britain, *Report of the Select Committee on Transportation* 1812, vol II, 341; and Balmain to Banks, 24/5/1802, HRA IV, I, 35.
27 Commission of Judge-Advocate Bent, Jan 1/1/1809, HRA IV, I, 46.
28 See e.g. the commission of the First Judge-Advocate, David Collins, HRA IV, I, 1.
29 Collins 1788–1976; Atkins 1796–7, 1800–1810. See *Australian Dictionary of Biography* for details of the early judge-advocates. See too Castles, *op.cit.*, n.16, *passim*.
30 *Bigge Report*, II, 34; Eagar to Bathurst, 3/4/1823, HRA IV, I, 444.
31 This despite the fact that he had only practised for four years, Currey, *op.cit.*, n.18, 42.
32 *Inter alia*, he makes these complaints in four long reports to the Colonial Office. See Bent to Cooke, 7/5/1810, HRA IV, I, 48; Bent to Liverpool, 19/10/1811, *ibid.*, 57 esp. 62; Bent to Bathurst, 14/10/1814, *ibid.*, 100; and, Bent to Bathurst, 1/7/1815, *ibid.*, 122, in which Bent reports his refusal to draft port regulations as ordered by the governor.
33 See H.V. Evatt, *Rum Rebellion* (Angus and Robertson, Sydney, 1938), esp. ch.20.
34 Re seizure of stills, *ibid.*, re criminal libel, Currey, *op.cit.*, n.18, 17; re intimidation of civil magistrate, Evatt, *ibid*, 14, ch.VII; re prosecutions

of Macarthur, *ibid.*, n.107–130. See too T. G. Parsons, 'Was John Boston's Pig a Political Martyr?' (1985) *JRAHS* 71, 163, discussed in ch.2, above.
35 *Op.cit.*, n.33, esp. 123–139 and ch.48.
36 Memorandum by Governor King reporting Macarthur's statement, *HRA* IV, I, 43–4, cf. Windeyer, *op.cit.*, n.4, 644–7, on the king's power in Crown colonies.
37 Bentham's correspondence on the issue includes a letter from Romilly agreeing with the opinion and expressing his astonishment, *Bentham Papers*, BL20/8/1802, ff 601. He sent the same letter to Fox, Dumont and Abbott. He predicted that the colony would burst into flame when the issue came out and all the colonial officials would be ruined over and again by law suits, *ibid.* f. 603.
38 See works cited at n.19.
39 The incidents are described in detail in C. Currey, *op.cit.*, n.18. The appointment of Ellis Bent's brother Jeffery to the Civil Court in 1814 added fuel to the fire. Jeffery was a much more prickly character than his brother. Currey speculates that Ellis Bent may not have been so bold had it not been for the support of his brother, *ibid.*, ch.3. Cf. M. Ellis, *Lachlan Macquarie* (Angus and Robertson, Sydney, 1969) who slights the issues of principle involved in the Bents' opposition to Macquarie. John Ritchie, *Lachlan Macquarie* (Heinemann, Melbourne, 1971), sees the issues of principle in these disputes, esp. 144–66.
40 Bent to Bathurst, 1/7/1815, *HRA* IV, I, 122, at 125. The letter rehearses in great detail the issues and events referred to in the text.
41 Macquarie to Bathurst 24/2/1815, *HRA* VII, I, 394.
42 Bathurst to Ellis Bent, 11/12/1815, *HRA* IV, I, 170 at 172.
43 Currey, *op.cit.*, n.18, 95.
44 *Ibid.*, 130.
45 *Ibid.*, 131.
46 Bligh to Windham, 31/10/1807, *HRA* VI, I, 149; D. Hainsworth, *The Sydney Traders: Simeon Lord and his Contemporaries* (Melbourne University Press, Melbourne, 1981), 1–34 for a detailed treatment of the mechanics of wealth accumulation by the officers. See too Currey *op.cit.*, n.18, ch.1, and Evatt, *op.cit.*, n.33; and R. Fitzgerald and M. Hearn, *Bligh, Macarthur and the Rum Rebellion* (Kangaroo Press, Sydney, 1988).
47 See n.25 and accompanying text.
48 See ch.2.
49 D. Hainsworth, *op.cit.*, n.46, 1–11.
50 For example, M.H. Ellis, *op.cit.*, n.39, 376 describes the bitter social war waged between Macquarie and the officers of the 46th regiment. It is but one of numerous examples. Bigge devotes pages and pages of his report to Macquarie's attempts to 'force' emancipists on society.
51 See discussions of this policy in *Bigge Report*, I, 80–90, and M.H. Ellis *ibid.*, ch.17.
52 *Bigge Report, ibid.*

53 See *Australian Dictionary of Biography*, and Castles, *op.cit.*, n.16, 98–9, 106–7 and *passim*.
54 E. Bent to Cooke, 7/5/1810, HRA IV, I, 54.
55 E. Bent to Bathurst, 1/7/1815, HRA IV, I, 1404.
56 Emancipist merchant Simeon Lord, was made a member of the Civil Court by Macquarie in 1817. Mr Justice Field had confidence in his judgment but felt that his lack of literacy was a drawback, HRA IV, I, 780. For Bigge's criticism see *Bigge Report*, I, 82–3.
57 Second Charter of Justice, HRA IV, I, 77.
58 S. Woinarski, *op.cit.*, n.15, 588.
59 On litigiousness, see Bligh, *op.cit.*, n.43; E. Bent to J. Bent, 9/3/1810 and 2/5/1810, Letter Book NL, MS 195, ff.121–168 ; *Bigge Report*, II, 8; On Lord, see Hainsworth, *op.cit.*, n.46, 100.
60 A. de Tocqueville, *Democracy in America* 265.
61 A blow by blow account of the events is contained in J. Bent to Bathurst, 1/7/1815, HRA IV, I, 144. See too C. Currey, *op.cit.*, n.18, 109 ff; and M. Ellis, *op.cit.*, n.39, chs. 20–1.
62 Bent to Bathurst, *ibid.*, at 154.
63 *Ibid.*, 155.
64 *Ibid.*, 147.
65 *Ibid.*, 156.
66 *Ibid.*, 159.
67 *Ibid.*, 152–3.
68 Bent to Bathurst 4/11/1815, *ibid.*, 162; C. Currey, *op.cit.*, n.18, 119 ff.
69 *Ibid.*, 139 ff.
70 Bathurst to Bent, 12/4/1816, HRA I, IX, 112, cited in M.H. Ellis, *op.cit.*, n.39, 312–3.
71 *Ibid.*
72 4 Geo. IV. c 96.
73 These issues are discussed in ch.7.
74 Section 24.
75 Sections 24–5.
76 Section 29. Forbes reminded the Colonial Office that he had opposed this provision, presumably because of separation of powers problems. His opposition proved prescient. Cf. C.M.H. Clark who wrongly thinks that the local circumstances clause 'promised much intellectual sport in which Forbes could excel' and that the repugnancy clause was 'pleasing to his vanity', *A History of Australia* (Melbourne University Press, Melbourne, 1962), II, 38. Clark notes later that Forbes *asked* to be relieved of this duty, *ibid.*, 83.
77 Section 18.
78 Section 1. The provision for an Attorney-General, however, lightened some of the load borne in the preliminary stages of cases, drawing the informations, etc.
79 Section 2. The functions of these courts are explained in Castles, *op.cit.*, n.16, ch.7.
80 Sections 3, 9, 10 respectively

81 Section 4.
82 *Ibid.*
83 *Ibid.*
84 Section 6.
85 Section 8 and see ch.7.
86 Sections 13–16. Forbes' remarks are in HRA IV, I, 656.
87 Section 19. See chs. 5 and 7.
88 See ch.5.
89 Section 20.
90 The availability of the prerogative writs was implied from the fact that the Supreme Court was to have the same powers as the courts at Westminster. See Castles, *op.cit.*, n.16, where the point is discussed at greater length.
91 See James Macarthur's evidence, *Molesworth Report*, 221–2; Alexander Harris, *Settlers and Convicts* (Melbourne University Press, Melbourne, 1953), 81.
92 Forbes to Horton, 22/3/1827, HRA IV, I, 716–7.
93 HRA I, X, 634 discussed in F. Crowley, 'Working Class Conditions in Australia 1788–1851' (Unpublished PhD thesis, University of Melbourne, 1949), 269 ff.
94 See ch.7.
95 See ch.7.
96 See ch.5.
97 This is the Sudds-Thompson affair, described by C. Currey, *Sir Francis Forbes* (Angus and Robertson, Sydney, 1968a), ch.18.
98 See John Brewer, 'The Wilkites and the Law' in J. Brewer and J. Styles, *An Ungovernable People*, 128.
99 Darling to Hay, 2/9/1826, PRO, CO 323/146 f.193; 31/1/1827 *ibid.*, f 274; and 6/2/1827, PRO, CO 323/149 ff 166–8; and 9/2/1827, *ibid*, ff. 209–11.
100 See C. Currey, *op.cit.*, n.97, 202–35.
101 S.9 *Australian Courts Act* 9 Geo. IV, c.83.
102 Darling to Murray, 6/7/1829, HRA I, XV, 53.
103 HRA I, XV, 346.
104 HRA I, XIV, 767–9.
105 Murray to Darling, 8/11/1830, HRA I, XV, 810.
106 An honourable exception to this is Currey, *op.cit.*, n.97, ch. 31, who deserves to be read much more widely. I am indebted to him on this issue.
107 C.M.H. Clark, *op.cit.*, n.76, 38.
108 J. Hirst, *Convict Society and Its Enemies* (Allen and Unwin, Sydney, 1983), 304–5.
109 R. Hughes, *The Fatal Shore* (Knopf, New York, 1986), 304–5.
110 A.G.L. Shaw, *Convicts and the Colonies* (Melbourne University Press, Melbourne, 1977), 233–4.

111 Darling to Murray 8/11/1830, HRA I, XV, 810.
112 D. Hay, 'Property, Authority and the Criminal Law' in D. Hay et al., Albion's Fatal Tree (Pantheon, New York, 1975), 17.

Chapter 5

1   H. Fisher (ed.), The Collected papers of Frederick William Maitland, 468–9.
2   Hall to Murray, 2/5/1829, HRA I, XV, 64–5.
3   See two articles by David Philips, 'A New Engine of Power and Authority: The Institutionalization of Law Enforcement in England 1780–1830' in Gatrell, Lenman and Parker, Crime and the Law: The Social History of Crime in Western Europe Since 1500 (Europa, London, 1980), 155, esp. 160–1; and 'The Black Country Magistracy 1835–60' (1976) Midland History, 173 and D. Neal, 'The Role of the Justices of the Peace in Relation to Popular Protest in Eighteenth Century England' (unpublished, 1979).
4   First Charter of Justice HRA IV, I, 6.
5   Edw. 3 c.1 (1361). Their predecessors, Conservators of the Peace were created in the 12th century. Significantly in terms of central authority, the Conservators were elected by local freeholders but the justices were appointed by the king, Osborne, Justices of the Peace 1361–1848, (Sedgehill Press, Shaftesbury, 1960) 3.
6   R. Burn, The Justice of the Peace and Parish Officer (Sweet, London, 1837).
7   J. Plunkett, The Australian Magistrate, Or a Guide to the Duties of a Justice of the Peace for the Colony of New South Wales (Ann Howe, Sydney, 1835). Plunkett contained 428 pages and a 40-page appendix.
8   In theory at least, landed property gave its owner the leisure to consider the common good and to perform civic duties, J.G.A. Pocock, The Machiavellian Moment (Princeton University Press, New Jersey, 1875), 390. On the legal form of government in England, see J. Brewer and J. Styles, An Ungovernable People (Rutgers University Press, New Jersey, 1980), 13–14.
9   Quarter sessions could hear all criminal cases except those involving legal technicalities. In practice they did not hear capital cases, leaving these to assize judges from London. See A. Castles, An Australian Legal History (Law Book Co., Sydney, 1982), 69. Examples of the sorts of offences and punishments handed out in these 'petty sessions' may be found in the collection from contemporary accounts by J. Cobley, Sydney Cove 1788 (Hodder and Stoughton, London, 1962), 49, 136, 164, 260; and Castles, ibid, 67–89.
10 John Hunter, Governor Hunter's Remarks on the Causes of Colonial Expense of the Establishment of New South Wales (London, 1802), 51–2.
11 E. Le Roy Ladurie, Montaillou (Penguin, Harmondsworth, 1980).

12 R. Bendix, *Kings or People* (University of California Press, Berkeley, 1978), 176–200, esp. 199–200.
13 See ch.2.
14 For example, Hobsbawm and Rudé, *Captain Swing* (Norton, New York, 1968); E.P. Thompson, 'The Moral Economy of the English Crowd in the Eighteenth Century' (1971) *Past and Present* 50, 76; J. Walter, 'Grain Riots and Popular Attitudes to the Law' in J. Brewer and J. Styles, *op. cit.*, n.8, 470; Neal, *op.cit.*, n.3; and Philips, *op.cit.*, n.3.
15 A. Atkinson, 'Four Patterns of Convict Protest' (1979) *Labour History* 37, 28.
16 The Colonial Office could override the governor but it was rare, e.g., the censure of Governor Macquarie over the appointment of the emancipist Redfern, HRA I, X, 310.
17 For example, the *Australian* 8/7/29 titillated its readers in this way about a forthcoming commission but refrained from mentioning names.
18 They were Ellis Bent and John Wylde. For Bent see M. Philips, *A Colonial Autocracy* (P.S. King, Sydney, 1909), 76. For Wylde, see his evidence to Bigge, HRA IV, I, 811. A prominent free settler and magistrate, Alexander Riley, had given a similar criticism in evidence to the 1819 Committee of Inquiry in England. Cited in A.C.V. Melbourne, *Early Constitutional Development in Australia* (University of Queensland Press, St Lucia, 1963), 54–5.
19 See Macquarie's memorandum on Wylde's evidence to Bigge, HRA VI, I, 878–9.
20 They were Andrew Thomson and Simeon Lord in 1810 and Henry Fulton in 1812. Another emancipist, Redfern was appointed in 1819. Bigge discusses each of these appointments in elaborate detail, *Bigge Report* I, 80.
21 Stephen to Under Secretary Wilmot Horton, 27/3/25, HRA IV, I, 602–3.
22 Quoted in J. Bennett and A. Castles, *A Source Book of Australian Legal History* (Law Book Co., Sydney, 1979), 99.
23 HRA IV, I, 336.
24 A.H. King, *Richard Bourke* (Oxford University Press, Melbourne, 1971), 238–40.
25 HRNSW VI, 518 and H. Evatt, *Rum Rebellion* (Angus and Robertson, Sydney, 1938), 75.
26 See the account of the Ann Rumsby affair and subsequent dismissal of four magistrates by Brisbane in Currey, *Sir Francis Forbes: The First Chief Justice of the Supreme Court of New South Wales* (Angus and Robertson, Sydney, 1968a), 51–66.
27 For Bourke's dismissals, see M. Roe, *The Quest for Authority in Eastern Australia* (Melbourne University Press, Melbourne, 1965), 25–7; King, *op.cit.*, n.24, 238–40.
28 *Sydney Gazette* 28/3/1818.
29 *Bigge Report*, I, 80ff.

30 See Currey, *op.cit.*, n.26, 52–66.
31 For example, Great Britain, *Papers Relating to the Conduct of Magistrates in New South Wales in Directing the Infliction of Punishments Upon Prisoners in that Colony* and 6 Geo IV, No. 18 (1825) (NSW).
32 Hall explicitly directed editorials at England, for example, the editorials quoted below, n.37. He also reprinted with obvious pleasure an editorial by an English newspaper expressing horror at the illegal torture by the magistrates, *Monitor*, 24/11/1826. See too 22/12/1827.
33 Macquarie's response to Bigge's criticisms is reprinted in J. Ritchie, *The Evidence to the Bigge Reports* (Heinemann, Melbourne, 1971) II, 280.
34 Macquarie was alleged to have refused some of those suggested on the basis that they were Exclusives. He denies this and anyway eventually appointed most of them claiming his refusal stemmed from the fact that the extra numbers were not needed. In Ritchie, *ibid.*
35 *Bigge Report*, I, 80ff.
36 Bathurst to Macquarie, HRA IV, I, 338. See Ritchie, *Punishment and Profit* (Heinemann, Melbourne, 1970), 115–20. Hughes has a fine biographical sketch of Redfern's qualities, *The Fatal Shore* (Knopf, New York, 1986), 337–8.
37 For example, the *Monitor* 15/12/1826 and 22/12/1826 complains about the dominance of graziers in the magistracy and their desire to keep emancipists in perpetual slavery. See too the *Monitor*, 27/1/1829.
38 *Bigge Report*, I, 80, and Bent to Bathurst 1/7/15, HRA IV, I, 130.
39 Government and General Order (hereafter 'GGO') 7/12/1816.
40 GGO 9/1/1813.
41 See Macquarie's Police Regulations, HRA I, VII, 410. See too Circular to Magistrates 20/9/1814, cited in M. Ellis, *Lachlan Macquarie* (Angus and Robertson, Sydney, 1969), 324.
42 Ellis, *ibid.*
43 3 Wm. IV no. 3 (1832).
44 GGO 10/12/1814, HRA IV, I, 142.
45 For example, A. Harris, *Settlers and Convicts: Recollections of Sixteen Years Labour in the Australian Backwoods* (Melbourne University Press, Melbourne, 1953), 9; *Bigge Report* I, 100; New South Wales, *Report of the Committee on Police and Gaols*, Legislative Council, 1839, 73 (hereafter 'the 1839 Committee').
46 The 1839 Committee, *ibid.*
47 King, *op.cit.*, n.24, 162.
48 *Ibid.* 166; see Great Britain, *op.cit.*, n.31; Forbes, Memorandum 1/1/1823, HRA IV, I, 417; J. McLaughlin, 'The Magistracy in New South Wales 1788–1850' (Unpublished LlM thesis, University of Sydney, 1973). See 6 Geo. IV, No. 18 (1825) retrospective to 1788; 6 Geo. IV c.69; 7 Vic. No. 25. Plunkett, points out that unless partiality, corruption or malice is shown, the Supreme Court will lean in favour of the magistrates, *op.cit.*, n.7, 207.

49 When the colony was small this could be done. Governor Phillip (1786–1792) reviewed all sentences of the magistrates before they were carried out and frequently reduced them. See J. Cobley, *op.cit.*, n.9, 164.
50 In J. Ritchie, *op.cit.*, n.33, 280.
51 R. Therry, *Reminiscences of Thirty Years Residence in New South Wales and Victoria* (Sydney University Press, Sydney, 1974), 168. Bligh had complained in 1808 that magistrates had been stacking benches, HRA I, VI, 424. By 1820 areas and hierarchies began to be specified, HRA IV, I, 812.
52 The *Australian* 11/7/1828; McLaughlin *op.cit.*, n.48, 329 ff. also notes frequent neglect of office. On the appointment of stipendiaries, see too L. Barlow, 'A Strictly Temporary Office: New South Wales Police Magistrates 1830–1860' (Law in History Conference, La Trobe University, 1985), and the 1839 Committee.
53 The 1839 Committee in an Appendix provides details on these matters. See too L. Barlow, *ibid.*
54 D. Philips, 'A New Engine. Power and Authority', *op.cit.*, n. 3; D. Neal, *op.cit.*, n.3.
55 D. Philips, 'The Black Country Magistracy 1835–60', *op.cit.*, n.3.
56 The *Monitor*, 13/1/1827.
57 The 1839 Committee, 58.
58 McLaughlin, *op.cit.*, n.48, 426; the *Australian* 30/8/1826.
59 McLaughlin, *ibid.* English commentators habitually referred to French police as 'Fouché's spies' and equated them with paid police. They saw paid police as a threat to English liberty. See n.3. The Tory newspaper, the *Sydney Herald*, 16/11/1835, invoked Fouché's name against the stipendiary magistrates, see Barlow, *op.cit.*, n.52, 9. The *Sydney Herald* saw the stipendiaries as tools of the government, see Roe, *op.cit.*, n.27, 25–6.
60 The 1839 Committee, Evidence, 172.
61 From early in his term Bourke had advocated reduction in the number of police magistrates. He did reduce the number but felt the pressure for increases: Bourke to Stanley, 29/9/1833 HRA I, XVII, 224. England was even firmer in its reply, Stanley to Bourke 12/5/1834 HRA I, XVII, 430.
62 The 1839 Committee, 58–9.
63 The 1839 Committee, Appendix, gives the numbers. For the Colonial Office view, see Stanley to Bourke, 17/5/1834, HRA I, XVII, 430.
64 Barlow, *op.cit.*, n.52, 12–14.
65 For example, Gisborne and Busby, the 1839 Committee, Evidence, 73 and 168.
66 *Op.cit.*, n.45, 228.
67 See chs. 4 and 7.
68 A. Castles, 'The Judiciary and Political Questions: The First Austra-

lian Experience' (1975) *Adelaide L.R.*5, 294. The *Australian* of 28/10/1824 and 11/11/1824 attacked the *bona fides* of the magistrates on the issue. See ch.7.
69 Certiorari was refused on the basis that other remedies were available.
70 5 Wm IV No.22, s.3.
71 See n.48.
72 See Plunkett's statement, referred to in n. 48, and the account of *Hall's* case, below.
73 Plunkett, *ibid.*
74 The Molesworth Committee Evidence, 221–2. In questioning, Macarthur had to retract some of this. See too Governor Darling's complaints about the 'technicalities' adopted by the Supreme Court which hampered the magistracy, and provoked threats of resignation by magistrates, Darling to Wilmot-Horton, 26/3/1827, PRO CO 323/149, f.238. This 'technicality' involved illegal sentences imposed on convicts!
75 See the discussion of Macquarie's feud with Marsden, above. For instance, the magistrates refused to carry out his orders about convict musters and assignment of convicts, and imposed extremely heavy penalties in contrast with Macquarie's lenient policies. The tradition reached its highpoint in the Ann Rumsby affair under Governor Brisbane, Macquarie's successor. See Currey, *op.cit.*, n.26.
76 *Op.cit.*, nn. 31 and 48.
77 H. King, *op.cit.*, n.24, ch.17, details the opposition to Bourke by the magistrates, starting with the *Summary Jurisdiction Act* 1832 and culminating over the election for quarter sessions.
78 See the *Monitor*, 30/6/1826, 11/8/1826, 22/9/1826.
79 Hall to Murray 11/3/1829, HRA I, XV, 56.
80 This was an offence under 5 Geo. IV No. 3 (1825). Hall received a warning that he was liable to prosecution from the Principal Superintendent of Convicts, F.A. Hely. Wentworth told the Supreme Court that the governor's secretary had 'schooled' the magistrates to their course of action.
81 *Op.cit.*, n.79.
82 *Ibid.*
83 The *Australian* 3/7/29.
84 C. Currey, *op.cit.*, n.26, 364. See too B. Fletcher, *Ralph Darling: A Governor Maligned* (Oxford University Press, Melbourne, 1984), 283–6.
85 HRA I XV, 759. James Macarthur complained to the Molesworth Committee that the case and the award of damages had made the magistrates timid, *Molesworth Report*, 278.
86 For example, the Ann Rumsby case, in which Governor Brisbane's protégé, the magistrate Douglass, was the target. See n.26.
87 See above, pp.126–7 and ch.7.

88 *The Australian* 15/7/1826.
89 James Macarthur, a leading Exclusives spokesman during the 1830s admitted this in 1850. See M. Sturma, *Vice in a Vicious Society* (University of Queensland Press, St Lucia, 1983), 30.
90 See Eager's attack on Marsden in J. Ritchie, *op.cit.*, n.33, II, 234–6.
91 J. Pocock, *op.cit.*, n.8, 390.
92 C.M.H. Clark, *A History of Australia* (Melbourne University Press, Melbourne, 1962), III, 182.
93 Quoted by A. Atkinson, *op.cit.*, n.15, 44–8, at 46.
94 See D. Hay, 'Property, Authority and the Criminal Law' in Hay *et al.*, *Albion's Fatal Tree* (Pantheon, New York, 1975) 17, 55–6.
95 See above, pp.119–22.
96 *Bigge Report* I, 83.
97 *Ibid.*, 89.
98 Hall's views have been quoted. Other contemporary observers referred to respected magistrates as exceptions e.g. Harris, *op.cit.*, n.45, 9, 13, 72, 123, 132, 137, 192, 199 and Therry, *op.cit.*, n.51, e.g. 44–50, 168–172 make these points. See too McLaughlin, *op.cit.*, n.48 and the Report of the 1826 committee on the magistracy showing a pattern of illegal and brutal punishments going back at least to the early 1800s, Britain, *op.cit.*, n.31, and Currey, *op.cit.*, n.26, 156–164. Governor Bligh had said: 'Benches of magistrates and the Courts of Justice are mockeries of what they represent'. Bligh to Castlereagh *HRNSW* VI, 787. See too A. Atkinson, *op.cit.*, n.15, 44–8.
99 See Max Weber's analysis of power, authority and legitimacy in M. Rheinstein and E. Shils, *Max Weber on Law in Economy and Society* (Harvard University Press, Cambridge, Mass., 1954), 328.
100 G. Stewart, 'Convict Rebel: Ralph Entwistle' in E. Fry, *Rebels and Radicals*' (Allen and Unwin, Sydney, 1983) 27; cf. J. Hirst who argues that the rulers and masters of New South Wales were not much troubled by thoughts of rebellion, *Convict Society and Its Enemies* (Allen and Unwin, Sydney, 1983) 135.
101 Stewart, *ibid.*, 30.
102 Cobley, *op.cit.*, n.9, 136 and 164–5.
103 R. Therry makes the point about quarter-deck justice, *op.cit.*, n.51, 46.
104 Eager said that prior to Macquarie (1810), magistrates ordered floggings, ignoring distinctions between emancipists and convicts, J. Ritchie, *op.cit.*, n.33, 228–230. Harris claimed that the upper class became so used to treating the convicts as having no rights that they wanted to treat free people in the same way, *op.cit.*, n.45, 163.
105 6 Geo. IV No.9 (1828) finally resolved the defect 40 years after foundation.
106 Therry, *op.cit.*, n.51, 47–9; Harris, *op.cit.*, n.45, 132. *The Monitor*, 26/12/1826.
107 Therry, *ibid.*; and Roe, *op.cit.*, n.27, 41 ff. See too Hirst's account of a dispute between two magistrates over such a case, *op.cit.*, n.100, 176.

NOTES TO PAGES 135-138 235

108 3 Wm. IV No.3 (1832), s.27.
109 Harris, *op.cit.*, n.45, 13; Therry, *op.cit.*, n.51, 43 quotes the example of a convict sentenced to 50 lashes for not raising his hat. See too ch.2.
110 *Bench of Magistrates, Queanbeyan – Deposition Books 1838* AONSW Reel No. 677. The cases took place on 22/6/1838, 1/11/1838 and 29/1 1839. See D. Chambers, 'Lanyon as a Pastoral Property Between 1835 and 1870' (unpublished, Department of Territories, 1986). I am indebted to Sandra Blair for pointing this material out to me and for transcriptions of some of the cases.
111 *The Monitor* 26/12/1826.
112 Circular to magistrates, 20/9/1814, cited in M. Ellis, *op.cit.*, n.41, 324.
113 Ch.2.
114 A.J. Faunce J.P. to the Colonial Secretary, 2/21840, appendixed to New South Wales Inquiry into the Queanbeyan Bench, 1840 AONSW 4/2507. I am indebted to Sandra Blair for drawing this source to my attention.
115 A.H. King, *op.cit.*, n.24, 161.
116 Sections 27 and 26 respectively.
117 A.H. King, *op.cit.*, n.24, Ch.17.
118 M. Sturma, *op.cit.*, n.89, 22–6, 29–30.
119 See ch.6
120 A. Harris, *op.cit.*, n.45, 80–1. See too ch.6.
121 *Ibid.*, 114.
122 Hall to Murray, 2/5/1829, HRA I, XV, 65–6.
123 *Op.cit.*, n.15.
124 E.g. *The Australian* 8/7/1829, and see n.100.
125 For an account of this event see C.M.H. Clark, *op.cit.*, n.92, I, 171–4.
126 See G. Stewart, *op.cit.*, n.100, and J. Hirst, *op.cit.*, n.100, 134–5.
127 See A. Merritt's suggestive work on the application of master and servant legislation in 'The Historical Role of Law in the Regulation of Employment' (1982) *Australian Journal of Law and Society*, 56, esp. 72–75, and 'Forgotten Militants: The Use of New South Wales Masters and Servants Acts by and Against Female Employees' in I. Duncanson and C. Tomlins, *Law and History in Australia* (Latrobe University Press, Melbourne, 1982), 54. See too A. Atkinson, *op.cit.*, n.15; and P. Byrne, 'Women and the Criminal Law; Sydney 1810–1821' (1985) *Push From the Bush* 21, 2.
128 A. Atkinson, *op.cit.*, n.15, 39–43. James Wright had his barn burned by a disaffected convict worker.
129 *Ibid*, 43–48.
130 For example, see above Hall's successful civil action against the Sydney bench. Eager, in J. Ritchie, *op.cit.*, n.33, 228, mentions that suing a master for a debt was regarded as insolence. A. Harris, *op.cit.*, n.45, 74, claimed that to sue for wages would brand the plaintiff as a troublemaker whom masters would not employ. He remarks elsewhere on other obstacles to legal action, estimating (dubiously) that one out

of ten might be successful in civil suits, 81–2, 183 Another contemporary account confirms Harris, J. Tucker, *The Adventures of Ralph Rashleigh* (Currey O'Neil, Melbourne, 1981) 158–9.
131 See the New South Wales *Queanbeyan Inquiry*, *op.cit.*, n.114, and Harris,*The Emigrant Family*, (Australian National University Press, Canberra, 1967), 180–90. And see the series of articles in the *Monitor* 26/8/1826, 22/9/1826, 20/10/1826, 26/12/1826.
132 Currey,.*op.cit.*, n. 26, ch.XV; and see nn. 31 and 48.

Chapter 6

1 Quoted in E. Halévy, *A History of the English People in Nineteenth Century: England in 1815* (Barnes and Noble, New York, 1961),44. Secondary source material on policing in New South Wales during the transportation period is virtually non-existent. The only work of substance is an unpublished MA thesis by Hazel (A.H.) King for the period 1825–1851, 'Police Organisation and Administration in the Middle District of New South Wales 1825–1851'. My debt to this fine work will be apparent from the notes.
2 Hannibal Macarthur to P.P. King 18/4/23, *King Papers* I, ML, f 259.
3 With respect to justice of the peace, see D. Neal, 'The Role of Justices of the Peace in Relation to Popular Protest in Eighteenth Century England' (unpublished MS, 1979) and on police, D. Philips, '"A New Engine of Power and Authority": The Institutionalization of Law Enforcement in England 1780–1830' in Gatrell, Lenman and Parker, *Crime and the Law: The Social History of Crime in Western Europe Since 1500* (Europe, London, 1980). Although this was the formal position, paid informers, like the thief taker Jonathan Wylde and others who reported to the Home office, undercut this rhetoric to some extent.
4 See E. O'Brien, *The Foundation of Australia* (Sheed and Ward, London, 1937); D. Hay ' Property, Authority and the Criminal Law' in D. Hay et. al., *Albion's Fatal Tree* (Pantheon, New York, 1975), 17; cf. J. Langbein, 'Albion's Fatal Flaws' (1983) *Past and Present* 98, 96 and D. Hay, 'The Criminal Prosecution in England and Its Historians' (1984) *Modern L.R.* 47, 1.
5 These themes recur in the parliamentary debates on paid magistracy and police forces throughout the eighteenth century. Many of the parliamentarians were justices of the peace themselves and rejected the proposals out of hand. See D. Neal *op.cit.*, n.3 and D. Philips, *op. cit.*, n. 3. Bow Street Magistrates Court with its stipendiary magistrates and police from mid-eighteenth century and the Middlesex justices towards the end of the same century were the exceptions.
6 See ch. 5.
7 On the dismissal see GGO 25/5/1802 *HRNSW* IV, 771. Henry related his career in the police to Governor Macquarie in a Memorial dated 10/1/1810. He was requesting recognition of grants made to him by Colonel Patterson after Governor Bligh had been deposed. Henry had

supported the Rum Rebels. A copy of the memorial is in the author's possession.
8 J.J. Tobias, *Crime and Police in England 1700–1900* (1979)(Gill and Macmillan, London, 1979); cf. Philips, *op.cit.*, n. 3, 160.
9 HRA I, I, 138, and W. Tench, *Sydney's First Four Years* (Angus and Robertson, Sydney, 1961), 156.
10 D. Collins, *An Account of the English Colony in New South Wales* (London, 1798), 78.
11 HRA I, I, 780.
12 Phillip to Sydney, 1/2/1790, HRA I, I, 134.
13 F. Crowley, *Working Class Conditions in Australia 1788–1851* (unpublished PhD thesis, University of Melbourne, 1949), 160.
14 New South Wales, *Report of the Committee on Police and Gaols* (Legislative Council, Votes and Proceedings, 1839) 35, (hereafter the 1839 Committee).
15 On Castle Hill, see C.M.H. Clark, *A History of Australia* (Melbourne University Press, Melbourne, 1962), I, 171–3; on The Rum Rebellion see H. Evatt, *Rum Rebellion* (Angus and Robertson, Sydney, 1938); and on Bathurst see G. Stewart, 'Convict Rebel: Ralph Entwistle' in E. Fry, *Rebels and Radicals*, (Allen and Unwin, Sydney, 1983) 27.
16 Government and General Order (GGO) 9/11/96, HRA I, I, 701.
17 Quoted in Swanton, *A Chronological Account of Crime, Public Order and Police in Sydney 1788–1810* (Australian Institute of Criminology, Canberra, 1983) 22.
18 Collins, *op.cit.*, n.10.
19 The 1839 Committee, 61.
20 There is a reference to farm constables too in A. Harris, *The Emigrant Family* (Australian National University Press, Canberra, 1967), 103. The reference there is to a convict who had served out his time as a farm constable. However, in Wright's case there appears to have been an expectation that the farm constable should not be a convict.
21 Not until 1832 were the offences specified in legislation after Governor Bourke became concerned about the illegal punishments being administered. See ch.5.
22 There are several instances of exemplary public executions, and reprieves with the noose around the neck of the condemned in the early years of the colony, Collins, *op.cit.*, n.10. Even by the 1820s the rate of executions in New South Wales was much higher than in England. See R. Therry, *Reminiscences of Thirty Years Residence in New South Wales and Victoria* (Sydney university Press, Sydney, 1974), 16. See too M. Sturma, 'Public Executions and the Ritual of Death' (1983) *Push from the Bush* 15, 3 and pp.52–3 above.
23 Evidence of D'Arcy Wentworth to Commissioner Bigge, in J. Ritchie, *The Evidence to the Bigge Reports* (1971) I, 41 and 60, (hereafter 'D. Wentworth'). He was the father of W. C. Wentworth, the Emancipist leader.
24 *Ibid.*

25 See Tobias, *op.cit.*, n.8, 43–6 for a description of the Bow Street system.
26 At certain times the Provost Marshall, traditionally head of the military police, had responsibilities for the police. See B. Swanton *et al, Police Source Book* (Australian Institute of Criminology, Canberra, 1983).
27 D.Wentworth, *op.cit.*, n.23, 44.
28 D.Wentworth, *op.cit.*, n.23, 41.
29 GGO 10/1/1810 quoted in Swanton, *op.cit.*, n.17, 32.
30 D. Wentworth, 48.
31 *Ibid.*, 47. See too *Bigge Report* II, 60–90.
32 *Ibid.*, 43.
33 The 1839 Committee, 59. Justices of the peace testifying to the 1835 and 1839 Committees said they preferred ticket-of-leave holders because they had more leverage over them; e.g., the 1835 Committee, 430.
34 An example is quoted for 1798 by Swanton *op.cit.*, n.17, 86–7 cf. *Bigge Report* I, 106. J.C. Byrne speaks from the point of view of a victim of police corruption in 'Twelve Years Wanderings in The British Colonies from 1835–1847' extracted in R. Ward and J. Robertson, *Such Was Life: Select Documents in Australian Social History 1788–1850* (Ure Smith, Sydney, 1969), 244–8. See too A. Harris, *Settlers and Convicts* (Melbourne University Press, Melbourne, 1953), 47, 56.
35 *Bigge Report* I, 106; Governor's Despatch to the Secretary of State for the Colonies, Sep.–Dec. 1826, Vol 8, ML; the 1835 Committee 430; the 1839 Committee 51.
36 Henry Kable was dismissed as chief constable at Sydney in 1802 because of his breaches of port regulations, *HRNSW* IV, 771. A fellow constable was flogged for trying to extort money from a prisoner. Between May 1825 and October 1826, out of a force of 50 there were 57 dismissals and 25 resignations. In 1844, out of a force of between 95 and 104, there were 82 dismissals (mostly drunkenness), 85 resignations and 5 deaths. See A.H. King, *op.cit.* n.1, 200, 217. The London Metropolitan Police had similarly high figures for the 1830s. See King, *ibid*, 30 and Tobias, *op.cit.*, n.8.
37 King, *ibid.*, App.K.
38 *Bigge Report* I, 106–7.
39 *Bigge Report* II, 82–83.
40 *Ibid.*, 85.
41 *Ibid.*, I, 106.
42 *Bigge Report* I, 79. The 1835 Committee 424; King, *op.cit.*, n.1, 187.
43 New South Wales, *Votes and Proceedings* 1825, Legislative Council, 18.
44 Enclosure to Governor's despatch Sep-Dec. 1826.
45 *Ibid.*, 508.
46 *Op.cit.*, n.3.
47 King, *op.cit*, n.1, 180.
48 For example, the 1835 Committee, 434.

49 On Day's investigations, see Atkinson and Aveling, *Australians 1838* (Fairfax, Syme and Weldon, Sydney, 1987), 389–92.
50 See King, *op.cit.*, n.1, 282 ff. See below.
51 The 1835 Committee 434.
52 The 1839 Committee 34–5.
53 King, *op.cit.*, n.1, App.M.
54 Appendix to 1839 Committee, Art. 3.
55 HRA I, XVI, 71.
56 The 1839 Committee, 35.
57 *Ibid.*
58 For example, HRA I, II, 403. See too Hobart to King 30/1/1802, regretting treatment of the 'natives' and directing him 'to use every occasion of cultivating a good understanding with them', PRO CO 324/66 f.192. See also H. Reynolds, *Frontier* (Allen and Unwin, Sydney, 1987a).
59 They are R v. *Jack Congo Murrell* and the trial of the Myall Creek Massacre defendants, discussed in A. Castles, *An Australian Legal History* (Law Book Co., Sydney, 1982), ch.18, esp. 522 ff. See also ch. 2. On the legal status and attitudes towards Aborigines, see H. Reynolds, *The Law of the Land* (Penguin, Melbourne, 1987), 1–79.
60 Saxe-Bannister to Darling, 9/9/1826, PRO CO 323/146 f.208. Darling complained to Hay, 11/9/1826, about Saxe-Bannister's rudeness, *ibid.* See ch.2, n.71.
61 N. Townsend, 'Masters and Men and the Myall Creek Massacre' (1985) *Push From the Bush* 20, 4; A. Atkinson and M. Aveling, *op.cit.*, n.49, 54–63, 392–4.
62 Castles *op.cit.*, n.59, 521–2. For the narrative of Nunn's killings, see Atkinson and Aveling, *op.cit.*, n.49, 38–45.
63 Quoted in King, *op.cit.*, n.1.
64 The 1835 Committee, 433.
65 The 1839 Committee, 28.
66 M. Sturma, *Vice in a Vicious Society* (University of Queensland Press, St Lucia, 1983b), 72.
67 King, *op.cit.*, n.1, 310–11.
68 *Ibid.*
69 *Ibid.*, App.M.
70 *Ibid.*, 206, cf. the 1839 Committee 26, which was still recommending that this be done.
71 4 Wm. IV No. 7.
72 The 1835 Committee, 427–8, praised Rossi for the way in which he had assimilated the Sydney police to the London model.
73 For example, section 15 required the police to attend to people beating carpets, flying kites, and dumping rubbish in the streets of Sydney. Section 36 prohibited dumping dead animals in Sydney Cove.
74 For example, section 32 required gutters on eaves.
75 Section 55 ff.
76 Section 45.

77 11 Geo. IV No. 10.
78 6 Wm. IV No. 6.
79 See ss.1, 4 and 5.
80 King, op.cit., n.1, App.M.
81 Ibid.
82 See Appendix 2 and 3.
83 The 1839 Committee, 2, 25, 51, 54. The slight increase was to allow costables to purchase uniform clothing. The reward system was undermined to some extent by the practice of naming the chief constable as informant, and hence recipient of the reward. The practice was criticised by the Committee, 56–7, for this reason. Not all offences carried rewards, and not all rewards were of equal value. Economic rationalists, as they were, the constables seem to have directed their energies to the most lucrative offences. See the 1839 Committee 57–8, and Sturma, op.cit., n.66, 143, where the author suggests that abolition of the moiety system for drunkenness after 1850 caused a drop in arrests for that offence. James Wright made allegations that constables took bribes in relation to floggings and tickets-of-leave, *New South Wales, Inquiry into the Queanbeyan Bench, 1840*, AONSW 4/2507.
84 For example, convicts from Queanbeyan would be taken to Yass, a distance of about 40 miles, where there was a medical officer to oversee floggings of more than 50 lashes.
85 King, op.cit., n.1, 276–7.
86 Ibid., App.F.
87 The 1839 Committee 62–4.
88 Ibid.
89 Ibid.
90 King, op.cit., n.1, 271–2 and see R. Therry op.cit., n.22, 16. See ch.2.
91 F.X. Prieur, *Notes of a Convict of 1838* (Ford, Sydney, 1949), recollects a fight among the police and soldiers meant to be guarding him! See R. Ward and Robertson op.cit., n.34, 124.
92 King, op.cit, n.1, 281.
93 The 1839 Committee, Evidence, 172. See also F. Rossi, HRA I, XII, 679.
94 For example, the 1835 Committee, 421, 429, 433; and the 1839 Committee, 58–9, App.,18.
95 The 1839 Committee, 58–9.
96 The 1839 Committee appends the following table:

Magistrates for New South Wales

	1836	1837	1838	1839
Civil	117	137	144	194
Military	28	34	29	15
Unpaid	145	171	173	209
Plus paid	30	25	29	29
	165	196	202	238

97 Evidence to 1835 Committee, 329.
98 King, *op.cit*, n.1, 263.
99 See preceding table.
100 Evidence to the 1839 Committee, 168.
101 The 1839 Committee, 60.
102 Evidence of W. Gunn to the 1835 Committee, 326.
103 Evidence of E.A. Wilson to the 1839 Committee, 51, 54.
104 These charges had been brought by one of the honorary magistrates, James Wright. The complaints reveal a personal dimension going beyond any disinterested concern about the standard of policing in the district. See below.
105 New South Wales, *Inquiry into the Queanbeyan Bench, 1840*, AOSW 4/2507.
106 See his request for a police magistrate in, Wright to the Colonial Secretary, 24/8 1835, AONSW CSIL 4/2290. The inquiry into Wright's treatment of his convicts is included in the Inquiry into the Queanbeyan Bench, see above, and dated 21/2/1840.
107 But see Harris, *op.cit*. n.34, 228; and the quote from Busby to the 1839 Committee, n.100 above.
108 A. Harris, *op.cit.*, n.20, 180–90. Harris went on to say that Mr Hurley JP was an exception among the magistrates and that it was not until the legal profession in Sydney had extracted large sums of damages from some magistrates that the problems really abated.
109 *Molesworth Report* evidence, 7.
110 *Op.cit.*, n.34, 166 ff.
111 *Ibid.*, 39.
112 *Ibid.*, 75, 80, 83, 142, 165.
113 *Ibid.*, 81, 181, 227.
114 James Tucker, *The Adventures of Ralph Rashleigh* (Currey O'Neil, Melbourne, 1981), 163.
115 *Inquiry Into the Queanbeyan Bench, op.cit.*, n.105.
116 James Demarr, 'Adventures in Australia Fifty Years Ago', extracted in Ward and Robertson, *op.cit.*, n.34, 248–52. One of Harris's informants, a free-born man who had been in the colony for 12 years, told of an average of two arrests per year, *op.cit.*, n.34, 81.
117 'Twelve Years Wanderings in the British Colonies from 1835–1847', extracted in Ward and Robertson, *ibid*, 244–248. See too Harris, *ibid*.
118 The *Australian* 27/2/1829.
119 *Bigge Report* II, 83. Bigge points out defects arising from failure to appoint a general superintendent, I, 79; the 1835 Committee, 42; King, *op.cit.*, n.1, 187–8. The 1825 Committee, 18; King, *op.cit.*, n.1, 92; the 1835 Committee, 424; and, the 1839 Committee, 24.
120 King, *ibid.*, 323.
121 The 1839 Committee, 24.
122 See D. Neal, *op.cit.*, n.3 ; and D. Philips, *op.cit.*, n.3. Peel used it too in debate over the New Police, and see too Tobias, *op.cit.*, n.6, 77.
123 The 1835 Committee, 424.

124 The 1839 Committee, evidence, 172.
125 M. Roe, *The Quest for Authority in Eastern Australia 1835–51* (Melbourne University Press, Melbourne, 1965), 41.
126 E.S. Hall to Murray, 2/5/1829, HRA I, XV, 64–5, quoted at the opening of ch. 5.
127 See ch.5.
128 L. Barlow, '"A Strictly Temporary Office": New South Wales Police Magistrates 1835–1860' (unpublished paper, 1985).
129 J. Hirst, *Convict Society and Its Enemies*, (Allen and Unwin, Sydney, 1983), 149.
130 *Op.cit.*, n.2.

Chapter 7

1 *Commentaries*, IV, 342–3. The Latin translated is: 'No free man may be executed, imprisoned, exiled or punished in any other way, except by the judgment of his peers or through the law of the land'. This has been taken to guarantee trial by jury, although the literal translation appears to countenance other forms of trial.
2 HRA I, X, 56–7. The petition was signed by 1261 'Merchants, Settlers, & c'.
3 *Ibid.*
4 King to Hobart, 7/8/1803, HRNSW V, 187. The earliest calls for jury trial go back to 1791, see J. Bennett, 'The Establishment of Jury Trial in New South Wales' (1959–61) *Sydney L.R.* 3, 463 at 464.
5 On Lilburne and other seventeenth-century political proponents of the jury, see T.A. Green, *Verdict According to Conscience* University of Chicago Press, Chicago, 1985), 202ff.; C. Hill, *The World Turned Upside Down* (Penguin, Harmondsworth, 1975), 271; and D. Neal, 'The Political Significance of the Jury' in D. Challinger, *The Jury* (Australian Institute of Criminology, Canberra, 1986), 61. On the eighteenth century, see John Brewer, 'The Wilkites and the Law' in J. Brewer and J. Styles, *An Ungovernable People* (Rutgers University Press, New Jersey, 1980), 136; and E.P. Thompson, *The Making of the English Working Class* (Pelican, Harmondsworth, 1968), 87–8.
6 See chs.3 and 4.
7 J. Brewer, *op.cit.*, n.5, 154–7.
8 Alexis de Tocqueville, *Democracy in America* (Anchor, New York, 1969), 729, the original of which had been published only two years previous to Macarthur's own book. Cited in James Macarthur, *New South Wales: Its Present State and Future Prospects* (London, 1837), 111.
9 W.C. Wentworth, *A Statistical, Historical and Political Descriptions of the Colony of New South Wales and its Dependent Settlements in Van Diemen's Land* (Doubleday, Sydney, 1978).
10 De Tocqueville, *op.cit.*, n.8, 274–6.
11 Quoted in M. Sturma, *Vice in a Vicious Society* (University of Queensland Press, St Lucia, 1983), 30.

NOTES TO PAGES 170-174 243

12 England's rulers had a range of devices to avoid juries. One of these was the passage of summary offences (e.g. riot legislation) which had drawn criticism from Blackstone in the middle of the eighteenth century, *Commentaries* IV, 277-8. Special juries, development of the equity jurisdiction, judicial usurpation of the jury function, and engineering the venue of trials constitute other examples of attempts by government to bypass the jury system in England.
13 On these colonial politics from the mid-1830s, see in particular, M. Roe, *The Quest for Authority in Eastern Australia* (Melbourne University Press, Melbourne, 1965). See too J. Hirst, *Convict Society and Its Enemies* (Allen and Unwin, Sydney, 1983), 194-27.
14 For example, A.C.V. Melbourne saw it in terms of social status for emancipists trying to live down their convict past, *Early Constitutional Development in Australia* (University of Queensland Press, St Lucia, 1963), 86, 125 and *passim*. See too W. McMinn, *A Constitutional History of Australia* (Oxford University Press, Melbourne, 1979), 18. R. Connell and T. Irving, *Class Structure in Australian History* (Longman Cheshire, Melbourne, 1980), 34-6, correctly identify the political significance of the magistracy but they see the jury issue as a contest over minor authority missing the wider significance of the issue. Cf. M. Sturma, *op.cit.*, n.11, 20-21, who does see the wider significance of the issue.
15 See for example, in the early colony, Settlers Address to Bligh, 1/1/1808, *HRNSW* VI, 411; H. Evatt, *Rum Rebellion* (Angus and Robertson, Sydney, 1938); T. Parsons, 'Was John Boston's Pig a Political Martyr?' (1985) *JRAHS* 71, 163. The independence of the colonial courts is discussed in ch.4. The core of the rule of law conception does not require juries but the English variant does, see ch.3.
16 On the twelfth-century origins of the jury, see Pollock and Maitland, *The History of English Law* (Cambridge University Press, Cambridge, 1968), I, 138-153, II, 621-32. On jury selection, see A. Manchester, *Modern Legal History* (Butterworth, London, 1980), 86-99. On English abuses, see E.P. Thompson, *Writing By Candlelight* (Merlin Press, London, 1980), 99-104; Thompson cites a book by Bentham, *Elements of the Art of Packing*. On juries generally, see W Cornish, *The Jury* (Allen Lane, London, 1968), T. Green, *op.cit.*, n.5. On the independence of juries, see D. Neal, *op.cit.*, n.5.
17 The position is discussed in n.26. See *HRA* I, I, 721.
18 Phillip to Sydney 16/5/1788 and 5/6/1789 *HRA* I, I, 35 and 108.
19 See Parsons, *op.cit.*, n.15.
20 King to Hobart, 7/8/1803, *HRNSW* V, 187.
21 Sydney Settlers Address to Bligh, 22/9/06, *HRNSW* VI, 188; Hawkesbury Settlers Address to Bligh, n.d., *HRNSW* VI, 190; Bligh to Windham 31/10/07, *HRNSW* VI, 355.
22 The case is described by Evatt, *op.cit.*, n.15, 75-6, 84. The complaints are in Johnston to Gordon 8/10/1807 *HRNSW* VI, 652 and Fitz to Chapman 15/10/1807 *ibid.*, 305.

23 Ibid., 410.
24 Bligh to Windham, 31/10/1807, HRNSW VI, 355.
25 Bligh to Castlereagh, 21/10/1808, HRNSW VI, 787.
26 See Judge-Advocate E. Bent who advocated civil juries, Bent to Cooke 7/5/1810 HRA IV, I, 48 and 57; Judge Advocate Wylde wrote that power of the governor to select the panel was a matter of public apprehension, Wylde to Bathurst 23/7/21 HRA IV, I, 357-8; Bigge accepted the force of the point, *Bigge Report* II,54-5; similarly Eagar to Bathurst 3/4/1823 HRA IV, I, 444-5. The right of challenge was given in s.4 *New South Wales Act* 1823. The editor of the *Monitor*, Hall, accused Governor Darling of departing from the roster system, Hall to Murray 19/5/1830 HRA IV, I, 632. The commanding officer of the garrison denied this, Snodgrass to de la Condamine 2/7/1830; both the Chief Justice and Mr Justice Stephen commented on the impropriety of the system in two cases where Governor Darling was prosecuting his press critics, see Currey, Sir *Francis Forbes* (Angus and Robertson, Sydney, 1968), 258-9, 362-3. These cases prompted the British Government to provide for jury trials in cases involving the governor or the Executive Council, see below.
27 Bent to Cooke, 7/5/1810, HRA IV, 1, 48 and 57 and in response to Bathurst's refusal, *ibid.*, 100.
28 Great Britain, *Report of the Select Committee on Transportation* 1812.
29 HRA IV, I, 77.
30 Bathurst to Bent, 11/12/1815, HRA IV, I, 170. See ch.4.
31 Andrew Thompson, William Redfern, Henry Fulton and Simeon Lord, all emancipists, were appointed magistrates by Macquarie. See ch.5
32 See works cited n.34.
33 See ch.4, n.99 for Darling's entreaties to England for competent lawyers to match Wentworth and Wardell.
34 A.C.V. Melbourne, *William Charles Wentworth* (University of Queensland Press, St Lucia, 1963a). See too *Australian Dictionary of Biography* entry; C.M.H. Clark, *A History of Australia* (University of Melbourne Press, Melbourne, 1962), II, ch.3; A. Castles, *An Australian Legal History* (Law Book Co., Sydney, 1982), 125-7; and R. Hughes, *The Fatal Shore* (Knopf, New York, 1986), 361-7. On the jury issue in the politics leading up to the American Revolution, see Lovejoy, D.S., 'Two American Revolutions 1689 and 1776' in J.Pocock (ed.) *Three British Revolutions* (Princeton University Press, New Jersey, 1980), 244 and J. Murrin,, 'The Great Inversion, Or Court Versus Country: A Comparison of the Revolution Settlements in England (1688-1721) and America (1776-1816)' in *ibid.*, 368. Wentworth was later prepared to threaten a Botany Bay tea party if the Emancipist claims were not met. The lessons of the American Revolution were still fresh in minds of those involved in the contemporary politics.
35 *Sydney Gazette*, 23/1/1819.
36 Macquarie to Bathurst, 23/3/1819, HRA I, X, 52.

37 Eagar became the honorary Emancipist spokesman in London for the next twenty years. He is a strange character but his support for egalitarian principles and devotion to the Emancipist cause are admirable. See his rebuttal of Bigge in J. Ritchie, *The Evidence to the Bigge Reports* (Heinemann, Melbourne, 1971), II, 200 esp. 231-3. See too N. McLachlan, 'Edward Eagar, A Colonial Spokesman in Sydney and London' (1961-3) *Hist. Studs.* 431, cf. Clark, *op.cit.*, n.34, I, 355-7, who has no kind word for Eagar.
38 HRA I, X, 57-8.
39 The Act is 30 Geo 111, c.47. See *Bigge Report* II, 8-9.
40 30 Geo 111, c.47.
41 After referring to the effect of the court's decision in perpetuating party division, they pray for the King's consideration of 'the Condition in which we your Majesty's Petitioners are placed in by this State of the Law, as interpreted and acted upon by the courts of Civil Judicature in this Territory, . . .'. They also complained of the lack of substance in the courts' objection: and '. . . for this one single reason the names of Your Petitioners have not been inserted in any General Pardon under the Great Seal of England, without which Ceremony the Courts of Civil Judicature in this Territory have, as aforesaid, adjudged that the Instruments of remission granted by the Governors of this Colony are of no force, effect or Validity whatever, . . .' HRA I, X, 554, 556. Field told Bigge that had he been in the colony at the time he would have prosecuted the author of the resolutions for contempt of court. See A. Melbourne, *op.cit.*, n.14, 80. The Commissioner of Inquiry into the state of the colony, Bigge, testifies to Field's partiality and to dislike for him among the Emancipists. He recommends his recall, J. Ritchie, *op.cit.*, n.37, II, 171.
42 HRA I, X, 549.
43 Clark, *op.cit.*, n.37, 359-60.
44 *Bigge Report* II.
45 Ellis reports clandestine meetings between Macarthur and Bigge, and Macarthur's loan of a fine horse to the Commissioner. See M.H. Ellis, *John Macarthur* (Angus and Robertson, Sydney, 1973), 456. Bigge and Macquarie clashed over the appointment of the emancipist, Redfern, to the magistracy, and ceased to be on speaking terms, C.M.H. Clark, *op.cit.*, n.34, I, 337-9. Eagar accuses Bigge of strong prejudice against emancipists. Ritchie, *op.cit.*, n.37, II, 201.
46 *Bigge Report*, II, 8.
47 Quoted in M. Ellis, *op.cit.*, n.45, 470.
48 Bigge refers, for example, to an interview with Sir John Jamison, chairman of the meeting, in which Jamison expected trial by jury to be introduced on the same principles as existed in England. Bigge wants us to infer that Jamison knew the legal intricacies of the effect of pardons, a subject to perplex the lawyers for some years, whereas Jamison, who was not a lawyer, may well have been referring only to the

property qualification. Bigge then says that in addition to the requirements laid down in England, it was understood at the meeting that those still under sentence would not be eligible. This leads to the inference that they understood that the other class, emancipated convicts, would be eligible to serve. In 1819, of course, most people thought the governor's pardon fully restored people to their legal rights, see *Bigge Report* II, 36–7. Evidence to Bigge discloses that one signatory, Blaxland, did not know whether emancipists were eligible for jury service in England, though it was discussed by the committee, and that a magistrate, Bell, signed the petition but did not agree with trial by jury. Ritchie, *op.cit.*, n.37, I, 87–8 (Blaxland 92–3, and Bell, 63). Cf. Eagar to Bathurst, 3/4/1823, denying Bigge's propositions, HRA IV, I, 458. Eagar also claimed, contrary to Bigge, that trial by jury was of primary importance in the petition and that the other issues were secondary.

49 *Bigge Report* II, 38–9.
50 Cited in Ritchie, *op.cit.*, n.37, II, 17. Eagar accuses Bigge of distorting figures in another context to minimise the claims of the Emancipists by only counting males in the emancipist population, Ritchie, *ibid.*, 213. Also in this vein by omitting people in the towns, HRA IV, I, 458. He says 600 was the number plus whoever arrived subsequently.
51 For Eagar's comments, see J. Ritchie, *ibid.*, 223.
52 4 Geo. IV, c.96.
53 Apparently this occurred extremely rarely.
54 Section 19.
55 The *Australian*, 28/10/1824 and 11/11/1824. On these events, see A. Castles 'The Judiciary and Political Questions' (1975) *Adelaide L.R.* 5, 294.
56 21/10/1824.
57 28/10/1824.
58 11/11/1824.
59 The phrase is borrowed from Evatt, *op.cit.*, n.22.
60 The *Sydney Gazette* 4/11/1824.
61 18/11/1824.
62 Letters from Anticipo and Algernon in the *Australian* 23/9/1825.
63 The *Australian* 23/9/1825.
64 Melbourne, *op.cit.*, n.14, 122.
65 Forbes to Wilmot-Horton, 7/11/1824 DCL *Catton Papers*, ABC WH 2753–5.
66 However that may have been, the intention of the legislature was not apparent from the words of the statute, in which case it was open to the Chief Justice to find that Quarter Sessions should be conducted on the same basis as in England, namely with juries.
67 See generally, A. Melbourne, *op.cit.*, n.14, 146.
68 Cited in M. Ellis, *op.cit.*, n.45.
69 See Melbourne, *op.cit.*, n.14, 148–51.
70 9 Geo IV, c.93.

71 *The Jury Act* 1829 (NSW), amended in 1830.
72 There had been marked controversy over prosecutions for criminal libel by Governor Darling, before a court in which he selected the officers of the military panel. See again n.26.
73 The Act is 4 Wm. IV, No.12. The politicking surrounding the passage of this legislation is discussed in J. Bennett, *op.cit.*, n.4, 473–6.
74 *Op. cit.*, n.8.
75 *Ibid.*, ch.3.
76 *Ibid.*, 106–7.
77 Macarthur had been cross questioned about why the magistrates could not strike the names of people who were unfit from the jury lists. He replied that they were afraid to do so for fear of being sued. When pressed on this he conceded that there was no such cause of action but complained that the magistrates felt harassed by the Supreme Court, *Molesworth Report* 224, 276.
78 *Ibid.*, App., 194.
79 3 Vic. No.11. Trial by assessors in civil cases was abolished in 1844, 8 Vic. No.4.
80 The Act granted a legislative Assembly of 36 of whom 24 were elected and 12 nominated, 5 and 6 Vic. c.76 (1842). Section 5 stipulated the property qualification.
81 *Op. cit.*, n.8, 270–6.

Chapter 8

1 Section 5 *New South Wales and Van Diemens Land Act* 5&6 Vic. The qualification was ownership of landed property worth 200 pounds or a house with an annual rent of 20 pounds. The qualifications for jury service were higher at 300 and 30 pounds respectively, s.2 *Juries Act* 2 Will. IV, No.3. Convicts under sentence were not entitled but otherwise emancipists were not barred.
2 E.P. Thompson, *Whigs and Hunters* (Pantheon, New York, 1975), 258–69.
3 *Commentaries*, I, 130.
4 E.P. Thompson, *op.cit.*, n.2; Hay, 'Property Authority and the Criminal Law' in D. Hay *et al.*, *Albion's Fatal Tree* (Pantheon, New York, 1975), 17. The debate is discussed in ch.3.
5 Quoted at the opening of ch.3.
6 H. Nenner, *By Colour of Law* (University of Chicago Press, Chicago, 1977).
7 Weber makes a distinction between power and authority but sees clearly that the claim to monopoly on the use of physical coercion lies behind political authority, M. Rheinstein and E. Shils (eds.), *Max Weber on Law in Economy and Society* (Harvard University Press, Cambridge, Mass., 1954), 328 ff.
8 A. Gramsci, *Selections from the Prison Notebooks* (International Publishers, New York, 1971), 55–6, 80, 245–50.

9 Philip Selznick crystallised this point for me in commenting on an early draft for this work.
10 Bathurst to Bent, 12/14/1816, HRA I, IX, 112.
11 Weber, *op.cit.*, n.7, see ch.12, 'Domination', esp. 328 ff.
12 E.P. Thompson, *op.cit.*, n.2., 258–69.
13 Hay, 'Property Authority and the Criminal Law' in D. Hay *et al.*, *op. cit.*, n.4., 17.
14 Michael Roe's *Quest for Authority in Eastern Australia 1835–51* (Melbourne University Press, 1965) has an excellent treatment of this for the period from 1835.

Bibliography

Anderson, P., *Arguments Within English Marxism* (New Left Books, London, 1980).
Annette, J., and Sugarman. D, "Taking Stock: Some Reflections on Recent Work On the History of Law, Labour and Crime' (paper presented to the History of Law, Labour and Crime Conference, Warwick University, 1983).
Aplin, G. (ed.), *Sydney Before Macquarie: A Difficult Infant* (University of New South Wales Press, Sydney, 1988).
Atkinson, A., 'The Place of John Macarthur and His Family in New South Wales before 1842' (unpublished MA thesis University of Sydney, 1971).
—, 'Jeremy Bentham And The Rum Rebellion' (1978) *JRAHS* 64, 1.
—, 'Four Patterns of Convict Protest' (1979) *Labour History (Australia)* 37, 28.
—, 'British Whigs and the Rum Rebellion' (1980) *JRAHS* 66, 73.
—, 'Myall Creek' (1985) *Push from the Bush* 20, 1.
Atkinson, A. and Aveling, M., *Australians 1838* (Fairfax, Syme and Weldon, Sydney, 1987).
Australian Dictionary of Biography (Melbourne University Press, Melbourne, 1966).
Aylmer, G.E., *The Struggle for the Constitution: England in the Seventeenth Century* (Blandford Press, London, 1963).
Backhouse, J., *A Narrative of a Visit to the Australian Colonies* (London, 1843).
Barlow, L., 'A Strictly Temporary Office: New South Wales Police Magistrates 1830–1860' (unpublished paper presented at the Law in History Conference, La Trobe University, 1985).
Barrow, R.H., *Slavery in the Roman Empire* (Barnes and Noble, New York, 1968).
Barthes, R., *Mythologies* (Cape, London, 1972).
—, 'Myth Today' in S. Sontag (ed.), *A Barthes Reader* (Hill and Wang, New York, 1982).

Beattie, J.M., *Crime and the Courts in England 1660–1800* (Oxford University Press, Oxford, 1986)
Beaumont G. de, and Tocqueville A. de, *On the Penitentiary System in the United States and Its Application in France* (Southern Illinois University Press, Carbondale, 1964).
Beirne P., and Quinney, R. (eds.), *Marxism and Law* (John Wiley, New York, 1982).
Bendix, R., *Kings or People* (University of California Press, Berkeley, 1978).
Bennett, J.M., *A History of the Supreme Court of New South Wales* (Law Book Co., Sydney, 1974).
Bennett, J., 'The Status and Authority of the Deputy Judge Advocates of New South Wales' (1958) *Sydney L.R.* 2, XX.
—, 'The Establishment of Jury Trial in New South Wales' (1961) *Sydney L.R.* 3, 463.
Bennett J. and Castles, A. (eds.), *A Source Book of Australian Legal History* (Law Book Co., Sydney, 1979).
Bent, E., *Letter Book*, NLA, MS. 195.
Bentham, J., *A Plea for the Constitution* (London, 1803).
Bentham, J., *Bentham Papers*, BL, Add MS 33543.
Berlin, I., *Four Essays on Liberty* (Oxford University Press, Oxford, 1969).
Bettelheim, B., *The Informed Heart* (Paladin, London, 1970).
Bigge Report, see Great Britain.
Blackstone, W., *Commentaries on the Laws of England*, 4 vols. (University of Chicago Press, Chicago, 1979, first published 1765).
Blainey, G., *The Tyranny of Distance: How Distance Shaped Australia's History* (Sun Books, Melbourne, 1966).
—, *A Land Half Won* (Macmillan, Melbourne, 1980)
Blair, S., 'George Howe and Early Printing in New South Wales' (1985) *Waysgoose Journal of Australian Printing Historical Society* 1.
—, 'The Felonry and the Free' (1985) *Labour History* 1.
—, 'The First Australian Printery' (1985) *Heritage Australia* 1.
Brewer, J. and Styles, J., (eds.), *An Ungovernable People: The English and Their Law in the Seventeenth and Eighteenth Centuries* (Rutgers University Press, New Brunswick, 1980).
Brewer, J., 'English Radicalism in the Age of George III' in J.G.A. Pocock (ed.) *Three British Revolutions* (Princeton University Press, Princeton), 323.
Brown, D., and Zdenkowski G., *The Prison Struggle* (Penguin, Melbourne, 1982).
Buckland, W.W., *The Roman Law of Slavery* (Cambridge University Press, Cambridge, 1908).
Burke, E., *Speech on Conciliation with America* (Selby, F. ed.) (Macmillan, London, 1985).
Burn, R., *The Justice of the Peace, and Parish Officer* (Sweet, London, 1873).
Byrne, P.J., 'Women and the Criminal Law: Sydney 1810–1821' (1985) *Push from the Bush* 21, 2.

Campbell, E., 'Prerogative Rule in New South Wales 1788–1823' (1964) *JRAHS* 50, 161.
Campbell v Hall (1774) 1 Cowp. 204.
Carroll, J., 'Original Sin or Paradise Regained?' (1987) *Quadrant*, 10.
Carson, W., 'Book Review of E.P.Thompson, *Whigs and Hunters*' (1977) *Contemporary Crisis* 1, 225.
Castles, A.C., 'The Judiciary and Political Questions: The First Australian Experience, 1824–1825' (1975) *Adelaide L.R.* 5, 294.
—, *An Australian Legal History*. (Law Book Co., Sydney, 1982).
Catton Papers, Derby Central Library.
Challinger, D. (ed.), *The Jury*, (Australian Institute of Criminology, Canberra, 1986).
Chambers, D., 'Lanyon as a Pastoral Property Between 1835 and 1870' (unpublished, Department of Territories, Canberra, 1986).
Clark, C.M.H., 'The Origins of the Convicts Transported to Eastern Australia 1787–1852' (1956) *Hist. Studs.* 7, Pt.1, 121; Pt.2, 314.
—, *A History of Australia* (Melbourne University Press, Melbourne, 1962).
—, *Select Documents in Australian History* (Angus and Robertson, Sydney, 1962).
Clarke, M., *His Natural Life* (Penguin, Melbourne, 1980, first published 1870).
Cobley, J., *Sydney Cove 1788* (Hodder and Stoughton, London, 1962).
—, *The Crimes of the First Fleet Convicts* (Angus and Robertson, Sydney, 1970).
Cohen S., and Scull, A. (eds.), *Social Control and the State* (Blackwell, Oxford, 1983).
Coke, E., *Institutes of the Laws of England* (Clarke, London, 1823).
—, 'Prohibitions del Roy' (1607) 12 Co. Rep. 63; 77 ER 1343.
Collins, D., *An Account of the English Colony in New South Wales* (London, 1798).
Colquhoun, P., *A Treatise on the Police of the Metropolis* (London, 1806).
Connell R.W. and Irving T.H., *Class Structure in Australian History: Documents, Narrative and Argument* (Longman Cheshire, Melbourne, 1980).
Cornish, W., *The Jury* (Allen Lane, London, 1968).
Craton, M., *Testing the Chains: Resistance to Slavery in the British West Indies* (Cornell University Press, Ithaca, 1982).
Craton, M., Walvin, J., and Wright, D., *Slavery, Abolition and Emancipation* (Longman, New York, 1976).
Crowley F., *Working Class Conditions in Australia 1788–1851* (unpublished PhD thesis, University of Melbourne, 1949).
Cunningham, P., *Two Years in New South Wales* (Libraries Board of South Australia, Adelaide, 1966, first published 1827), 2 vols.
Currey, C.H., *Sir Francis Forbes: The First Chief Justice of the Supreme Court of New South Wales* (Angus and Robertson, Sydney, 1968a).
—, *The Brothers Bent* (Sydney University Press, Sydney, 1968b).
Darling R., *Letters to R. Hay* PRO, CO 323/146 and 323/149.

David, P.A., Gutman, H.G., Sutch, R., Temin, P., Wright, G., *Reckoning with Slavery* (Oxford University Press, Oxford, 1976).

Diamond, S., 'From Organization to Society: Virginia in the Seventeenth Century' (1958) *American Journal of Sociology* 457.

—, *The Creation of Society in the New World* (Rand McNally, Chicago, 1963).

—, 'The Rule of Law versus the Order of Custom' (1971) *Social Research* 38, 42.

Dicey, A., *Introduction to the Study of the Law of the Constitution* (Macmillan, London, 1939. first published 1885).

Dickinson, H., *Liberty and Property: Political Ideology in Eighteenth Century Britain* (Methuen, London, 1977).

Dietze, G., *Two Concepts of the Rule of Law* (Liberty Fund, Indianopolis, 1973).

Drescher, S., 'Public Opinion and the Destruction of British Colonial Slavery' in J. Walvin (ed.), *Slavery and British Society 1776-1846* (Macmillan, London, 1982)

Dugan v Mirror Newspapers (1979) 142 CLR 583.

Duncanson, I.W. and C.L. Tomlins (eds.), *Law and History in Australia* (La Trobe University Press, Melbourne, 1982).

Durkheim, E., *The Division of Labour in Society* (Free Press, New York, 1933).

Dworkin, R., *Taking Rights Seriously* (Harvard University Press, Cambridge, Mass., 1977).

Ekirch, A., *Bound for America: The Transportation of British Convicts to the Colonies, 1708-1775* (Oxford University Press, Oxford, 1987).

Ellis, M.H., *Lachlan Macquarie: His Life, Adventures and Times with Reference Notes and Bibliography* (Angus and Robertson, Sydney, 1969).

—, *John Macarthur* (Angus and Robertson, Sydney, 1973).

Evans, L., and Nichols, P., *Convicts and Colonial Society* (Cassell, Sydney, 1976).

Evatt, H.V., *Rum Rebellion* (Angus and Robertson, Sydney, 1938).

Fielding, H., *History of Joseph Andrews* (Bell, London, 1913).

Fine, B., *Democracy and the Rule of Law* (Pluto Press, London, 1984).

Fisher, H.A.L. (ed.), *The Collected Papers of Frederick William Maitland* (Cambridge University Press, Cambridge, 1911).

Fitzgerald, R. and Hearn, M., *Bligh, Macarthur and the Rum Rebellion* (Kangaroo Press, Sydney, 1988).

Fladeland, B., '"Our Cause Being One and the Same": Abolitionists and Chartism' in J. Walvin (ed.), *Slavery and British Society 1776-1846* (Macmillan, London, 1982)

Fletcher, B., *Landed Enterprise and Penal Society* (Sydney University Press, Sydney, 1975).

—, *Ralph Darling: A Governor Maligned* (Oxford University Press, Melbourne, 1984).

Forbes, F., 'Trial by Jury' *Forbes Papers* ML, A741.

Foster, W.C., Howard, W.L., and David B.T., *The Story of Hartley and Its Court-House* (Sydney, 1937).

BIBLIOGRAPHY 253

Foucault, M., *Discipline and Punish: The Birth of the Prison* (Vintage, New York, 1979).
Frederickson G.M. and Lasch, C., 'Resistance to Slavery' (1967) *Civil War History* 13, 315.
Friedmann, W., *The Planned State and the Rule of Law* (Melbourne University Press, Melbourne, 1948).
—, *Law in a Changing Society* (Penguin, Harmondsworth, 1972).
Frost, A., *Convicts and Empire: A Naval Question* (Oxford University Press, Melbourne, 1980).
Fry, E., (ed.), *Rebels and Radicals* (Allen and Unwin, Sydney, 1983).
Fuller, L.L., *The Morality of Law* (Yale University Press, New York, 1964).
Gatrell V.A.C., Lenman, B. and Parker G. (eds.), *Crime and the Law: The Social History of Crime in Western Europe Since 1500* (Europa, London, 1980).
Genovese, E., *Roll, Jordan, Roll: The World the Slaves Made* (Pantheon, New York, 1972).
—, 'Slavery in the Legal History of the South and the Nation' (1981) *Texas L.R.* 59, 969.
Giddens, A., *A Contemporary Critique of Historical Materialism* (University of California Press, Berkeley, 1981).
Glasson, J., *Letters to His Parents* (courtesy of Mr and Mrs C. Alexander, Sydney).
Goffman, E., *Asylums: Essays on the Social Situations of Mental Patients and Other Inmates* (Anchor, New York, 1962).
Goodhart, A., 'The Rule of Law and Absolute Sovereignty' (1958) *University of Pennsylvania L.R.* 106, 943.
Goveia, E., *Slave Society in the British Leeward Islands at the End of the Eighteenth Century* (Yale University Press, New Jersey, 1965).
—, *The West Indian Laws of the Eighteenth Century* (Caribbean University Press, Bridgetown, 1970).
Grabosky, P.N., *Sydney in Ferment: Crime, Dissent and Offical Reaction, 1788 to 1973* (Australian National University Press, Canberra, 1977).
Gramsci, A., *Selections from the Prison Notebooks* (Q. Hoare and G. Howell-Smith, eds.), (International Publishers, New York, 1971).
Grant, J., *Letter to His Mother and Sister* 2/5/1804, NLA MS. 737.
Grant, J., *Letters from John Grant* SRO Seafield Muniments, GD 248/351/7/27.
Grant, J., *Peel Papers* BL Add MS. 40357 ff 37-45 (John Grant).
Great Britain, *Report of the Select Committee on Transportation* (House of Commons, 1812).
Great Britain, *Report of the Commissioner of Inquiry into the State of the Colony of New South Wales* (House of Commons, 1822), 3 vols, (*The Bigge Report*).
Great Britain, *Papers Relating to the Conduct of Magistrates in New South Wales, in Directing the Infliction of Punishments Upon Prisoners in that Colony* (House of Commons, 1826).
Great Britain, *Report of the Select Committee on Slavery* (House of Commons, 1832) (IUP, 'Slavery').

Great Britain, *Report from Select Committee on Transportation* (House of Commons, 1837) (IUP, 'Transportation', 2), (*The Molesworth Report*).
Great Britain, *Petition from New South Wales* (House of Commons, 1840) (IUP, 'Australia', 6) 159.
Green, B., *Norwich Castle: A Fortress for Nine Centuries* (Jarrold, Norwich, 1970).
Green, T.A., *Verdict According to Conscience: Perspectives on the English Criminal Trial Jury, 1200–1800* (University of Chicago Press, Chicago, 1985).
Greenberg, D.F. (ed.), *Crime and Capitalism: Readings in Marxist Criminology*, (Mayfield, Palo Alto, 1981).
—, 'Crime, Law Enforcement and Social Control in Colonial America' (1982) *American Journal of Legal History* 26, 293.
Gutman, H., *Slavery and the Numbers Game* (University of Illinois Press, Urbana, 1975).
Hainsworth, D.R., *The Sydney Traders: Simeon Lord and His Contemporaries 1788–1821* (Melbourne University Press, 1981).
Haldane, R., *Police in Victoria 1836–1980* (Victoria Police Department, Melbourne, 1980).
Hale, M., *The History of the Pleas of the Crown* (Professional Books, London, 1971, first published, 1736).
Halévy, E., *A History of the English People in the Nineteenth Century : England in 1815* (Barnes and Noble, New York, 1961).
Hall, S., Critcher, C., Jefferson, T., Clarke, J. and Roberts, B., *Policing the Crisis: Mugging, the State, and Law and Order* (Macmillan, London, 1978).
Hamlin, A. and Pettit, P. (eds.), *The Good Polity* (Blackwell, Oxford, 1989).
Hancock, W.K., *Australia* (Jacaranda Press, Sydney, 1961).
Harris, A., *Settlers and Convicts: Recollections of Sixteen Years Labour in the Australian Backwoods* (Melbourne University Press, Melbourne, 1953, first published 1847).
—, *The Emigrant Family* (Australian National University Press, Canberrra, 1967, first published 1849).
Hart, H.L.A., 'Positivism and the Separation of Law and Morals' (1957–8) *Harvard L.R.* 71,593.
—, *The Concept of Law* (Oxford University Press, Oxford, 1961).
—, *Punishment and Responsibility: Essays in the Philosophy of Law* (Oxford University Press, Oxford, 1968).
Haskins, G.L., *Law and Authority in Early Massachusetts* (Archon Books, New York, 1968).
Hay D., et.al, (eds.), *Albion's Fatal Tree: Crime and Society in Eighteenth Century England* (Pantheon, New York, 1975).
—, 'The Criminal Prosecution in England And Its Historians' (1984) *Modern L.R.* 47, 1.
Hayek, F.A., *The Road to Serfdom* (University of Chicago Press, Chicago, 1960).
—, *The Constitution of Liberty* (University of Chicago Press, Chicago, 1960).
Hazzard, M., *Punishment Short of Death: A History of the Penal Settlement at Norfolk Island*, (Hyland House, Melbourne, 1984).

Higman, B., *Slave Population and Economy in Jamaica 1807–34* (Cambridge University Press, Cambridge, 1976).
Hill, C., *The World Turned Upside Down: Radical Ideas During the English Revolution* (Penguin, Harmondsworth, 1975).
—, *Intellectual Origins of the English Revolution* (Oxford University Press, Oxford, 1980).
Hill-Reid W.S., *John Grant's Journey: A Convict's Story* (Heinemann, London, 1957).
Hindus, M., *Prison and Plantation: Crime, Justice and Authority in Massachusetts and South Carolina 1767–1878* (University of North Carolina Press, Chapel Hill, 1980).
Hirst, J., *Convict Society and Its Enemies: A History of Early New South Wales* (Allen and Unwin, Sydney, 1983).
—, 'Or None of the Above' (1988) *Hist. Stud.* 22, 519.
Historical Records of Australia.
Historical Records of New South Wales.
Hobsbawn, E.J. and Rudé, G., *Captain Swing* (Norton, New York, 1968).
Holmes, O.W., *The Common Law* (Macmillan, 1968, first published 1881).
Holt, J., *Memoirs T. Crofton Croker* (ed.), (Henry Colburn, London, 1838).
Horwitz, M.J., 'The Rule of Law: An unqualified Human Good?' (1977) *Yale L.J.* 86, 561.
Howard, J., *Prisons and Lazarettos, vol I: The State of the Prisons in England and Wales, with Preliminary observations and an account of some Foreign Prisons and Hospitals* (Patterson Smith, 1973, first published 1777).
Hughes, R., *The Fatal Shore: A History of the Transportation of Convicts to Australia 1787–1868* (Knopf, New York, 1986).
Hume, D., *Essays: Moral, Political and Literary* (Oxford University Press, Oxford, 1963).
Hunt, A., 'Dichotomy and Contradiction in the Sociology of Law' in Beirne and Quinney (eds.), *Marxism and Law*(John Wiley, New York, 1982), 74.
Hunter, J., *Governor Hunter's Remarks on the Causes of Colonial Expense of the Establishment of New South Wales* (London, 1802).
Ignatieff, M., *A Just Measure of Pain: The Penitentiary in the Industrial Revolution 1750–1850* (Macmillan, London, 1978).
Ingleton, G., *True Patriots All* (Angus and Robertson, Sydney, 1952).
Innes, J., 'The King's Bench Prison in the Later Eighteenth Century: Law, Authority and Order in a Debtors' Prison' in Brewer and Styles (eds.), *An Ungovernable People* (Rutgers University Press, New Brunswick, 1980), 250.
James, C.L.R., 'The Slaves' in L. Comitas and D. Lowenthal, *Slaves Free Men, Citizens: West Indian Perspectives* (Doubleday Anchor, New York, 1973).
Jennings, I., *The Law and the Constitution* (University of London Press, London, 1933).
Jones, H., 'The Rule of Law and the Welfare State' (1958) *Columbia L.R.* 58, 143.
Jones, W.J., *Politics and the Bench: The Judges and the Origins of the English Civil War* (Allen and Unwin, London 1971).

Kent, John to E.S. Hall (from Moreton Bay) 10/8/33, NLA MS. 3310.
King Papers, ML MS. 710.
King, A.H., 'Police Organization and Administration in the Middle District of New South Wales 1825–51' (unpublished MA thesis, University of Sydney, 1956a).
—, 'Some Aspects of Police Administration in New South Wales 1825–1851' (1956b) *JRAHS* 205.
—, 'The Humanitarian Leanings of Governor Bourke' (1961) *Hist. Studs.* 10, 19.
—, *Richard Bourke* (Oxford University Press, Melbourne, 1971).
King P, 'Decision Makers and Decision Making in the English Criminal Law, 1750–1800' (1984) 27 *Historical Journal* 27.
Krygier, M., 'Law as Tradition' (1986) *Law and Philosophy* 5, 237.
Kuhn, T.S., *The Structure of Scientific Revolutions* (University of Chicago Press., Chicago, 1962).
Ladurie, E. LeRoy, *Montaillou*, trans. B. Bray (Penguin, Harmondsworth, 1980).
Landon, M., *The Triumph of the Lawyers: Their Role in English Politics 1678–89* (University of Alabama Press, Tuscaloosa, 1970).
Langbein J., 'Albion's Fatal Flaws' (1983a) *Past and Present* 98, 96.
—, 'Shaping the Eighteenth Century Criminal Trial: A View from the Ryder Sources' (1983b) *University of Chicago L.R.* 50, 1.
Linebaugh, P., 'The Tyburn Riot against the Surgeons' in Hay et al. (eds.), *Albion's Fatal Tree* (Pantheon, New York, 1975), 65.
Liston, C., 'Sir Thomas Brisbane in New South Wales' (1985) *JRAHS* 71, 91.
Locke, J., *Second Treatise of Government* (Bobbs-Merrill, New York, 1952, first published, 1690).
Lovejoy, D.S. 'Two American Revolutions 1689 and 1776' in J.G.A. Pocock (ed.), *Three British Revolutions* (Princeton University Press, Princeton, 1980), 244.
Loveless, G., *The Victims of Whiggery* (Cox, Kay, Hobart, 1946, first published 1837).
Lumb, R.D., 'Aboriginal Land Rights: Judicial Approaches in Perspective' (1980) *Australian Law Journal* 63, 273.
Macarthur, J., *New South Wales: Its Present State & Future Prospects* (London, 1837).
Mackay, D., *A Place of Exile: The European Settlement of New South Wales* (Oxrord University Press, Melbourne, 1985).
McKinnon J., *Convict Bushrangers in New South Wales, 1824–1834* (unpublished MA thesis, La Trobe University, 1979).
McLachlan, N., 'Edward Eager (1787–1866): A Colonial Spokesman in Sydney and London' (1961-3) *Hist.Studs*. 431.
McLaughlin, J.K., 'The Magistracy in New South Wales 1788–1850' (unpublished LM thesis, University of Sydney, 1973).
McMartin, A., *Public Servants and Patronage: The Foundation and Rise of the New South Wales Public Service, 1786–1859* (Sydney University Press, Sydney, 1983).

BIBLIOGRAPHY 257

McMinn, W.G., *A Constitutional History of Australia* (Oxford University Press, Melbourne, 1979).
McQueen, H., *A New Britannia* (Penguin, Melbourne, 1970).
Manchester, A.H., *Modern Legal History of England and Wales 1750–1950* (Butterworth, London, 1980).
Marx, K., *Capital* (Foreign Languages Publishing House, Moscow, 1957).
—, *Grundrisse* (Vintage, New York, 1973).
Marx, K., and Engels, F., *The Communist Manifesto* (Penguin, Harmondsworth, 1967).
Mayhew, H., *London Labour and the London Poor* (A.K. Kelly, London, 1968, first published 1851).
Melbourne A.C.V., *Early Constitutional Development in Australia* (University of Queensland Press, St Lucia, 1963).
—, *William Charles Wentworth* (University of Queensland Press, St Lucia, 1963).
—, *Early Constitutional Development in Australia* (University of Queensland Press, St Lucia, 1963).
Meredith, J. and Whalan, R., 'A Poet in revolt: Francis MacNamara' in E. Fry (ed.), *Rebels and Radicals* (Allen and Unwin, Sydney, 1983), 37.
Merivale, H., *Colonisation and the Colonies* (Longman, London, 1861).
Merritt, A., 'The Nature and Function of Law: A Criticism of E.P. Thompson's Whigs and Hunters' (1980) *British Journal of Law and Society*, 7, 194.
—, 'The Historical Role of Law in the Regulation of Employment-Abstentionist or Interventionist?' (1982) *Australian Journal of Law and Society*, 56.
—, 'Forgotten Militants: Use of the New South Wales Masters and Servants Acts by and against Female Employees 1845–1930' in I. W. Duncanson and C. L. Tomlins (eds.), *Law and History in Australia* (La Trobe University Press, Melbourne, 1982), 54.
Mockler, A., *Lions Under the Throne* (F.Muller, London, 1983).
Molesworth Report, see Great Britain.
Montesquieu, Baron de, *The Spirit of the Laws*, (Collier, New York, 1949).
Morgan E.S., *American Slavery, American Freedom* (Norton, New York, 1975).
Morgan, K., 'The Organisation of the Convict Trade to Maryland: Stevenson, Randolph & Cheston, 1768–1775' (1985) *William and Mary Quarterly* 42, 201
Morgan, P.D., 'Work and Culture: The Task System and the Work Low Country Blacks, 1700–1880' (1982) *William and Mary Quarterly* 39, 563.
Morris, H., 'Persons and Punishment' (1968) *The Monist* 52, 475.
Morris, T.D., '"As If the Injury was Effected by the Natural Elements of Air or Fire": Slave wrongs and the Liability of Masters' (1982) *Law and Society Review* 16, 569.
Mostyn v Fabrigas (1774) 1 Cowp. 161.
Mouledous, J.C., 'Organizational Goals and Structural Change: A Study of the Organization of a Prison Social System' (1963) *Social Forces* 41, 283.
Mudie, J., *The Felonry of New South Wales* (Whaley and Co., London, 1837).

Murrin, J., 'The Great Inversion, or Court versus Country: A Comparison of the Revolution Settlements in England and America 1776–1861' in J.G.A. Pocock (ed.), *Three British Revolutions* (Princeton University Press, Princeton, 1980), 368.

Neal, D.J., 'The Role of Justices of the Peace in Relation to Popular Protest in Eighteenth Century England' (unpublished MS. University of California, Berkeley, 1979).

—, 'Law and Authority in New South Wales,1788–1840 – The Magistracy' (1985) *Law in Context* 45.

—, 'The Political Significance of the Jury' in D. Challinger (ed.), *The Jury* (Australian Institute of Criminology, Canberra, 1986).

—, 'The Campaign for Trial by Jury in New South Wales, 1788–1840' (1987) *Journal of Legal History* 107.

—, 'Free Society, Penal Colony, Slave Society, Prison?' (1987) *Hist. Studs.* 22, 497.

Neale, J., *The Cutlass and the Lash* (Pluto Press, London, 1985).

Nenner, H., *By Colour of Law: Legal Culture and Constitutional Politics in England 1660–1689* (University of Chicago Press, Chicago, 1977).

Nepean, E. to Lord Sydney ML MS. An 53/1.

New South Wales, *Report on Police* (Legislative Council, NSW, Votes and Proceedings, 1825).

New South Wales, *Governor's Despatch to the Secretary of State for Colonies* Vol 8, Sep–Dec 1826, ML A1197.

New South Wales, *Report of the Committee on Police and Gaols* (Legislative Council, NSW, Votes and Proceedings, 1835).

New South Wales, *Report of the Committee on Police and Gaols* (Legislative Council, NSW, Votes and Proceedings, 1839).

New South Wales, *Inquiry into the Queanbeyan Bench, 1840*, AONSW 4/2507.

New South Wales, *Colonial Trials and Court Records, Benches of Magistrates – Deposition Books 1838–44*, AONSW 4/5650, Reel No. 677 and 4/5648, Reel No. 2731.

New South Wales, *Court of Petty Sessions: Muswellbrook, Letters Sent, 1838–51*, AONSW 5/4781, Reel No. 2731.

Nichol, W., 'Ideology and the Convict System in New South Wales, 1788–1820' (1986) *Hist. Studs.* 22, 1.

Nicholas, S. (ed.), *Convict Workers* (Cambridge University Press, Cambridge, 1988).

Oakeshott, M., 'The Rule of Law' in *On History and Other Essays* (Blackwell, Oxford, 1983).

O'Brien, E., *The Foundation of Australia (1786–1800): A Study in English Criminal Practice and Penal Colonisation in the Eighteenth Century* (Sheed and Ward, London, 1937).

Osborne, B., *Justices of the Peace 1361–1848* (Sedgehill Press, Shaftesbury, 1960).

Paley, W., *The Principles of Moral and Political Philosophy* (London, 1814, first published 1785).
Parsons, T.G., 'Was John Boston's Pig a Political Martyr?' (1985) *JRAHS* 71, 163.
—, 'The Commercialisation of Honour: Early Australian Capitalism 1788-1809 in G. Aplin (ed.), *Sydney Before Macquarie* (University of New South Wales Press, Sydney, 1988), 120.
Patterson, O., *Slavery and Social Death: A Comparative Study* (Harvard University Press, Cambridge, Mass., 1982).
Peel, R., *Peel Papers*, BL Add MSS. 40357.
Perkins, E., 'Roll, Jordan, Roll: A Marx for the Master Class' (1976) *Radical History Review* 3, 41.
Petchesky, R.P., 'At Hard Labor: Penal confinement and Production in Nineteenth-Century America' in D.F. Greenberg (ed.), *Crime and Capitalism: Readings in Marxist Criminology* (Mayfield, Palo Alto, 1961).
Philips, D., 'The Black Country Magistracy 1835-60' (1976) *Midland History*, 161.
—, *Crime and Authority in Victorian England: The Black Country 1835-1860* (Croom Helm, London, 1977).
—, '"A Just Measure of Crime, Authority and Blue Locusts": The Revisionist Social History of Crime and the Law in Britain 1780-1850' in S. Cohen and A. Scull (eds.), *Social Control and the State* (Blackwell, Oxford, 1983)50.
Phillips, M., *A Colonial Autocracy: New South Wales under Governor Macquarie 1810-1821* (P.S. King and Son, Sydney, 1909).
Picciotto, S., 'The Theory of the State, Class Struggle and the Rule of Law' in P. Beirne and R. Quinney (eds.), *Marxism and Law* (John Wiley, New York, 1982), 169.
Plunkett J.H., *The Australian Magistrate, or A Guide to the Duties of a Justice of the Peace for the Colony of New South Wales* (Anne Howe, Sydney, 1835).
Pocock, J.G.A., *The Ancient Constitution and the Feudal Law: A Study of English Historical Thought in the Seventeenth Century* (Cambridge University Press, Cambridge, 1957).
—, 'Burke and the Ancient Constitution – A Problem in the History of Ideas' (1960) *Historical Journal* 125.
— *The Machiavellian Moment: Florentine Political Thought and the Atlantic Republican Tradition* (Princeton University Press, Princeton, 1975).
— *Three British Revolutions: 1641, 1688 and 1776* (Princeton University Press, Princeton, 1980).
Pollock F. and F.N. Maitland, *The History of English Law*, Cambridge University Press, Cambridge, 1960.
Poulantzas, N., 'Law' in P. Beirne and R. Quinney (eds.), *Marxism and Law* (John Wiley, New York, 1982), 185.
Preyer, K., 'Penal Measures in the American Colonies: an Overview' (1982) *American Journal of Legal History* 26, 326.

Prieur, F.X., *Notes of a Convict of 1838* (Australian Historical Monographs vol. VI (new series), Ford, Sydney, 1949).
R v *Jack Congo Murrell* (1836) 1 Legge 72.
Raz, J., *The Authority of Law : Essays on Law and Morality* (Clarendon Press, Oxford, 1979).
Redhead, S., 'Marxist Theory, the Rule of Law and Socialism' in P. Beirne and R. Quinney (eds.), *Marxism and Law* (John Wiley, New York, 1982), 328.
Rees, J., *The Social Foundation of the Rule of Law* (unpublished paper, University of California, Berkeley, 1980).
Reynolds, H., *Frontier* (Allen and Unwin, Sydney, 1987).
—, *The Law of the Land* (Penguin, Melbourne, 1987)
—, *The Other Side of the Frontier* (Penguin, Melbourne, 1982).
Rheinstein, M. and Shils, E., (eds.), *Max Weber on Law in Economy and Society* (Harvard University Press, Cambridge, Mass., 1954).
Ritchie, J., *Punishment and Profit* (Heinemann, Melbourne, 1970).
—, *The Evidence to the Bigge Reports: New South Wales Under Governor Macquarie* (2 vols, Heinemann, Melbourne, 1971).
—, 'Towards Ending an Unclean Thing: The Molesworth Committee and the Abolition of Transportation to New South Wales 1837–40' (1976) *Hist. Studs.* 17, 144.
—, *Lachlan Macquarie: A Biography* (Melbourne University Press, Melbourne, 1986).
Robinson, P., *The Hatch and Brood of Time: A Study of the First Generation of Native-born White Australians, 1788–1828* (Oxford University Press, Melbourne, 1985).
Robson L., *The Convict Settlers of Australia: An Enquiry into the Origin and Character of the Convicts Transported to New South Wales and Van Diemen's Land 1787–1852* (Melbourne University Press, Melbourne, 1965).
Roe, M., 'Colonial Society in Embryo.' (1956) *Hist. Studs.* 7, 149.
—, *The Quest for Authority in Eastern Australia, 1835–51* (Melbourne University Press, Melbourne, 1965).
Rossi F.N., *First Police Magistrate*, 7/10/26 ML MSS. A1197,516
Rossi Papers (2 vols) 1801–71, ML A 723.
Rudé G., *Protest and Punishment* (Oxford University Press, Oxford, 1978).
Rutman, D. (ed.), *The Old Dominion* (University Press of Virginia, Charlottesville, 1964).
Schedvin, C.B. and Schedvin, M.B., 'The Nomad Tribes of Urban Britain: A Prelude to Botany Bay' (1978) *Hist. Studs.* 10, 254.
Schwoerer, L., 'The Bill of Rights: Epitome of the Revolution of 1688–89' in J.G.A. Pocock (ed.) *Three British Revolutions* (Princeton University Press, Princeton, 1980), 224.
Shaw A.G.L., *Convicts and the Colonies: A Study of Penal Transportation from Great Britain and Ireland to Australia and Other Parts of the British Empire* (Melbourne University Press, Melbourne, 1977).
—, *Heroes and Villains in History* (Sydney University Press, Sydney, 1966).

BIBLIOGRAPHY 261

Sheldon, R.G., 'Convict Leasing: An Application of the Rusche-Kirkheimer Thesis to Penal Changes in Tennessee, 1830–1915' in D. Greenberg (ed.), *Crime and Capitalism: Readings in Marxist Criminology* (Mayfield, Palo Alto, 1961), 95.
Silver A., 'The Demand for Order in Civil Society: A Review of Some Themes in the History of Urban Crime Police and Riot' in D. Bordua (ed.), *The Police: Six Sociological Essays* (Wiley, New York, 1967) 1.
Smith, Adam, *Lectures on Jurisprudence*, R.L.Meek, D.D. Raphael, P.G. Stein (eds.) (Oxford University Press, Oxford, 1978).
Smith, A.E., 'Transportation of Convicts to the American Colonies in the Seventeenth Century' (1934) *American Historical Review* 39, 232.
Somerset v Stewart 1 Lofft. 1, 98 ER 499 (1772).
Sontag, S. (ed.), *A Barthes Reader* (Hill and Wang, New York, 1982).
Stampp, K.M., *The Peculiar Institution* (Knopf, New York, 1956).
Stone, J., *Legal System and Lawyers' Reasoning* (Maitland, Sydney, 1964).
Stone, L., 'The Results of the English Revolutions of the Seventeenth Century' in J.G.A. Pocock (ed.), *Three British Revolutions* (Princeton University Press, Princeton, 1980), 23.
Sturma M., 'Public Executions and the Rituals of Death' (1983) *Push from the Bush* 15, 3.
—, *Vice in a Vicious Society: Crime and Convicts in Mid-Nineteenth-Century New South Wales* (University of Queensland Press, St Lucia, 1983).
—, 'Policing the Criminal Frontier in Mid-Nineteenth Century Australia, Britain and America' in M. Finnane (ed.), *Policing Australia: Historical Perspectives* (University of New South Wales Press, Sydney, 1989).
Summers, A., *Damned Whores and God's Police* (Penguin, Melbourne, 1975).
Swanton B., *A Chronological Account of Crime, Public Order and Police in Sydney 1788–1810* (Australian Institute of Criminology, Canberra, 1983).
Swanton B., Harrigan, G. and Biles, D. (eds.), *Police Source Book* (Australian Institute of Criminology, Canberrra, 1983).
Sykes, G.M., *The Society of Captives: A Study of a Maximum Security Prison* (Princeton University Press, New Jersey, 1968).
Tench W., *Sydney's First Four Years* (L.F. Fitzhardinge (ed.), (Angus and Robertson, Sydney, 1961, first published, 1793).
Therry, R., *Reminiscences of Thirty Years' Residence in New South Wales and Victoria* (Sydney University Press, Sydney, 1974).
Thompson, E.P., *The Making of the English Working Class* (Peguin, Harmondsworth, 1968).
—, 'The Moral Economy of the English Crowd in the Eighteenth Century' (1971) *Past and Present* 50, 76.
—, *Whigs and Hunters: The Origin of the Black Act* (Pantheon Books, New York, 1975).
—, *Writing By Candlelight* (Merlin Press, London, 1980).
Tobias, J.J., *Crime and Police in England 1700–1900* (Gill and Macmillan, London, 1979).
Tocqueville, A. de, *Democracy in America* (Anchor, New York, 1969).

Townsend N., 'Document: Bourke's Comments on the Molesworth Committee' (1982) *Push from the Bush* 12, 65.
—, 'A "Mere Lottery": The Convict System in New South Wales Through the Eyes of the Molesworth Committee' (1985) *Push from the Bush* 21, 58.
—, 'Masters and Men and the Myall Creek Massacre' (1985) *Push from the Bush* 20, 4.
Tucker, J., *The Adventures of Ralph Rashleigh* (Currey O'Neil, Melbourne, 1981).
Tushnet, M., 'The American Law of Slavery 1810–1860: A Study In the Persistence of Legal Autonomy' (1975) *Law and Society Review* 119.
—, *The American Law of Slavery 1810–1860: Considerations of Humanity and Interest* (Princeton University Press, Princeton, 1981).
Ullathorne, W., *The Horrors of Transportation Briefly Unfolded to the People* (Dublin, 1838).
Unger, R.M., *Law in Modern Society* (Free Press, New York, 1976).
Vamplew, W. (ed.), *Australians: Historical Statistics* (Fairfax, Syme and Weldon, Sydney, 1987).
Walicki, A., 'Marx and Freedom' (1983 Nov.) *New York Review of Books*, 50.
Walker, G., *The Rule of Law* (Melbourne University Press, Melbourne, 1988).
Walter, J., 'Grainriots and Popular Attitudes to the Law: Maldon and the Crisis of 1629' in Brewer and Styles (eds.), *An Ungovernable People: The English and their Law in the Seventeenth and Eighteenth Centuries* (Rutgers University Press, New Brunswick, 1980), 47.
Walvin, J. (ed.), *Slavery and British Society 1776–1846* (Macmillan, London, 1982).
Ward R. and Robertson J., *Such Was Life: Select Documents in Australian Social History 1788–1850* (Ure Smith, Sydney, 1969).
Ward, R., *The Australian Legend* (Oxford University Press, Melbourne, 1978).
—, *Finding Australia* (Heinemann, Melbourne, 1987).
Weber, M., *Economy and Society*, (University of California Press, Berkeley, 1978).
—, *The Protestant Ethic and the Spirit of Capitalism* (Scribners, New York, 1958).
Wentworth Papers on Police, 1810–27 ML DI.
Wentworth, W.C., *Statistical, Historical and Political Descriptions of the Colony of New South Wales and its Dependent Settlements in Van Diemen's Land* (Doubleday, Sydney, 1978, first published, 1819).
White, R., *Inventing Australia: Images and Identity 1788–1980* (Allen and Unwin, Sydney, 1981).
Winch, D., *Adam Smith's Politics* (Cambridge University Press, Cambridge, 1978).
Windeyer, V., *Lectures on Legal History* (Law Book Co., Sydney, 1957).
—, 'Responsible Government – Highlights, Sidelights and Reflections' (1957) *JRAHS* 52, 257.

—, '"A Birthright and Inheritance": The Establishment of the Rule of Law in Australia' (1962) *University of Tasmania L.R.* 1, 635.

Woinarski, S., *The History of Legal Institutions in Victoria* (unpublished LlD thesis, University of Melbourne, 1942).

Wood, G., 'Convicts' (1922) *JRAHS* 8, 177.

Index

Aborigines, 9, 17–8, 32, 43, 58, 78–80, 91, 143, 150–4, 161, 164–5, 190, 191, 193, 239n
— Myall Creek massacre, 79–80, 150–4
— and police, 143, 150–4, 164–5, 191
— and rule of law, 17–8, 58, 78–80, 91, 191
American Revolution, 7, 10–11, 71, 72, 170, 221n

Bathurst, Earl, 30–1, 55, 96–7, 103–4, 175, 188, 194
Beccaria, Cesare, 13, 142
Bent, Ellis, 54, 95, 95–6, 100, 101, 168, 174–5, 194, 195
Bent, Jeffery, 16, 77, 78, 101–5, 175–6, 179, 192, 195
Bentham, Jeremy, i, 10, 14, 30, 42, 45, 95, 243n
Bigge, John, 31, 93, 150, 179–80, 182
Bill of Rights, xi, 23, 24, 65, 71, 72
Blackstone, William, x, xi, 6, 13, 23, 29, 71–4, 77, 80, 167, 168, 176, 191, 192, 225n
Bligh, Governor William, 16, 18, 21, 22, 78, 92–4, 97–8, 120, 121, 128, 145, 168, 173–5, 193
Bourke, Governor Richard, 19, 50, 120, 121, 122, 123, 124, 128, 137, 134–5, 144, 163, 184, 186, 191
Brisbane, Thomas, 120–2, 126, 128, 148, 163, 183
Burton, William, 78, 185
Bushranging, 31, 54, 137, 150, 155, 161, 164

Charles I, 72, 113, 193
Clark, Manning, 31, 47, 62, 112, 132
Clarke, Marcus, 53
Coke, Edward, 62, 66, 71–2, 86, 107, 176, 225n
Courts, xi, 5–7, 16, 17, 18–19, 21–3, 28, 32, 53, 54–5, 63, 64, 67, 69, 71–2, 75–8, 79–80, 81–3, 85–113, 115–40, 171–6, 181–3, 184, 185, 186, 190–6
— civil jurisdiction, 5, 75–6
— criminal jurisdiction, 54–5, 167, 168, 194
— magistrate's court, 75–6, 108–113, 115–40, 146–8, 156, 159
— quarter sessions, 181–3, 184, 185
— Supreme Court, 16, 53, 77, 82, 108–113, 116, 121, 126–31, 171–6, 185
— use by convicts, 50–1, 75–6, 134
Cromwell, Oliver, 13, 61, 62, 74, 96, 193
Crossley, George, 93, 99–102, 178, 225n

Darling, Governor Ralph, 17, 19, 20, 27, 28, 78, 79, 82, 86, 108–13, 129–31, 149–152, 177, 191, 192, 195, 207n
Day, Edward, 150–1

Eagar, Edward, 19, 55, 57, 93, 100, 102, 110, 176, 177, 178–81, 184, 186, 195, 204n, 207n,
Evatt, Herbert, xi, 21–2, 23, 63, 86, 94
Emancipists, 12, 18–21, 24, 54–6, 62, 77–8, 80–1, 99–105, 108, 116–7, 131–3, 168–71, 175–6, 177–87, 191–2, 195–7
— definition, 18–19
— lawyers, 16, 101–5, 175–6, 178, 179, 192

INDEX 265

— magistrates, 55, 100, 122, 132–3, 176
— standing to sue, 5–7, 80, 99, 106, 110, 127, 132, 176, 178–80, 191–2, 225n
— petition, 20, 24, 167, 176, 177–9
English Civil War, 24, 62, 65, 93, 173, 193
Exclusives, 12, 18, 19, 20, 55–6, 77–8, 81, 99, 105, 108, 116–7, 120–1, 126, 128, 131–3, 139–40, 158, 168–71, 175, 179, 182, 185–7
— definition, 18
Executions (see Punishment, capital)

Field, Barron, 6, 110, 178–9, 207n, 228n, 246n
Flogging, 7, 36–7, 39, 42, 43, 49–52, 108–9, 129, 134–6, 139, 156, 160, 211–2nn, 216n, 234–5n, 240n
— of convicts, of slaves, 36–7
Forbes, Francis, xi, 31, 41, 69–70, 71, 78, 86, 87, 101, 107, 108, 109, 110–3, 128, 164, 173, 177, 183, 195, 206n
Foucault, Michel, 42, 45
Free society, 9–10, 14, 23, 27–9, 31–3, 33–4, 44, 56–9, 62, 80–1, 86, 88, 108, 117, 142, 196–7, 207–8n
French Revolution, 10–11, 71, 74, 142

Gipps, George, 80, 136, 138, 152, 153, 154, 164, 191
Glorious Revolution, 65, 71, 73, 86, 176, 193
Governor's power, 16, 20, 21, 22, 23–5, 32, 36, 43, 56, 62–3, 64, 76, 77, 78, 81, 85–90, 92, 113, 116–7, 119–25, 127–8, 128–31, 134, 135–7, 138, 139–40, 143–4, 146–7, 151–4, 158, 160–1, 171, 172–4, 178, 181, 186, 190, 191, 207–8nn, 232n
Grant, John, 31, 58, 61, 62, 75, 77, 195

Habeas Corpus, 23, 24, 57, 71
Hale, Mathew, 61, 62, 176, 193
Hall, Edward S., 19, 77, 111, 115, 116, 122, 129–33, 136, 137, 140, 163, 192, 195, 245n
Hay, Douglas, x, xii, 63, 64, 112, 193
Harris, Alexander, 51, 109, 126, 138, 160, 161, 195
Hirst, John, xi, 31, 35, 36, 38, 47, 50, 52, 112, 207–8n
Holmes (Kable), Susannah (see Kable, Susannah)
Hughes, Robert, 28, 31, 63, 112
Hunter, Governor John, 21, 76, 92–3, 118, 168, 173, 175

Judges, 54, 71, 77, 80, 81–2, 85, 88, 89–90, 93–4, 95–7, 99–106, 109–12, 119, 129–30, 168, 174–6, 178, 181, 196
Juries, 10, 17, 19–20, 24, 32–3, 34, 54–9, 71, 72, 77–8, 80, 81, 85, 90, 91, 93, 99, 104, 106, 107, 108, 110, 126–7, 129, 130, 132, 137, 167–87, 189, 192, 195, 196, 207n, 222n, 247–9nn
— grand jury, 8, 54, 79, 89, 138, 178
Justice of the Peace (see Magistrates)

Kable, Henry, 1–8, 16, 18, 29, 33, 66, 143, 144, 177, 189, 195–6, 236n, 238n
Kable (Holmes), Susannah, 1–8, 16, 29, 66, 177, 189, 195–6
King, Governor Philip, 21, 75, 92–3, 99, 168

Lawyers, 19, 71–2, 75, 77, 82, 88, 92, 93, 95, 99–103, 105, 109, 110, 138, 140, 175–6, 178, 196
Legal reasoning, 66, 69–70, 110–3, 193, 195
Legal rights, 6–7, 23, 27, 29–30, 34–5, 42, 45, 63, 71, 77–8, 81, 86, 90–2, 110–1, 127, 177–9, 182, 209n, 218n
Liberty, x, xi, 23, 27–9, 45–6, 53–4, 56–7, 64–5, 72, 85, 86, 87, 141–3, 145, 162, 163–4, 167–8, 171, 176, 179, 182, 192, 219n
Locke, John, 27–9, 73

Macarthur, Hannibal, 134, 141–2, 164
Macarthur, James, 18, 55–6, 78, 109, 127, 169–70, 185–6
Macarthur, John, 18, 19, 21, 78, 94, 168, 170, 173, 174–5, 180, 191, 195, 206n
Macquarie, Governor Lachlan, 19, 20, 24, 54, 76, 78, 81, 92, 94–7, 98–106, 121, 122, 123, 128, 146, 163, 171, 175, 178–9, 186, 191, 206–7n
Magistrates, 93, 115–40, 149, 155, 157–61
— conflict with Supreme Court, 108–13, 121, 126–31, 138
— illegalities, 108–9, 123, 129, 138–9, 142, 192, 215n
— police magistrates (stipendaries), 124–6, 147, 149, 157–61
— supervision by Governor, 138–40, 147
— supervision by police, 146–8, 155
Magna Carta, xi, 23, 24, 54, 63, 71, 72, 76, 77, 80, 171, 176, 187, 223n
Marsden, Samuel, 118, 120–2, 124, 131

Molesworth Committee, 38, 58, 78, 127, 161, 185, 196
Mounted Police (see Police)

Nepean, Evan, 88–9
New South Wales Act, 87, 90, 92, 94, 106–9, 126, 181–3
New South Wales Corps, 18, 21, 75, 94, 99, 112, 168, 173–4, 186
Newspapers, 20–1, 24, 63, 77, 82, 108, 110–12, 140, 177, 182, 196

Paine, Thomas, 11, 76
Penal colony, 9, 17, 23, 28–9, 30–3, 44–59, 87, 90–1, 134, 137, 146, 164, 171, 186, 208n
Philips, David, 48, 150
Phillip, Governor Arthur, 8, 76, 143, 144, 145, 172–3
Police, 141–66
— Border, 151–4, 163
— and magistrates, 137–8
— constables, 5, 13, 146
— convict/emancipist/ticket-of-leave, 9, 141, 143–4, 148
— Mounted, 80, 144, 150–4, 163, 191
— paid police, 13, 65, 71, 72, 74, 125, 141–2
— military as, 21, 144–5
— Night Watch, 143–4
— numbers, 43, 53–4, 145, 147, 148, 150–1, 155, 156–7, 161–2, 164–5
— supervision of, 82–3, 117, 123, 131, 137, 140, 142, 144, 146–7, 152–3, 161, 162–4
— and rule of law, 63, 79, 116, 142–3, 164–5, 190–1, 195
Population of New South Wales, 15, 33–4, 44, 49–50, 52–3, 54, 155–6, 200–1, 205n
Power, 14, 20, 22, 37, 39, 46, 51–2, 54, 56, 57, 65–6, 68, 74–5, 77–81, 85, 92, 104, 105, 108–9, 112–3, 115–7, 121–2, 130–1, 132, 137–40, 142–3, 154, 163–5, 168, 177, 185–7, 189–91, 193–4, 195
Prison, 7, 12–14, 41–4, 213n
Punishment, 12–14, 31–2, 39, 41–6, 49–53, 56–7, 89, 136–7, 138–9, 142, 146, 148, 156–7, 159, 160, 165, 194, 196–7, 207n
— capital, 12–14, 52–3
— flogging (see Flogging)
— Norfolk Island, 52
— road gangs, 52

Redfern, William, 121, 177, 179
Representative legislature, 10, 19, 25, 55–6, 57, 59, 108, 109–10, 169–70, 177, 183–4, 185–7, 189, 192, 197
Robson, Lloyd, 31, 47–9, 182
Rule of law, 17–8, 22, 23–5, 29, 33, 56, 57, 61–84, 86, 88, 91, 93, 96, 102–5, 108–13, 116, 122–3, 127–8, 129–31, 137, 138, 140, 142–3, 153–4, 157, 161, 163, 165, 168, 171, 176, 189–97
Rum Corps (see New South Wales Corps)
Rum Rebellion, 18, 21, 22, 25, 63, 78, 94, 98, 101, 144–5, 171, 173–5, 191, 193–4

Saxe-Bannister, S., 17, 19, 79
Shaw, Alan, 31, 47–9, 62, 112
Slavery, xi, 11–12, 15, 29–30, 31, 34–41, 44–5, 51, 57, 66, 67, 111, 119, 136, 137, 139, 170, 178, 196
— access to courts, 34–8
— anti-slavery movement, 11–12, 29, 170, 177, 196
— slave rights, 29–30, 34–5
Smith, Adam, 85, 87
Stephen, James, 70, 112, 120, 153, 183, 218n, 225n
Sturma, M., 31
Supreme Court (see Courts)

Thompson, E.P., x, xii, 63, 68, 192–5
Tocqueville, Alexis de, 169–70, 187
Twiss, Horace, 112–3

United States of America, xi, 1–3, 7–8, 10–11, 13, 23, 25, 32, 34, 35, 36, 39, 42–3, 44–5, 67, 87, 111, 177, 203n, 204n, 221n

Wardell, Robert, 19, 20–1, 82, 108, 110, 112, 138, 140, 177, 182
Wentworth, D'Arcy, 146–8
Wentworth, William C., 18, 19, 20–1, 25, 46, 71, 77, 82, 108, 110, 112, 129, 138, 140, 169, 170, 176–7, 182, 192, 195
West Indies, xi, 10, 11–12, 31, 34, 35–41, 55, 57, 136, 178
Wilkes, John, 21, 74, 110, 142, 168, 192, 196
Windeyer, Charles, 125, 147, 157, 161, 162
Wright, James, 51, 135–6, 138, 147, 157–8, 159–61, 163
Wylde, John, 110